The First Treaty of World War I

Ukraine's Treaty with the Central Powers of February 9, 1918

STEPHAN M. HORAK

EAST EUROPEAN MONOGRAPHS, BOULDER
DISTRIBUTED BY COLUMBIA UNIVERSITY PRESS, NEW YORK

1988

EAST EUROPEAN MONOGRAPHS, NO. CCXXXVI

*This posthumous volume
is dedicated to the memory of
Stephan M. Horak*

TABLE OF CONTENTS

INTRODUCTION

Complying dutifully with established tradition in the enterprise of publishing, this introduction intends to set three main points of departure: (1) to justify the monograph's publication and its place among the growing number of works on Eastern European affairs, especially in the English language; (2) to place the events discussed here into proper perspective and into the context of a crucial period in European history that shaped the destinies of several nations; (3) to explain the circumstances and factors foreboding the failure of a large nation to establish itself as an independent state and to take its place in the family of European nations. The history of the Ukrainian people, while not a familiar topic in western historiography, offers a unique case study of the reasons why some nations fail to establish statehood, despite the presence of seemingly favorable conditions.

The first objective can be satisfied easily. The events discussed here involved, in various degrees, all the major European powers in the First World War, influenced events in Russia, and became decisive in the fate of the largest East European nation—Ukraine. Yet the treaty of Brest-Litovsk between the Central Powers and independent Ukraine remains mostly ignored, as is the March 3, 1918 treaty with Soviet Russia. Only two works in English, by John S. Reshetar and Oleh Fedyshyn, provide limited treatment of the treaty. There is only one work in German on the subject, by Peter Borowsky, in addition to three doctoral dissertations and a few articles and brief essays. Not surprisingly, Soviet historiography found it important enough to produce several monographs on the subject.

Indeed, there are many valid reasons compelling Soviet historians to deal with the events of 1918 and to direct them in support of Moscow's interpretation.

Ukraine's treaty with the Central Powers can be placed best within two larger contexts of European history. First, the treaty contributed to and was a factor of the war itself. Second, it arose out of the Russian revolution of 1917 and exemplified the extension of the revolution into the national realm. Ukraine, like Soviet Russia, concluded a peace treaty that relieved the Central Powers of the nightmare of a two-front war and briefly inspired their hope of victory. The treaty helped ease the immense burden of providing large quantitues of foodstuffs badly needed in Germany and especially in the Dual Monarchy. Certainly, many lives were saved as a result of the treaty. For that Ukraine was "rewarded" with international recognition as an independent state and it was freed from Soviet Russian occupation by the German and Austrian armies. This made Ukraine's independent existence in fact as well as name possible for almost two years.

At the same time, Ukraine's predicament, as an outgrowth of the Russian revolution, illustrated an exercise in self-determination as understood within the traditional definition and as offered in Lenin's concept "national in form, socialist in context." However even this restricted exercise in national self-determination had been entrusted exclusively to the Bolsheviks.

Born of chaos, war, and revolution the young Ukrainian state was denied sufficient time by Soviet Russia and by Ukraines' new friends from Berlin and Vienna to experiment, to mature and to solidify itself. Inexperienced in political, military, and economic matters, the young government had to master the complexities of its commitment to both socialism and nationalism. This confluence of two powerful trends of modern history on the Ukrainian soil makes the case an intriguing one.

A few words about the format and structure of this monograph are in order. The work is not intended to present either a history of the Ukrainian revolution or an all inclusive account of Soviet Russian-Ukrainian relations of the 1917-1919 period. These subjects have been well covered by other authors. Nor is this monograph a presentation of Germany's *Ostpolitik.* That subject has already been discussed in *Germany's Drive to the East and the Ukrainian Revolution, 1917-1918* by Oleh Fedyshyn and complemented by Dmytro Doroshenko's work, *Ukraine und das*

Reich: Neun Jahrhunderte deutsch-ukrainischer Beziehungen im Spiegel der Deutschen Wissenschaft und Literatur. The theme of this monograph focuses upon the Brest-Litovsk treaty and its immediate consequences for the fate of Ukraine. Its origin is reviewed against the general historical background consisting of German-Ukrainian encounters and the development of the Ukrainian national rebirth that culminated in the events of 1917-1918. Such a structure should better explain the meaning and consequences of the meeting in Eastern Europe of three very different forces: the conservative Central Powers, Russian Communism, and Ukrainian Nationalism. In fact, Ukraine became the first battleground in history on which all three fought for survival and victory. Moreover, the outcome of that confrontation determined equally the future of Ukraine, of Eastern Europe, and of Europe as a whole. Had Ukraine survived as an independent nation, it would have influenced differently the fates of both Eastern and Western Europe for decades to come. Precisely because the clash of these diverse alternatives the Brest-Litovsk treaty with U-kraine should have attracted the historian's attention and consequently provided additional motives for the presentation of this monograph.

My personal interest in the Brest-Litovsk treaty can be traced back to my doctoral dissertation at the Erlangen University in 1949. After several decades and after having had a chance to do more research at the archives in Vienna, Koblenz and Bonn, and after becoming familiar with the literature published since on that and related subjects, I have decided to introduce this neglected treaty into historical literature.

Generous financial aid from the Shevchenko Scientific Society helped me in my effort to gain access to various depositories. My wife, as always, typed and retyped the manuscript. After many years of teaching at Eastern Illinois University I am pleased to dedicate this work to all my students past and present.

October 1986   Stephan M. Horak

CHAPTER I

HISTORICAL SETTING AND MEETING

The delegates of the Ukrainian Central Rada arriving in Brest-Litovsk on January 4, 1918, to meet with the representatives of Germany, Austria-Hungary, Bulgaria, and Turkey certainly were not the first Ukrainians facing Germans, Bulgarians or Turks. They were by no means strangers, for the past provided all sides with numerous contacts. Some had been peaceful, some had come during protracted warfare, and some had even been alliances, as was the case with the Ottoman Empire and its subjects —the Crimean Tartars during the sixteenth and seventeenth centuries. This neighborly relationship has been discussed in numerous Ukrainian histories and monographs. Perhaps this may have contributed to a rather sympathetic attitude from the Turkish delegation towards the Ukrainian representatives and their cause during the negotiations.

Similarly, Ukrainian-Bulgarian religious, cultural and literary contacts, beginning with the Kiev Rus' period,[1] was especially rekindled by the prolonged stay of Mykhailo Drahomanov in Sofia during his years of exile.[2] The old historical Bulgarian-Russian friendship could hardly have been a factor in Brest-Litovsk since Bulgaria fought the war on Germany's side, hence, the Ukrainian interest was not in jeopardy, on the contrary, the Bulgarian-Ukrainian relationship during the negotiations and afterwards remained friendly throughout the period of Ukraine's independence.

1

Yet, since Turkey and Bulgaria have played only minor roles in Brest-Litovsk and in the subsequent events, apart from a normal political and economic relationship with Ukraine, the partners that dominated the flow of events were Germany and Austria-Hungary. Of these two, Germany's role and presence in Ukraine became a determining and dominant factor, although Vienna continued to be very present in Brest-Litovsk and then in the South Ukraine through the occupational army.

As far as Germany was concerned, and specifically the German-Ukrainian meetings and encounters, there was a centuries-old tradition. While sharing no common frontiers no visible hostilities of the past had lasting consequences. On the contrary, one can even speak of positive aspects extending into such areas as religion, culture, scholarship, literature, and mutually prevailing views. Some negative experiences caused by Germans in the service of Tsarist Russia were usually identified with Russian policy rather than with the image of the German nation.

The nine-centuries long acquaintance, as revealed by Dmytro Doroshenko,[3] commenced in the tenth century with Princess Olha's dispatch of a special envoy to Emperor Otto (958-959) requesting that he send a bishop and clergy to Kiev. Bruno von Querfurt, the first German who traveled to Kiev in 1007 as Monk Bonifacius reported in his memoirs[4] about Grand Prince Volodymyr. Among other German chroniclers and travelers reporting on Kiev Rus' were Tiethmar von Merseburg (976-1018), and Lambert von Hersfeld. By far the most numerous contacts were made during the sixteenth and seventeenth centuries and caused by the rise and existence of the Cossack State. Much information can be found in the memoirs and works of Siegmund Freiherr von Herberstein (1566-1620), Laurentius Müller († 1598), Erich Lassota von Steblau,[5] Johann Mayer's travel through Ukraine in 1651, the historian Samuel Puffendorf (1632-1694),[6] Johannes Herbinius (1633-1679),[7] and Ulryk Werdum's (1632-?) account of his travel through Ukraine in 1671.[8] Much material can also be found in German newspapers and other publications about Hetman Ivan Mazepa, especially in N. H. Hundling's *Der jetzige Zustand von Europa* (Halle, 1712).

The incorporation of the Cossack Ukraine into the Russian Empire resulted in the decline of the German interest in Ukraine during the eighteenth and nineteenth centuries. Although Ukraine had disappeared from the political map of Europe, information about the land and the people continued to attract some interest among the Germans. This interest was often seen through "Russian eyes," due to the growing friendly Russian-Prussian and Russian-Austrian relations leading to Poland's partitions, and of course, because of the German presence in Russia, including the dynastic ties. On the other hand, Austria's annexation of the Ukrainian-populated provinces of East Galicia and Bukovina after 1772, increased markedly the German and Austrian interest in the Ukrainian problem, leading to the numerous publications.

Much of the eighteenth-century literature on Ukraine in the German language came from the pen of Germans in the employ of Russian institutions, consequently their views reflected Russian policy and interest. Among the best-known works of Friedrich-Christian Weber, Christopher Hermann Manstein (1711-1756), August Ludwig Schlözer (1735-1809) that were commissioned by Catherine II, a work of note on Ukraine is *Neuverändertes Russland* (Leipzig, 1766-1772). Another, Johann Benedikt Scherer, wrote: "Ukraine once possessed its own princes who ruled over Great Russia from Kiev."[9] Yet the foremost German-Hungarian historian contributing to Ukraine's history and its popularization was Johann Christian Engel (1770-1814). This rationalist authored *Geschichte der Ukraine und der ukrainischen Kosaken* (Halle, 1796) which has been recognized by Mykhailo Hrushevskyi and Borys Krupnytskyi as the "first scholarly work on Ukrainian history to be very close to our own scientific prerequisite."[10] His work remained for a long period of time the most dependable source of information about Ukraine for the Western and especially the German reading public.

German interest in Ukraine continued throughout the nineteenth century, often inspired by the incorporation of Galicia into the Habsburg empire. The fame and the tradition of the Cossack Ukraine served as an attractive topic for several authors: Johann Paul Pöhlmann, Carl von Plotto, Franz von Gretmüller and Dr. Ernst Hermann. The best description of Ukraine by travelers were those of Loulau Thürheim (1788-1864), Moritz von Engelhardt and Dr. Friedrich Parrot, August von Behr, Johann Heinrich Blasius (1809-1870) and Freiherr von Haxthausen (1792-1866), to name just a few.

The Ukrainian issue in some way began to reflect European international diplomacy, especially during the last quarter of the nineteenth century. Rapidly deteriorating relations between Russia and Germany and Austria-

Hungary brought new interest for Ukraine as exemplified in the thought of the philosopher Eduard von Hartmann (1842-1906).[12] Possibly instigated by Otto von Bismarck himself, Hartmann proposed the creation of the "Kingdom of Kiev" which would lead to the weakening of Russia and would prevent her expansion toward the Balkan peninsula. Admittedly, his concept was not motivated by Ukrainian national aspirations; nonetheless, it coincided with the prolonged process of the Ukrainian national rebirth during the second half of the nineteenth century.

Ukraine found also much attention in Sarmaticus' (pseud.) book, *Von der Weichsel zum Dnjepr. Geographische, kriegsgeschichtliche und operative Studie* (Hannover, 1886) extolling the positive Ukrainian traits, in contrast to the rather negative portrayal of the Russians. From among other authors of the period concerned with Ukraine Friedrich Bodensteddt, Dr. A. J. Braver, and the linguist Dr. Carl Abel deserve special mention.[13]

From the perspective of the early twentieth century, one may conclude that Ukraine and her people were not strangers to the Germanic world. The encounters of the previous centuries became even more intensive during the nineteenth century due to the immediate contacts of both worlds within the Habsburg empire.[14] Here, for the first time, Ukrainians were exposed to German history, culture, literature, political thoughts and institutions not only in schools but through direct participation in all spheres of the Empire's life and activities. Through translations and available monographs association was reciprocal. Vienna emerged as the prime meeting place, whereas German universities welcomed Ukrainian students in increasing numbers. Of course, neither Austria-Hungary nor Germany could have ignored the rise of Ukrainian national consciousness, the spread of national rebirth followed by political activism in Galicia as well as in Ukraine under Russian rule. Indeed, the Ukrainian question was rapidly becoming a European issue involving not only two great powers —Austria-Hungary and Russia, but also geographically as well as economically important territory. Ukraine was the famous "bread-basket" of Europe and soon would become Russia's asset and also a trouble-spot. Between 1909 and 1913 Ukraine produced annually ten percent of the world's output of grain (250 million tons). Eighty percent of Russia's grain export came from Ukraine.[15]

Not surprisingly, the twentieth century witnessed a rise of German and Austrian interest in the Ukrainian question, reflected in the number and substance of the literature published. Of course, World War I served as the immediate cause. The pioneering task belongs to Paul Rohrbach, a publicist, who even before the war held a sympathetic interest for the Ukrainian political struggle, and the well-known historian Otto Hoetzsch. Soon, Ukrainian topics became popular with German newspapers, journals, and monographs.[16] Rohrbach, the prolific and influential Baltic German author,[17] was the first to treat the Ukrainian issue as a political one. He favored Ukraine's independence and linked the German interest with the Ukrainian cause. His concept, envisioning the break-up of the Russian empire through the independence of Ukraine and of the other nationalities, thereby removing Russia from Central Europe, assumed special importance due to his employment with the Center for Foreign Services, a division within the Foreign Office (Auswärtiges Amt—AA). This position offered him a chance to influence somewhat the thinking of German government officials as well as German public opinion in general.

Of no lesser importance in informing Germans about Ukraine was a work by Professor Otto Hoetzsch, *Russland: Eine Einführung auf Grund seiner Geschichte von 1904 bis 1912* (Berlin, 1913). There, in a special chapter "The Ukrainian Question," Hoetzsch stressed the separateness of the Ukrainians from the Russians. The Ukrainians were "purer Slavs," and possessed of a uniquely "democratic spirit." Hoetzsch pointed to their growing political and national aspirations, which in a period of rumblings within the Russian empire could be employed accordingly. This quite prophetic prediction became a reality by 1917/18, an event that should not have surprised the German political establishment, especially due to the steady increase of publications and the activities of such men as Axel Schmidt, Silvio Broedlich-Kuhrmahlen, Professor Paul Förster, Johann von Ardesch, Hans Hartmayer, Karl Nötzel, Georg Cleinow, Otto Kessler, Professor Albrecht Penck, Professor Hans Übersberger, and many others.[18]

A few samples would illustrate the formation of German thinking about Ukraine's importance in the context of the war with Russia and a new potential for Germany's policy. J. von Ardesch in an article "The Ukrainian Question" in *Hamburger Nachrichten* (September 6, 1914) had considered Ukraine to be the most important factor of European policy. Professor Förster in *Tägliche Rundschau* (October 23, 1914), discussing the consequences of the war, insisted on the independence of Ukraine as a means to weaken Russia. Hans Hartmeyer in the Berlin weekly *Das Neue*

Deutschland (nos. 14-17, 1915) equated an independent Ukraine with Germany's basic interests. Similarly, Dr. Karl Nötzel in his brochure[19] insisted on Ukrainian independence as an instrument of defense against the continuous Russian danger to Germany and Austria-Hungary. During 1916 Albrecht Panck, Paul Rohrbach, General Baron K. Gebsattel, and several others, had toured Germany with public lectures on the importance of Ukraine for Germany and her foreign trade. Otto Kessler in his pamphlet[20] provided detailed statistical data on Ukraine's agricultural production and export with the assurance that the Central Powers would welcome an independent Ukraine. Dr. Paul Ostwald's publication,[21] having outlined the Ukrainian national awakening, proposed a personal union between a free Ukraine and Austria-Hungary. One of the most active supporters of the Ukrainian cause, Axel Schmidt, having revealed Russia's political plans, concluded that only the loss of Ukraine will diminish and restrict Russia's expansion in Europe, and especially the peril to Germany's Berlin-Bagdad commercial connection.[22] The well-known geo-politician, Professor Albrecht Penck, in an essay "Ukraine,"[23] insisted that Ukraine's tectonic structure is characteristic of that of Central Europe and not of Eastern Europe. Equally so Ukrainians in their social-economic habit are similar to the Czechs and Poles. Therefore, Ukraine's destiny should be the restoration of her seventeenth-century independence and the return to the Central-European civilization. Economically Ukraine possessed all the prerequisites for an independent state.

Considering the amount of knowledge about Ukraine during the first three years of the war, one could expect that that knowledge would be used by politicians at a time when they would have to deal with the U-krainian state in 1918. By that time Germany and her allies had been provided an opportunity to conclude the first peace treaty of World War I. In light of such potential development the treaty with Ukraine, together with the subsequent German behavior and policy in Ukraine until November 1918, can also be used for a comparative study with the Versailles Peace Treaty and with the post-World War I policies of the victorious Entente powers. This would make the Brest-Litovsk treaty a testing factor with far-reaching consequences in European modern history.

CHAPTER II

UKRAINIAN DRIVE TOWARDS STATEHOOD

The period of the Ukrainian Cossack State (Hetmanate) during the seventeenth and eighteenth centuries was neither the first nor the last in the over one thousand-year-old history of the Ukrainian people. Ukrainian historians of that period have seen the Cossack State as a successor to Medieval Kiev Rus'.[1] Hetman Bohdan Khmelnytskyi called himself "Autocrat of Rus' by the grace of God," and intended to liberate the entire Rus' people from Polish rule as far as Lublin and Cracow. Thus the Patriarch Paisic of Jerusalem bestowed upon him the title "Prince" (*kniaz'*) of Rus'." Hetman Ivan Vyhovs'kyi signed a treaty in 1658 at Hadiach by which Ukraine joined the Polish Commonwealth as the Grand Rus' Principality. It became, along with Poland and Lithuania, a separate political entity, united with others through the person of the king.

The very idea of national consciousness and of statehood survived the final liquidation of the Littlerussian College in 1781 in Ukraine and the incorporation of the Hetmanate into the Russian empire. With the dismantling of the political and administrative framework of the Cossack State, together with the cleverly implemented policy of denationalization, the Ukrainian national identity suffered enormous setbacks, especially within the national elite—the former Cossack elders, the nobility, and civil servants. The traditional national loyalties were often exchanged for tsarist rewards of advancement and material advantages.

7

In fact, as many Ukrainian national historians agree, the Ukrainian national situation of the first half of the nineteenth century worsened more during the second half of the eighteenth century. While they differ on the causes and forms, most of them agree that the collapse of will on the part of the nobility and the educated elite made it easier, or perhaps possible, for the Russian regime to reduce the whole Ukrainian problem to past memories, folklore, and ethnographic curiosity and to voluntary cultural russification. However, deeply rooted dissatisfaction, the national character, and especially awareness of the negative impact of the Russian rule over Ukraine survived in various quarters of the society. Eyewitness accounts report: "Ukraine is not blessed with good fortunes despite the kindness of nature. The political sun does not warm her as much as the heavenly one. She is exhausted from having suffered various hardships and from the sense of the loss of her liberty of by-gone centuries."[2] One Russian traveler wrote:

> Regretably I have to end the report on Ukrainian morality with an unpleasant characteristic: I must speak about their abhorrence toward the Great-Russian. . . . One can hear often 'Good man, but moskal.' But that is not all. They convey these feelings to their children and do scare them with the Muscovites (moskaliamy). By invoking that name a frightened child stops weeping.[3]

Still another observer, the German John G. Kohl, during the 1830s reported:

> The contempts which the people of Littlerussia feel in regard to the people of Greatrussia is so strong that one can rightly characterize it as national hatred. Since the 17th century when this country was first brought under Muscovite Tsardom these feelings have not diminished, on the contrary, they have increased. . . . Littlerussians are saying that until their subjugation by Moscow they were free people and serfdom was unknown to them. The Russians made one-half of the population serfs. Before, Littlerussia had its hetmans and its own constitution and privileges, but all that was wiped out by backward tsarist reforms. The battle of Poltava is being remembered and compared with the battle remembered by the Czech people at White Mountain. Should the Russian empire disintegrate in the future

there is no doubt that the Littlerussians will organize a separate state. They have their own language, their historical memories, they seldom mix with the Russians and there are ten million of them.[4]

The existence of national consciousness below the "official surface" and in the privacy of homes was of little significance, unless it could be translated and reactivated by either a man of historical greatness or by an extraordinary combination of events. All of these stimuli were absent in the first half of the nineteenth century while the Ukrainian situation continued to worsen, especially under the oppressive regime of Nicholas I. Taras Shevchenko identified the period as the time of silence, stretching from the Black Sea and the Caucasus to the Baltic Sea.

By the middle of the nineteenth century a Ukrainian "great awakener," a poet, appeared on the scene of the nation's darkened landscape—Taras Shevchenko. His *Kobzar* (Collection of Poems), his appeal and vision of freedom came in time to reverse the trend of decline in will and spirit. He ordered his countrymen to read, to learn and to respect the native wisdom. Instead of portraying the hopelessness, Shevchenko assured the people that they will get their George Washington, yet not through prayers and pacifist inaction but through struggle and blood: "Fight to win," and learn "how to rule" since only in "one's home there is one's justice, strength and freedom."

Yet his generation of serfs and servile-minded individuals neither understood him nor had the courage to follow his "commandments." Therefore in his prophetic wisdom he addressed himself to the future generations, too. Nonetheless, the process of national awakening was slow; it had to pass through Romanticism, typified by periods of "Ukrainophilism," "*khlopomanstvo*" (devotion to the peasantry), "Populism," and only then to merge into Socialism and Nationalism of the late nineteenth and early twentieth centuries.

Even before nationalist ideology began to spread, the Austrian Consul in Kiev, Edward Serdiaczek reported in 1893 to Vienna:

> The Littlerussian national movement is growing as before, however, it maintains extreme caution. . . . I personally know numerous administrators and teachers who, in private conversations reveal their anti-government feelings . . . .It is interesting to observe that

increasingly historical and ethnographic studies are published in the Russian language about Littlerussia. This is understandable due to the censorship prohibiting the use of the Littlerussian language. Secret circles are spreading throughout the country contributing to the rise of Littlerussian patriotism.[5]

Quite identical information was forthcoming from a Russian author, S. N. Shchegolev. Apart from his anti-Ukrainian bias, his book reflects the impression that on the eve of World War I the whole of "South Russia," was undermined with Ukrainian national activities.[6] The special value of this book was not in its becoming a sort of "guide for the police," but more in its contribution to the understanding of the Ukrainian "miracle of 1917."[7]

While it remains debatable how deep and how far the national idea had penetrated the masses, its slow development was not a sign of Ukrainian inability or even of the superficiality of the movement, as portrayed by antagonists. The responsibility for its lethargic growth rests first of all with the severity of the Russian suppressive measures typified by Piotr Valuev's decree and the Ems *ukaze* (1863 and 1876), prohibiting publication and import of books in the Ukrainian language. These were practices rather unknown in the histories of other European empires. The Russians' extreme anti-Ukrainian measures and policy could only partially be counterbalanced by West Ukrainians in Galicia under the Habsburg rule, especially through the activities of the Shevchenko Scientific Society, the establishment and existence of educational and cultural organizations and of the political parties gaining experience in political activism.

The appearance on the Ukrainian political scene of Mykhailo Drahomanov (1841-1885)[8] at the crucial stage of its development proved to be of great importance, in addition to the impact of the Russian socialist movement upon Ukrainian students and the intelligentsia. His intellectual strength, his excellent education and scholarly ability, in addition to his journalistic skill, influenced enormously the political outlook of a whole generation.[9] His political and social programs exhibited Liberalism, Cosmopolitanism, Internationalism, Socialism and Federalism as well as anti-Nationalism, which he expressed often and freely in contrast to Shevchenko's glorification of the past and of nationalism. Perhaps at any other period of Ukrainian history Drahomanov's contribution to political and social thought would have been welcomed and justified. However, considering his enormous influence upon the formation of Ukrainian thinking, his role at that time proved a negative factor. His work became a force that deeply divided the intelligentsia of this stateless people, and disarmed them with slogans instead of preparing them for the national ideals in the spirit of G. Mazzini. His preaching of "socialist federative communes" (*hromady po vsii Ukraini*) hardly could mobilize the whole people for one national cause. Drahomanov, an exponent of European Utopian Socialism, in fact asked Ukrainians to forget even the modest program of the Cyril and Methodius Brotherhood of 1847-48, which spoke of a federation of all Slavic nations, with Ukraine becoming an equal partner in it. His animosity toward Ukrainian nationalism forced Ivan Franko to distance himself from him and to expose him as "gente Ukrainus, natione Russus."

While many Ukrainians became confused with Drahomanov's exercise of a "great vision," and thus were lost for the national cause, there were others who committed themselves to the national priority. For one, U-krainian students at St. Petersburg University in 1883 organized a "U-krainian Social-Federalist" group that accepted a federative system providing that each nationality of the Russian empire would be free to either remain in such a federation or to proclaim an independent state. In 1891 the newly created "Brotherhood of Tarases" committed itself to Shevchenko's insistence on political independence despite Drahomanov's denial for the need of sovereignty.[10] Among the members were Ivan Lypa, Mykola Mikhnovs'kyi, Mykhailo Kotsiubyns'kyi, Borys Hrincenko, Mykola Voronyi; some of them subsequently emerged as national leaders.[11] The *Tarasivtsi* program demanded separation and independence of Ukraine, but to socialist members the idea of independence was simply a "Ukrainian Don Quixote-ism."[12] The majority of the organization made public their views in *Pravda* (April 1893):

> Humanity consists of races, nationalities and nations. . . . We know that the Russian state is a superficial aggregate of many nations united only by the powers of the autocrat, therefore the very idea of absolutism is dead, only the nation is a living body. The very existence of the Ukrainian people demonstrates that Ukraine existed, is, and will remain always a separate nation and like any other nation

Ukraine is in need of national freedom. . . . Ukraine is suppressed, therefore we, Ukraine's children, like sons of a nation, are nationalists and first of all we concern ourselves with the restoration, with our people's national liberty. For us conscious Ukrainians exists only one Ukrainian-Ruthenian people. . . . We strive to increase and to spread in Ukraine a national spirit, to regenerate and to promote among the intelligentsia and the people national feelings. . . . We wish to bring about changes which will foster, in contrast to the existing situation, a free development and a complete satisfaction of the moral, social and political needs of the people.

This eloquent expression and dedication to the national cause written in the style of Mazzini's "Young Italy" program, could have gained broad acceptance among the masses provided a sufficient number of patriots would have been willing to join that group. Yet too many joined the Russian radicals and helped them to popularize socialist programs in Ukraine.

The last decade of the nineteenth and the first decade of the twentieth century witnessed a somewhat brighter picture in Habsburg-ruled Galicia where Ukrainians, less affected by the powerful Russian radical movement and in close contact with Western European culture and political conditions, partially compensated for all the setbacks of their brethren in Dnieper Ukraine. There, in a truly "Ukrainian Piedmont," despite obstacles from the hostile Poles and Vienna's hesitation, Ukrainians had matured politically in a different direction. In 1890, the Radical Party emerged, which one year later, after the death of Drahomanov, committed itself to political independence. While Mykhailo Pavlyk remained loyal to Drahomanov's internationalism, a co-founder of the party, Ivan Franko chose to side with the nationalists. His critics were rebuffed in the article "Outside of the boundaries of the possible" in *Literaturno-Naukovyi Vistnyk* (1900): "We have to feel with our hearts our ideals, we must explain with reason to ourselves, we must use all power and means in order to get nearer to our national ideal."

In the same year, on July 15, in a meeting in Lviv (Lemberg), Ukrainian students resolved: "Only an independent national state will secure for the Ukrainian people full freedom of development."[13] But the campaign for the West Ukrainian minds and hearts was not an easy one either.[14] In addition to a strong Russophile movement generously financed by the Russian Panslavists, there was also a lack of an educated elite, in addition to a high percentage of illiterate peasants. Also, the diversity of political, social, and economic orientations among the intelligentsia was detrimental. For instance, the renowned Julian Bachynskyi in his *Ukraina irredenta* (1895) advised Ukrainians of the importance of evolutionary strategy, expecting that the economic development in Ukraine would force Russia to accommodate Ukrainian political aspirations. This reasoning of "one step forward, two steps back," apart from the uncertainty as to expected results, hardly could stimulate the political activism sorely needed at that time. This was understood by the most eloquent spokesman of nationalism, Mykola Mikhnovs'kyi, from the Russian Ukraine. This "Ukrainian Mazzini" had initiated a new chapter in the history of the formation of Ukrainian political thought and had laid a theoretical foundation for modern nationalism. His work *Samostiina Ukraina* (Lviv, 1900) remained the textbook for the Nationalists. The book stresses two basic themes: (1) The devastating consequences of the Russian rule led to spiritual serfdom, national decay and psychological submissiveness; (2) The only resolution for the subjugated nation lay in an armed uprising against the oppressor. To Mikhnovs'kyi,

> The existence of an independent state is the main condition for a nation's being, . . . the sovereign state represents the natinal ideal in international relations. . . . The Ukrainian nation went through a long and difficult interval in its history. The interlude began in 1654, when the Ukrainian Cossack republic accepted political union with the Muscovite state. From that time on, the Ukrainian nation slowly faded politically as well as culturally and became nationally exhausted. In 1876, the issue of a *ukaz* condemned our nationality to die. In the schools our children are made the enemies of our people. Even in the church our enemy's language prevails.

As soon as Mikhnovs'kyi's view became known, a number of RUP members of socialist conviction began to attack him, forcing him and his followers to set up a separate organization, the Ukrainian National Party. To the socialists' attack he answered: "Let the frightful and apostates go to our enemy camp, there is no place for them among us. All those in U-kraine who are not with us are against us. Ukraine for Ukrainians."

Now the dividing lines separating Socialists from Nationalists would not only widen, but would soon lead to the most devastating results affecting Ukraine's future. Retrospectively, it was Mikhnovs'kyi's nationalism and not socialism that could have better prepared Ukrainians for their confrontation with Russia, and especially with the Bolsheviks under the leadership of the great tactician Lenin. Socialism did not prove itself to be an effective instrument in the complex process of rebuilding the Ukrainian national state.

By 1905, the nationalists were outnumbered by socialists within the RUP's organization, which subsequently split up into the Ukrainian Socialist Democratic Workers Party (which limited its program to Ukrainian autonomy), and the Ukrainian Socialist Democratic Union, led by D. Antonovych (which proclaimed itself a branch of the Russian Socialist Democratic Workers Party in Ukraine). Antonovych in an article "Non-existing question" in *Pratsia* (1905) stated that "The national problem is an invention of the bourgeoisie to blind the class-conscious of the proletariat, and as the proletariat is concerned this question does not exist."[15] After 1908, several members of the Union joined the Bolsheviks,[16] and the newly organized Ukrainian Socialist Revolutionary Party having copied its program from the Russian S. R., joined a common front with them in activities which helped spread their programs in Ukrainian villages.

At the other end of the political spectrum, Mikhnovs'kyi and his followers formed the Ukrainian National Party in 1902, which remained the strongest national party until 1917, only to merge in that year with the Ukrainian Party of Independent Socialists. The party's program, known as the "Ten Commandments," prepared by Mikhnovs'kyi demanded among other things:

> One Ukraine, undivided from the Carpathian Mountains to the Caucasus, independent, free and democratic Ukrainian Republic—that is an all-Ukrainian national ideal; Ukraine for Ukrainians! Therefore remove from Ukraine all foreign oppressors; everywhere and always use the Ukrainian language. Do not become a renegade or traitor. Respect the patriots of your native country; hate the enemies and traitors of your country.

Consequently, the party's attention turned to the working class and its economic interest which was proclaimed to be of national concern in order to neutralize the socialist propaganda, especially among Ukrainian workers.

National honor and respect for workers requires that on the Ukrainian territory the struggle against exploitation will become the workers' responsibility. . . . The Ukrainian worker should know that his liberation is the task of Ukrainian workers and no one else. The Ukrainian workers' union will protect against capitalists and Russians alike.

The National Party paid equal attention to the interest of the intelligentsia and peasantry. After 1905 it began to publish pamphlets and newspapers in the Ukrainian language, *Khliborob* in Lubny city, and *Slobozhanshchyna* in Kharkiv. Moreover, the members of the party set up an underground militant organization, *"Oborona Ukrainy,"* for terrorist activities against all symbols of the Russian presence in Ukraine including destruction of monuments and state buildings. New opportunities for Ukrainian activities opened after the 1905 revolution in Russia.

Literature, often a medium of nationalism, began to appear. The principal examples were the works of O. Oles', S. Cherkasenko, and H. Chuprynka. Strikes in support of Ukrainian schools spread across Ukraine, the rise of *Prosvita* Houses and especially the establishment of the Ukrainian Scientific Society in Kiev were the best testimonies to the strength of the Ukrainian national movement and its future potential. The popular commitment to nationalism between 1905 and 1908 challenged and questioned sceptics and adversaries of the idea of national independence.

On the political level Ukrainians succeeded in sending forty-four representatives to the First Duma, and forty-seven to the Second in spite of an elaborate indirect electoral system. Exactly this increased Ukrainian visibility brought about a new wave of Russian oppressive measures. The "Black Hundreds" and Piotr Stolypin's reaction generated various prohibitive means and forced many Ukrainians into exile. Again, as after the 1860s, this setback was somewhat alleviated by Ukrainian achievements in Galicia and by concentration on economic activities mainly in organizing cooperatives. By remaining less vocal politically until 1917, Ukrainians did what other nations did before them; they built social, economic, cultural, and educational structures for the future.

* * *

The Ukrainian people faced World War I and the subsequent turn of events in a state that could best be characterized as only "half-prepared" for national statehood. In the words of John S. Reshetar, "In 1917 the rebirth of the Ukrainian nation was not an accomplished fact. Relatively few of the inhabitants of Ukraine were fully conscious of their nationality. Two and a half centuries of union with the Russians had left their mark."[17] The small number of intelligentsia, torn apart by ideological, social and political views, a still largely peasant-structured society with russified and polonized cities, and the lack of friends and allies abroad were the most serious obstacles with which Ukraine had to contend.

Of no lesser importance was the quality of leadership available in those eventual years. One could suggest that with the proper leadership, the right time and with favorable conditions present, even a "half-prepared" nation had a chance to maintain its regained statehood. However, lacking two out of three such requisites, and facing two formidable enemies—the Poles in the West and Soviet Russia in the North, the odds prevailed. Exactly within this "game of numbers" a still powerful Germany could have become the decisive force in pushing the pendulum of events to the Ukrainian side.[18]

The Ukrainian reaction to the collapse of the tsarist regime in Russia in early March 1917 and the growing revolution there came relatively quickly and with the promise of playing a major role in the formation of a new future. Lacking representation in the Fourth Duma and in the Russian power-structure, Ukrainians had been left with only one alternative—to build up their own political apparatus from the bottom. On March 17, 1917, Ukrainian activists reactivated in Kiev the Society of Ukrainian Progressives which initiated the creation of a new representative body, including representatives of the Ukrainian socialist parties. It was named the Central Rada (Council). Within a few weeks a large number of delegates of military, social, and political organizations joined the Rada creating *de facto* in a most uncertain period the first free representative institution of Ukraine. The renowned Professor Mykhailo Hrushevskyi was elected *in absentia* chairman of the Rada, which recognized the Provisional Government in Petrograd and expressed its belief that "in a free Russia all legal rights of the Ukrainian people will be guaranteed."[19] On April 22, addressing itself to the "Ukrainian nation, peasants, workers, soldiers, townspeople, clergy and intelligentsia," the Rada assured the thirty million Ukrainians that soon "they will live among friendly free nations and should build for themselves a new free life."[20]

The Progressives issued an appeal to Ukrainians urging them to proceed with ukrainization, education, culture and a press, and promised to work for autonomy for Ukraine in a federally-structured new Russia. On April 17-21, the first All-Ukrainian National Congress gathered in Kiev attracting nine hundred delegates from a variety of newly-emerging organizations. The adopted resolution demanded territorial autonomy, federation as a new order for Russia with frontiers among the states based on ethnographic principles and Ukraine's participation in any future peace conference. The Congress increased the Rada's membership to one hundred fifty and added much to its respectability. Taking advantage of the prevailing freedom, Ukrainian newspapers began to emerge in great numbers spreading good news and national spirit from Kiev across the country. Clearly, the prevailing atmosphere in Ukraine during the Spring of 1917 reflected a typical national character more than a socialist revolution.

The ukrainization of the army on March 22, and the creation of the "Supreme Military Council" as well as General Pavlo Skoropadskyi's ukrainization of his regiment, unmistakably pointed to the coming of a national revolution. Moreover, the Rada demand in its First and Second universals for political autonomy supports the foregoing contention.

Still another event of that early period conveyed the message to Petrograd. On March 29 a "celebration of freedom" took place in Kiev attracting over 100,000 participants marching under 320 Ukrainian yellow and blue national flags including tens of thousands of Ukrainian soldiers, students, workes, and civil servants. Hrushevskyi urged the participants not to rest until autonomy for Ukraine was secured. A resolution of that mass meeting recognized the Central Rada as the representative institution of the Ukrainian people and demanded from the Provisional Government recognition of Ukrainian autonomy.

The Central Rada's road to statehood was a difficult undertaking. Prevailing war conditions, the Provisional Government's refusal to act on the pressing national issue, and the Rada's hesitation to act more forcefully were some of the obstacles.

In order to function as a representative organ the Central Rada set up a so-called Little Rada (*Mala Rada*) composed of the Rada's Presidium and twenty-five other members, and the General Secretariat as the executive branch with the Social Democrat Volodymyr Vynnychenko as head of the Secretariat, or General Secretary. With a majority of Social Democrats, the Secretariat became an instrument for socialist policies and programs. Together with the Social Revolutionary Party, the socialists emerged as the dominant majority in the Rada, resulting in the social and political radicalization of this first Ukrainian "government." This in turn led to long-term consequences in both the domestic and foreign affairs areas and the Rada's failure to resolve the internal problems, to unify the country and finally to defend it.

The Central Rada was in charge of Ukrainian affairs from April 21, 1917 to April 28, 1918. Its existence can be divided into two phases: (1) From its inception to January 22, 1918; (2) From January 22 to April 28, 1918. The first period symbolized by three universals, elevating the Ukrainian political and national aspirations to the level of autonomy within a "Federative Democratic Russian Republic" (which in fact never materialized) and coincided roughly with the existence of the Russian Provisional Government and the war against the Central Powers. Securing *de facto* autonomy for Ukraine as can be understood from the text of the Second universal of July 16 was the most important accomplishment.

The fall of the Provisional Government and the Bolshevik seizure of power in Russia together with the ensuing uncertainty placed the Rada in a new position demanding a new clarification of the status of Ukraine. This was done with the Third universal of November 20, proclaiming the creation of the Ukrainian People's Republic (*Ukrains'ka Narodna Respublyka*). Becoming officially then a state entity, the Rada decided to preserve the federal form with the nonexistent Russian Republic; "a federation of equal and free peoples."[21]

Having become officially a state-nation and without the co-federative Russian republic, the Rada, instead of providing the young state with all the instruments of defense and government such as a national army, an administration and a police force, began to introduce socialist programs. The socialization of land, control of industry, abolishment of capital punishment hardly could contribute to the solidification and stabilization of the country nor could these programs provide the government with the instruments of control and enforcement of the Rada's laws and regulations. Equally so, the promise to continue a war in which Ukrainians had no interest, except dying for Russia, multiplied the Rada's problems. Its large number of proclamations, decrees, and legal acts became an impressive catalog of good intentions that could not be translated into realities.

Yet the Rada had a mandate to represent and to govern the Ukrainian people as proven by the results of the election of November 1917 to the All-Russian Constituent Assembly, the only free election in Russian history. The Ukrainian political parties received eighty percent of the votes with only ten percent for the Bolsheviks. Therefore, it was up to the Rada to act accordingly and forcefully in light of events in Russia, the Bolshevik propaganda and the chaotic situation in Ukraine. The Rada misread the events in Russia, the nature of the Bolshevik regime and the significance of the Bolshevik activities in Kiev and Kharkiv, where a tiny minority of the Ukrainian Bolsheviks proclaimed a Ukrainian Socialist Soviet Republic on December 30. Only the Russian attack in December forced the General Secretariat to recognize officially the volunteer military units, remnants from the former 34th Corps commanded by General Skoropadskyi. By January, the Central Rada managed to send to the northern front two battalions, the Galician Batallion of *Sichovi Striltsi,* and the Auxiliary Student Battallion that was wiped out by the Bolshevik Red Guard on January 30, 1918 at Kuty. Some two thousand defenders were no match for the 20,000 man Soviet Russian army.

With their illusions coming to a tragic end, with Lenin's ultimatum of December 7, and the invasion of Soviet troops under V. Antonov-Ovsiienko on December 25, the Rada, still with only a token force in retreat, proclaimed on January 22, 1918 Ukraine's independence with the Fourth universal.[22] With the enemy at the gate of Kiev, in addition to several Bolshevik uprisings in Ukrainian cities and progressive demoralization of several army units, Ukraine's independence was about to end. Only if an unexpected chain of events would have taken place in the obscure town on the north-western border of Ukraine—Brest-Litovsk—could her independence have been preserved. Remaining weak and socialist the Rada had to be saved, at least for a while, by the armies of the Central Powers as a consequence of the February 9, 1918 treaty. The Ukrainian government returned to Kiev in early March determined to continue its socialist policy under the protection of the German Imperial army.

CHAPTER III

ON THE EVE OF THE BREST-LITOVSK
PEACE CONFERENCE

The journey to Brest-Litovsk and the meeting of the representatives of
the countries involved was indeed extraordinary for it brought together
very different partners with seemingly common yet essentially opposite
expectations. Four delegations representing established "old regimes,"
—Germany, Austria-Hungary, the Ottoman Empire, and Bulgaria, had
nothing in common with the delegation of the Soviet Russian communist
regime, and only limited similarity existed between the Four and the
young socialists representing the newly emerged, yet not stabilized Ukrainian National Republic. Nonetheless, they all came and agreed to negotiate
an end to the long-lasting war that badly affected all of them at that time.
They also agreed to overlook their basic interests and intentions, to toler-
ate each other at the negotiating table, and finally to conclude agreements
ending the war and initiating a new, unknown, relationship. This particular
uncertainty was only multiplied by ongoing warfare on the Western and
Italian fronts. Brest-Litovsk certainly was not another Congress of Vienna
nor even a Congress of Berlin in 1878. It signaled a very new and different
period for the countries involved. None of them was aware what the future
would hold; whereas in Vienna and Berlin the makers of the settlement to
a certain degree were in a position to "foresee the future" since they were
able to determine the future, at least for the period immediately following
the negotiations.

Perhaps for this reason, some negotiators at the Brest-Litovsk meeting should have had the "foresight of great statesmen," which at the last moment could have turned the flow of history. Options and alternatives were available to all of them, but the settlement of other problems remained a big gamble that created big losers and big winners as well. History textbooks have provided a sufficient amount of information on the Brest-Litovsk treaty of March 3, 1918 between the Central Powers and Soviet Russia, but the treaty with Ukraine still warrants more attention as to its real as well as its potential importance.

In late November it became obvious that the survival of Ukraine depended on the support of the great powers. Consequently Oleksander Shulhyn, the acting foreign minister initiated contacts with the French Military Mission as to the possibility of securing France's support. He was also aware that in the absence of French backing Ukraine would come under German influence.[1] The Rada's pro-French orientation was encouraged by General Tabouis of France and British Major Fitzwilliams' call on Shulhyn offering their respective countries' assistance in the establishment of the new state. Shulhyn on his part requested recognition and exchange of diplomatic representatives. No action was taken until mid-December when Tabouis in a note of December 18 forwarded, on behalf of the French government, expressions of sympathy to the Ukrainian government for its efforts in continuing its resistance to the Central Powers and the desire to remain faithful to the Allies.[2] Tabouis' generous assurance that "France's sympathy toward Ukraine was realistic and real," was followed by a similar expression by Great Britain of "good will for Ukraine and her support in the struggle against the Central Powers, the enemies of democracy and humanity." This last was conveyed by Picton Bagge, the British representative in Ukraine.

On January 3, Tabouis informed Vynnychenko, the General Secretary, about his appointment as France's official representative to the Ukrainian government.[3] Vynnychenko and Shulhyn mistakenly thought that these notes amounted to *de-jure* recognition of Ukraine by the governments of France and Great Britain. In fact, this was officially denied by the French ambassador as well as the claim that both countries obliged themselves to support Ukraine morally as well as legally. Ambassador Noulens disavowed Tabouis' formulation of the stated position.[5] He even argued that France refused *de-facto* recognition of Ukraine, insisting that Ukraine lacked the attributes of a sovereign state. The entire confusion, clarification and claims of that period—December through January—revealed only France's and England's commitment to preserve an indivisible Russia as ally. This, of course, meant that neither had any intention of seeing Ukraine become an independent state.

Vynnychenko had to know this since in his conversation with Tabouis before January 3, he informed him about the negotiation with the Central Powers assuring him that Ukraine did not consider retreating from the position taken.[6] Doroshenko concluded that the Entente Powers' attitude and policy toward Ukraine was limited only to the desire of organizing several army units of Ukrainians to continue the war against the Central Powers along with the Czech and Polish military units. There was never expressed a sincere desire to support Ukraine in her existence; the situation was somewhat similar to the Provisional Government's commitment to continue the war, a fact that enormously contributed to its downfall. It was Ukraine's turn to fight the war without being recognized or promised any advantages. On the contrary, for Ukraine war served only as a self-destructive force. This became even more obvious with Lenin's peace propaganda and his dispatch of the Soviet delegation to Brest-Litovsk on December 2 without any consultation with the Central Rada. Moreover, lacking a strong army and facing the Soviet Russian threat and imminent invasion, the desire to end the war, as it has been stated already in the Third universal, became imperative. In other words, the Central Rada was forced to seek peace as a consequence of Russia's decision, her own inability to protect the country, and her own inability to control domestic affairs. Within this context of events and conditions, the Entente Powers' role became a secondary factor for they were in no real position either to act or to change the prevailing realities in Ukraine and in Soviet Russia.

The erstwhile Ukrainian interest in peace was of a general nature, i.e., and end to the war on all fronts as had been discussed in the Little Rada's meeting on December 4. There the concept of peace had been linked to Ukrain's becoming and remaining an independent state. No talk concerned a separate peace with the Central Powers. The Rada decided to send delegations with a peace proposal to the fronts (Romanian and German-Austrian—as well as to the Entente Powers and to inform the Council of the People's Commissars in Petrograd of its intent. The situation grew almost intolerable and even dangerous for Ukraine when the Soviet regime concluded an armistice with the Central Powers in Brest-Litovsk on December 15 in the name of "all Russia," i.e., Ukraine as well. It amounted to involvement of Ukraine into the process of negotiations without consultation and a complete disregard of the existence of the Central Rada.

Yet even this chain of events did not convince the Rada of the necessity of directly negotiating with the Central Powers. At the meeting of the Central Rada on December 25, Shulhyn insisted on the participation of all nationalities of Russia in negotiations, rejecting Soviet Russia's right to sign an agreement on behalf of all other peoples that would only enable German and Austrian troops to march against France and England, "We should stand for peace and democracy in the whole world." German historian Erwin Hölzle had to admit that, "in the largest country neighboring the German area of interest, in Ukraine foreign policy initially was anti-German."[8] On December 26, Vynnychenko assured the Central Rada, "that France, England, USA, Belgium and Romania would show an interest in the Ukrainian republic, and while remaining reserved all of them in due time extend us a helping hand."[9]

Six days after the peace negotiation between Soviet Russia and the Central Powers' officially began on December 22, the Rada, having heard a report by M. Liubynskyi, observer in Brest-Litovsk, decided to dispatch immediately an official Ukrainian delegation to participate in the ongoing negotiations. On January 3, the Ukrainin delegation headed by the young Vsevolod Holubovych left for Brest-Litovsk. They arrived without the detailed instructions, papers, supporting documents and material needed for any international negotiation. There was not even enough time to prepare the young delegates in the art of diplomacy. This fact should be remembered when discussing their difficulties, their performance and their accomplishment. Because of lack of time, neither the Secretariat nor the Rada itself could provide the delegation with elaborate and detailed guidelines. Only in an *ad hoc* meeting Hrushevskyi instructed them on the main issues and the position to be taken in negotiations. Among them the incorporation of Galicia, Kholmland, Bukovina, and Transcarpathian Ruthenia into Ukraine were to be demanded. He also provided them with an ethnographic map and a map of Ukraine's borders in the north-west. In the case of an Austrian-Hungarian refusal, Hrushevskyi insisted on the creation of a separate (Ukrainian) crownland within the Monarchy with broad autonomy.[10] This was, indeed, not only an ambitious all-Ukrainian undertaking, but also a great and difficult task, considering all the international as well as internal factors unfavorable for the Ukrainian cause.

* * *

Until late 1917 the Ukrainians from the Russian empire, including the Central Rada members, had not shown any special interest in establishing contacts with Germany and Austria-Hungary. They remained loyal to the Provisional Government and maintained pro-Entente sympathies in contrast to the West Ukrainians in Galicia who favored the Central Powers. This tendency became more acute with the outbreak of the war in 1914 and reflected their long-standing anti-Russian attitudes. Their anti-Russian stand was shared by the East Ukrainian emigrés residing in Lviv. On August 4 they organized a non-partisan Union for the Liberation of Ukraine (*Soiuz vyzvolennia Ukrainy*—SVU) under the leadership of Andrii Zhuk.[11] Undoubtedly, their activities and publications had caught Vienna's attention, thereby contributing to the importance of the Ukrainian problem in general, but especially the aim of creating an independent Ukraine. But the main promotor of the Ukrainian cause in Berlin and Vienna became the Supreme Ukrainian Council (*Holovna Ukrains'ka Rada*—HUR), composed of various political parties under the leadership of Dr. Kost' Levyts'kyi, head of the Ukrainian National Democratic Party and representative to the *Reichsrat* on August 1, 1914.[12] The council pledged to organize a Ukrainian military force, Ukrainian Sich Riflemen (*Ukrains'ki Sichovi Striltsi*) with Dr. Kyrylo Trylovskyi as head of the Military Directorate. By 1916 various Ukrainian military units formed into the Ukrainian Legion consisting of 2,500 men.[13] Overshadowed by political implications, its military value reflected the poignancy of the Ukrainian question.[14]

The resurfacing of Ukrainian political activity instantly alarmed the Poles. The viceroy of Galicia, Witold Korytowski, denounced the Ukrainians in Vienna as an unreliable element, pointing to the rapidly declining movement of the Russophiles as potential agents of Russia. At the beginning of the war he ordered mass arrests which were followed by executions mainly at the hands of Hungarian troops. Altogether, in the first weeks of the war, some 36,000 Ukrainians were hanged and several thousand more were placed in internment camps in Talerhof, western Austria.[15] Ukrainians, placing the blame on the Poles and Hungarians, continued to maintain a pro-Austrian and pro-German orientation as a lesser evil, especially after the appointment of an ethnic Austrian, General Collard, as Galicia's new viceroy.

On May 5, 1915, the General Ukrainian Council (*Zahalna Ukrains'ka Rada*) representing the Ukrainian political parties in Galicia and Bukovina was founded in Vienna. The council worked closely with the Union for the Liberation of Ukraine, having proclaimed as its aims the liberation of Ukraine and autonomy for Ukrainians in Austria. Simultaneously the S.V.U. began to organize Ukrainian military units from the prisoners of war with Vienna's official support. All this compounded the potential importance of Ukrainians especially in view of the prolonged war, Austria-Hungary's growing internal difficulties, Germany's desire to end the war at the eastern front, and the Polish problem involving equally Germany, Austria-Hungary and the Ukrainians.

On August 26, Levyts'kyi arrived in Berlin to the surprise of the Austro-Hungarian ambassador who immediately notified Vienna.[16] Levyts'kyi and the Polish Prince Andreas Lubomirski, a member of the Austrian *Herrenhaus,* were seeking contacts with the German Foreign Office and leading politicians. Their trip to Berlin did not have the support of the Dual Monarchy's Foreign Minister, Count Ottokar Czernin, who consented to it only at the request of the German ambassador in Vienna. In his reply to Ambassador Count Hohelohe Czernin nevertheless considered the "collaboration with the Ukrainians and the Poles to be in the interest of both states in order to win the war against Russia."[17] As for Levytskyi's appearance in Berlin, Czernin wrote, "I suppose he came to Berlin against the Polish oppression in East Galicia and to warn the Germans of the Polish danger.... In case of the German inquiries, you should inform them that the government and myself are determined not to hurt Ukrainians and to secure from them a broad autonomy."[18]

Having held talks with the German authorities, Levytskyi appeared at the Austrian embassy to report on his activities. Of special significance was Levytskyi's meeting with the Polish Count Bogdam Huten-Czapski, a member of the German General Staff in charge of the problem of non-

Russians, Poles, Ukrainians, Jews and others and of searching for means of turning them against Russia to make them useful for military and political activities.[19] To his surprise the meeting convinced Levytskyi that official Berlin was uninformed about Eastern Europe and that the government relied on a Pole who had no sympathy for the Ukrainian cause.[20]

There seems to be general agreement that until 1914 the German policy makers had neither knowledge nor interest in exploiting non-Russian nationalities for political or strategic purposes. After all, after 150 years of close and mostly friendly relations with the Romanovs, a complete turn-around could hardly be expected. Only with the outbreak of the war, the need for auxiliary means such as the national question slowly began to emerge. Yet it took another two years before Berlin committed itself openly to a policy aimed at the destruction of the Russian empire and in support of national movements. Moreover, the Polish issue that affected Ukraine played an important role in Germany's eastern policy.

As the German army advanced into Russia Berlin began to be faced with a new problem—non-Russian peoples and *nolens volens* was forced seriously to consider the new possibilities. The war made a German-Ukrainian meeting imperative despite the prevailing lack of interest on both sides save for several German Ukrainophiles such as Paul Rohrbach and Axel Schmidt who kept the Ukrainian issue alive. The evolution in that direction was inevitable, and only a question of format and time.[21] The same was true on the Ukrainian side, especially in Galicia as proven by Levytskyi's trip to Berlin, and S.V.U.'s contacts with Berlin.

On the other hand, Austria-Hungary bordering on Ukraine and consisting of some four million Ukrainians within its empire, and having occupied the Kholm district populated by Ukrainians, displayed a much greater interest in Ukrainian affairs. Additionally, a festering Polish-Ukrainian conflict kept Vienna involved.

The issue of the Kholmland, claimed by the Poles and Ukrainians, emerged as the first testing ground. At the end of October 1916, the Ukrainian National Council sent a memorandum to Vienna concerning the church situation, demanding the restoration of the Ukrainian Uniate Church there that was liquidated during Russia's rule over the land. While the German authorities sympathized with the Ukrainian claim,[23]

Vienna, under Polish pressure, endlessly hesitated to meet Ukrainian requests, leaving the problem unsolved until the end of the war. Austria's intention to play the Polish card, stipulated by the German-Austrian proclamation of an "independent Poland" on November 5, 1916, and the promise of autonomy for the Poles in Galicia, continued even after the outbreak of the Russian revolution. Fearful of the reaction of its own Ukrainian citizens, the Austrian government did not welcome the prospect of a common border with the Ukrainian state because "Austrian Ukrainians will gravitate towards their countrymen."[24] In a secret note of August 8 to Ritter von Stock of the High Command of the Army, the government insisted that it would not treat Ukrainians preferentially but rather in conjunction with the Polish question.[25] Vienna's quasi-benevolence towards Ukrainians obviously reflected a twofold intention—to please the Poles and at the same time to treat kindly Ukrainians and to hope that the Empire would survive the war and prolong its existence. This sum of arguments and intentions could have been undermined easily by major upsets. These came sooner than the Dual Monarchy anticipated in the form of the emergence of the Ukrainian National Republic, the Soviet Russian peace initiative and the gripping food shortage in Vienna. For these convincing and dangerous reasons the Austrian Foreign Minister Count Ottokar Czernin was sent to Brest-Litovsk to "bring home peace at any price," as ordered by Emperor Karl I.

* * *

Even before the arrival of the Ukrainian delegation at Brest-Litovsk on January 1, 1918 public and private German interests in Ukraine developed five specific theses:[26] (1) Recognition that Ukrainians are an independent nationality and not a "little-Russian" branch of Russianism. That their language is not a dialect but a separate idiom. (2) The process of national rebirth has progressed since Ivan Kotliarevskyi's time and was comparable to that of other nations of Central and Eastern Europe. This rebirth which began in 1798, was spreading and created a solid national movement in the Dnieper Ukraine. (3) This national movement aimed at the separation of Ukraine from Russia and a closer cooperation with the Central Powers. (4) The Russians and Poles are the natural enemies of Ukrainians. The anti-Polish tradition of the Ukrainians from

Galicia is growing. (5) Economically Ukraine is the center of the East. Her separation from Moscow would decide the outcome of the war in favor of the Central Powers.

Beyer's conclusion that despite Vienna's awareness of the importance of Ukraine her policies did not change as the German public expected,[27] remains convincing. Therefore, the arrival of Ukrainians at Brest-Litovsk was welcomed by the Germans but aroused uncertainty and even fear among the Austro-Hungarian representatives. Indeed, the Ukrainians arrived at the right time and in the right place. The rest was left to their diplomatic skill in exploiting German-Austrian differences on the Polish issue. The presence of the Russian Bolsheviks brought an entirely different package of intentions to the table.

CHAPTER IV

NEGOTIATING THE PEACE TREATY

In response to the Bolshevik regime's peace initiative of November 10 and after preliminary contacts since November 20, the delegates from Berlin and Petrograd arrived at Brest-Litovsk on December 2, 1917, to sign the first armistice of World War I. This unusual gathering of Imperial Germany, represented by Prince G. Hohenlohe and General Max von Hoffmann, with the Russian representatives—a worker, a sailor and a non-commissioned officer, among others (Adolf A. Joffe, Lev B. Kamenev, Gregory Y Sokolnikov, N.A. Obrukhov—worker, F. V. Olich—seaman, and R. N. Stashkov—peasant), in fact opened a new chapter in European history. It seemed that Germany would be rewarded for her assistance in Lenin's return to Russia with an agreement releasing her from the two-front war burden and might bring her closer to victory. It was a worthy prospect regardless of the suspicious partnership and Hoffman's "never to be forgotten lunch" with the crowd across the table.

Lenin's capacity to issue a deluge of decrees, beginning with the "Decree on Peace" of November 8, and one of December 5 to the "working and oppressed peoples of Europe" extolling the armistice and urging all governments to begin with peace negotiations, found a welcome reception in Berlin and Vienna, but was instantly rejected by France and Great Britain. The two democracies responded with a secret agreement of December 23, against the Bolshevik regime, in support of General Kaledin, and dividing Russia into two spheres of interest with Ukraine assigned to France. Concern about France's huge investment of capital in the mines of the Don region and the metallurgical industry in Ukraine, and also with Ukraine's political independence, played an essential role in her decision. To this end England and France decided on January 5 to dispatch their representatives to Ukraine, a decision that was applauded by Vynnychenko and the Francophile Shulhyn. The news about this decision was immediately forwarded to Vienna.[1]

The armistice was signed on December 15 and the attempt by the unofficial Ukrainian delegation to reach Brest-Litovsk failed due to the Bolsheviks' refusal to let them cross the front line, "because they would not have been able to reach Brest in time,"[2] and eventually to prevent the signing. Another reason for their refusal must be seen in the Soviet delegation's intention to act on behalf of "all Russia," including Ukraine, which in fact had not at that time legally separated itself from the "Russian federation." This step had been taken only on January 22, 1918 with the proclamation of the Fourth universal.

Even so the Decree of November 8 granted all nationalities the right to political independence and self-determination, the Soviet regime was the first one to violate its own acts. The Soviet delegation continued to speak on behalf of "all peoples" until the arrival of the official Ukrainian delegation. Lev Trotsky, head of the Soviet delegation, on January 10 much to its own regret and Soviet historiographical condemnation,[3] recognized the Ukrainians' right to represent the Ukrainian Republic. It had to be a painful experience for Trotsky to witness the implementation of the "right for self-determination" by the Ukrainians eagerly supported by the delegates of Imperial Germany in the face of the Soviet Russian regime's unwillingness to implement the stated intention.

Surely enough, the Soviet demand for a peace without annexations, indemnities and with self-determination for all, coincided with the then prevailing German, Austrian, and Ukrainian interests, even if for different reasons. In a way, one of the Bolshevik designs aimed at the destruction of their opponents was about to turn against their own interst.

The Central Powers' desire to achieve peace at the eastern front was much furthered with the note of the Ukrainian General Secretariat of

December 25 informing them about Ukraine's decision to participate in the negotiations[4] :

> With the Central Rada's proclamation of the Third universal of November 20, 1917, Ukraine achieved independent statehood.

In regard to the negotiations, in Brest, the note stated,

> (1) Democracy of the Ukrainian State strives toward world peace, to a general peace among all states involved in war. (2) Peace should be extended to all the people, including the small ones, peace should secure rightful self determination. . . . (7) The Ukrainian Democratic Republic is now in charge of its own front and therefore it will participate in international affairs in order to protect the interest of the Ukrainian people. This government must participate in all peace negotiations, conferences and congresses on an equal basis with other states. The political power of the People's Commissars does not extend over Ukraine.[5]

The main significance of the note lies with Ukraine proclaiming herself to be party to the war, and in rejection of the Soviet regime's claim to represent "the whole Russia." Legally, this empowered the Rada to become a partner of the negotiations dealing with the war, and such was the purpose of the Brest meeting.

The step taken by the General Secretariat had its immediate origin in the Soviet Russian ultimatum of December 17 that demanded troop movements across Ukraine to the area be stopped, and that complete freedom of action be given the Ukrainian Bolsheviks, which meant Petrograd's interference into Ukraine's internal affairs. The Rada's rejection of this provocative ultimatum on December 20 was answered with the declaration of war against the "counterrevolutionary Rada regime."[6] The Soviet Russian-Ukrainian war together with the small well organized local communists, made the Rada's position even bleaker and more receptive to the prospect of an agreement with the Central Powers.

Having failed to achieve a majority at the Ukrainian Congress in Kiev, the communists left for Kharkiv where they proclaimed the Ukrainian Socialist Soviet Republic on December 26, creating a "dual power" situation and providing themselves with a "legitimate" excuse for their opinion collaboration with Soviet Russia.[7]

The Rada's note of December 25, born out of desperation, found an instantly positive response by the Central Powers' governments, which too, had to act under the pressure of circumstances. The telegram dispatched to Kiev informed:

> Germany, Austria-Hungary, Bulgaria and Turkey hold it necessary to declare that they are to welcome the Ukrainian Democratic Republic to the peace negotiations in Brest-Livotsk. At the same time we declare that the Ukrainian delegation would have been welcomed to the armistice negotiations.[8]

With all the formalities behind, the Ukrainian delegation arrived at Brest-Litovsk on January 4, 1918, during the ten-day recess of the negotiations. The number of the negotiating parties had now increased to six, and in terms of the population they represented approximately 200 million people, i.e., half of Europe's population around 1914.

The Ukrainian representatives were Vsevolod Holubovych, Mykola Levytskyi, Mykola Liubyns'kyi, and Oleksander Sevriuk, a group of young people with an average age of 26. Hoffmann characterized them, "The young representatives of the Kiev Central Rada were not sympathetic to Count Czernin, and he disliked to negotiate with Liubyns'kyi and Sevriuk, who only recently passed students years." He himself admired these "young Ukrainians for their tough stand in negotiations with Czernin." In fact, it was Czernin with his previous indifference and a certain apprehension in regard to Ukrainians and the Ukrainian problem in general, who found himself on the defensive vis-a-vis the Ukrainian delegation. In his private meeting with Zalizniak who had attended the Stockholm convention of the Second International, Czernin nervously inquired whether the Ukrainian delegates desire peace as he was still uncertain as to their position, because "the Ukrainians have a choice with whom to go." This conversation alone precludes any suspicion of the existence of an Austrian-Ukrainian conspiracy, or for this matter, a German-Ukrainian intrigue, or of any previously contemplated secret arrangement.[10]

The appearance of the Ukrainians at Brest immediately created a new condition and changed the course of negotiations.[11] To the German delegates Richard von Kühlmann and General Max Hoffmann this meant putting extra pressure on the Soviet delegation, and for Count Ottokar Czernin, despite his personal considerations, hope emerged that Vienna be spared from imminent food shortage. Thus, the Ukrainian delegation had all reasons to expect successful negotiations leading to agreement, while finding itself in a favorable position to exploit the prevailing objective as well as subjective conditions and to secure the best terms possible. Two important issues were in their favor and served equally Ukrainian interests: the desire for immediate peace and the principle of self-determination accepted by all the parties involved, with Czernin being the only one notoriously fearful of the "nightmare"—national self-determination.

It was Czernin who in a meeting with Kühlmann and Hoffmann complained about self-determination: "I cannot bring into the debate the word self-determination for the Czechs, Ruthenians, and South Slavs will come to me demanding self-determination."[12] Germany, being less affected by this "modern dynamism," except for the Polish question still hanging in the air, had no such reservation. Contact with Ukraine was very much welcomed by Chancellor Georg von Herling and Field Marshall Erich Ludendorff, with only some tactical considerations,[13] and Kühlmann, in agreement with Hertling, decided to proceed towards an agreement with Ukraine without delay. He received Ukrainians with delight, "because their appearance offers the opportunity to play them off against the Petersburg delegation."[14]

The German military establishment, especially Hoffmann, viewed the emergence of Ukraine as a counterpoise to the newly created Poland and as a walled border against Bolshevism. But the most convincing argument determining the general's reasoning was the desire to eliminate the eastern front enabling the German military forces to concentrate on a decisive offensive in the West to bring the war to an end. This strategy was also linked to the possibility of securing critical economic resources from Russia and, subsequently, Ukraine. In that the position of the military coincided with that of the *Reichswirtschaftsamt* (R.W.A.— Office of Economics) and could not be ignored by the Foreign Office either. On the "bread issue" there was no disagreement between Czernin and Kühlmann, as admitted by Edmund von Glaise-Horstenau:

The importance of Ukraine for Austria-Hungary because of her ability to resist the Bolsheviks was much greater than that of Soviet Russia, which did not border on the Danubian Monarchy. Of special significance was the abundance of grain in the new state, which with justification was valued as the breadbasket of the Tsarist Empire.[15]

Armed with convincing reasons and after two days of talks between the German and Ukrainian delegations to get acquainted with each other, both sides were ready though still hesitant about beginning official negotiations. Germany's full recognition of the Central Rada's delegation came only after the Ukrainian threat to withdraw from the Brest negotiations and two days after Trostsky's recognition of their right to represent the Ukrainian people on January 10. An official of the German Foreign Officer, Diego von Bergen, a longtime sympathizer of the Ukrainian cause, insisted on the immediate conclusion of a treaty that would draw Ukraine into the German sphere of interest.[16]

Similar private meetings were arranged between Czernin and the Ukrainians on January 3-4. The Ukrainians requested not only official recognition of their delegation, but also legal recognition of Ukraine's independence in addition to the incorporation of the Kholmland and Pidliashia regions into Ukraine and a plebiscite in East Galicia, North Bukovina and Carpathian Ukraine.[17] Czernin responded to these demands on January 6. While avoiding direct official recognition of the old Austro-Russian frontier and non-interference in the Monarchy's internal affairs.[18] The rift between Austria-Hungary and Ukraine seemed not to fade away, even on the eve of the first plenary session.

Kühlmann presided over the first meeting which began on January 10 with delegates from all four Central Powers present, Soviet Russian and Ukrainian representatives seated in the middle. The official languages for the negotiations were German, Russian and French. At that session Holubovych delivered to Trotsky a note demanding official recognition of the Rada's delegation. Trotsky, on behalf of the Soviet delegation stated: "Since the Ukrainian delegation appeared here as in independent delegation we proposed to recognize her presence in peace negotiations, and no objections have been raised, I consider the problem to be taken care of."[19]

This recognition which now legally separated the Ukrainian representatives from the Russian, made the conference a meeting of six independent countries. Trotsky's action has been differently interpreted. According to Wheeler-Bennett, Trotsky did it at Kühlmann's insistence.[20] Sevriuk understood it as Trotsky's expectation of seeing the Ukrainians side with him against the Central Powers.[21] Contemporary Soviet explanation holds that:

> This declaration continued to be a trotskyist destructive policy which completely contradicted real conditions and realities. . . . It was obvious at that time that the power of the Ukrainian bourgois nationalists with each passing day was becoming illusory. On January 12 the Central Executive Committee of the Soviet Ukraine, created in Kharkiv, empowered the Chairman of the C.E.C., E. G. Medvedev to represent the interest of the Ukrainian People's Republic at the conference at Brest-Litovsk. All this was well known to Trotsky. . . . His recognition of the Central Rada's delegation proved to be a serious blow to the position of the Soviet delegation. From that time on the German block used the Rada's delegation against the Soviet representatives and began to collaborate with them. All this ended with the signing of the treaty between the Rada and the Central Powers.[22]

In this lengthy quotation there is no mention of the fact that the Soviet army was already invading Ukraine.

However, it was Trotsky who upon his arrival at Brest held lengthy "speeches to the window" in which self-determination of nations became a repetitious rhetoric and, facing the young Ukrainian socialists, he expected them to join the Soviet delegation against "the common enemy." To the Ukrainians' reasoning the enemy was attacking Ukraine from the North and not from the West. Moreover, unlike the Russian Bolsheviks, the Ukrainian socialists were not entirely committed to a Marxist socialist world revolution and their understanding of national self-determination differed very much from Lenin's formula—"national in form, socialist in substance." In reality this meant that the Rada's socialist "revolution" divorced itself from Lenin's revolution, making it possible to negotiate with Imperial Germany and the multi-national

Habsburg state about issues of mutual importance at that given moment in history. Ukrainians did not have any use for Lenin's "breathing spell" strategy for Soviet troops were about to destroy their country. Nonetheless, one of the delegates, M. Levytskyi, a member of the Ukrainian Socialist Democratic Party, at the beginning of the negotiations did some ideological soul-searching as to his "socialist purity," while in the same room with the representatives of the "old regime." His hesitation, however, disappeared after his meeting with the leadership of the German Social-Democratic Party (SPD) in Berlin. The SPD supported Germany's war effort, thereby placing the country's interest above "class conscience" as many other European socialist parties of the Second International had done. The SPD example had a greater impact on Levytskyi than the Russian Bolshevik propaganda. Previously, another delegate M. Zalizniak, attended the Stockholm meeting of the Second International. Both men, like most of their fellow party-members, except of Vynnychenko and a few others, lined up with the European socialist parties and not with Lenin.

A new turn of events affecting the Ukrainian delegation took place on January 23. When Trotsky left for Moscow on January 18 for new instructions, Adolf Joffe informed the Central Powers that the Kharkiv-based Ukrainian Soviet regime was sending its own delegates—E.G. Medvedev and V. M. Shakhrai would join the Russian delegation. Upon his return on January 30 Trotsky officially demanded that the Rada's representatives be replaced by the Kharkiv delegates. A strongly worded rebuff from Sevriuk on February 1 said:

> Having previously recognized the Ukrainian delegation as representatives of an independent state, Trostky is now trying to deny the Ukrainian delegation their right by referring to a yet unknown Kharkiv executive committee. . . . Therefore we are obliged to state the following: We agree with Trotsky as to the new situation in Ukraine, yet the changes are of a different nature than Trotsky thinks. The essence of the change is the fact that the Central Rada with the Fourth Universal[24] of January 22 proclaimed: From now on the Ukrainian National Republic becomes the independent, free and sovereign state of the Ukrainian people. . . . The Ukrainian Rada herewith expressed in this same universal her desire to live in

peace with all neighbors, but none of them has the right to inter-fere into the independent life of the Ukrainian republic. The Fourth Universal unmistakably clarifies the legal international position of the Ukrainian Republic.... On this ground we request the formal recognition of the delegation of the Ukrainian National Republic, to acknowledge her international position, her right and her delegation.[25]

Medvedev, speaking on behalf of the Kharkiv Executive Committee, had accused the Rada's delegation of secretly negotiating with the Central Powers and he repeated the threat that agreements reached with the Cen-tral Powers "will not be recognized by the Ukrainian people represented by his delegation." Trotsky, on his part, having referred to the instability in Ukraine, the absence of clearly defined Ukrainian borders, and to the decision of the Rada's delegation to leave the Russian delegation, asserted that the agreement reached with the Kievan Rada would be recognized only when approved by the Russian delegation.[26] Liubyns'kyi in turn cited Russia's multinational character, the former oppression of non-Rus-sian peoples and the changes which took place since 1917, accused the Bolshevik regime of its refusal to comply with the principles of self-deter-mination, for its use of propaganda and demagoguery, of disbanding the first freely elected Constituent Assembly and for the regime's oppressive policy under the protection of the Red Guard mercenaries. He reminded Trotsky that

The Ukrainian Central Rada, in fact, was the first government in Russia composed of socialists. It meant that the Ukrainian people, step by step, created their own state.... In the November elec-tions the Ukrainian parties won seventy-five percent of the votes cast for the Central Rada and the Bolsheviks less than ten percent, therefore, the Rada represents the great majority of the Ukrainian people. At the meeting of the Ukrainian Congress of workers, pea-sants, and soldiers in Kiev on December 3, 2000 delegates recognized the Rada and only eighty Bolsheviks went to Kharkiv to set up their own 'government.' So came into existence the Kharkiv regime and such is its base. Our future will be determined by the working people.[27]

Following Liubyns'kyi's presentation, the chairman of the session, Ottokar Czernin, on behalf of the four powers, recognized the Ukrainian National Republic as an independent, free and sovereign state entitled to conclude international agreements.[28] From then on, two separate negotiations would be conducted: The Central Powers and Soviet Russia, and the Central Powers and Ukraine.

While the Soviet Russian-Ukrainian conflict reached a point of no return, the Central Powers, and especially Germany, became aware of the difficulties in coming to terms with Trotsky. The need for a separate agreement with Ukraine favorable to the Central Powers became more acute in the face of a worsening situation in Ukraine.[29] At that point, no official proposals had been submitted either by the Ukrainian side or by the Central Powers.

In Kiev, the vacillating Social Democrat Vynnychenko resigned, having failed to protect Ukrainian territory and consistently opposing the formation of a Ukrainian army. The General Secretariat now passed into the hands of the Social Revolutionaries headed by Vsevolod Holubovych. Antonov-Ovsiienko's offensive continued from the East, with Poltava being taken on January 20 and Konotop on January 26. Another red unit under Michael Muraviev attacked Bakhmach on January 27 and from there the three Soviet Russian army units marched toward Kiev. On January 30, the Ukrainians suffered a crushing defeat at Kruty. On January 29 the local Bolsheviks staged an uprising in Kiev. For a while the Rada was saved by the Ukrainian Galician Battalion of the Sich Riflemen and by the units of the Free Cossacks. Yet it was too late for the meager force of some 3,000 men to stop the Soviet troops. On February 9 Muraviev's units entered Kiev after the Rada fled to Zhytomyr. Three weeks of Muraviev's reign of terror in Kiev resulted in over 5,000 Ukrainians being executed. Any inhabitant caught speaking Ukrainian became suspect in his own capital city Kiev. The Russian madness had turned into a blood bath, offering Ukrainians a practical lesson in Soviet internationalism and self-determination. Moreover, the previous Rada's pacifism and the government's misplaced priorities of relying on socialist solidarity and putting socialist reforms above the need to arm the nation led to the most tragic and disastrous consequences.

The Ukrainian Social Democrats had failed to take lessons from Lenin and Trotsky, who from the outset of their revolution had built the army and the *Cheka* as the safeguards of their seizure of power. By the middle of February the Rada's rule was limited to a small strip of territory along the Zhytomyr-Korosten-Sarny railroad. The deliverance had to come from the outsiders and the place to look for them was Brest-Litovsk.

Of course, the situation in which the Rada found itself was well understood by the Germans and Austrians. Immediately after the dramatic events of January 30, Czernin invited the Ukrainian delegates along with Kühlmann and Hoffmann and in their presence presented on behalf of the four powers the "Three Points," which in the words of Hoffmann amounted to a friendly ultimatum in a new formulation—"accept it or go home." The points, general in nature, suggested: (1) A declaration of an end to the war between the Central Powers and Ukraine and establishment of diplomatic relations. (2) Ukraine shall deliver to the Central Powers one million tons of grain and other foodstuffs. (3) All other matters shall be resolved and settled later on among the parties involved.[31]

Zalizniak and Sevriuk received the note in silence and not without indignation.[32] They could have expected less pleasantries and more realistic diplomacy. Consequently in their nightly conference they had to modify significantly their original demands, as formulated by Hrushevskyi before their departure. But having quickly learned the rules of diplomatic negotiations, their counter-proposal did not amount to a capitulation of the weak in the face of the powerful. They presented them on February 3, consisting of the following: (1) The future Ukraine's border in the Kholm region will be determined by ethnographic principles. (2) An unspecified amount of foodstuffs will be secured for the Central Powers in a separate agreement. (3) The East Galician issue will be resolved in an additional secret agreement with the understanding that East Galicia and Northern Bukovina would merge into a special crownland within the Dual Monarchy.[33] The situation of having nothing to loose, but everything to gain, worked this time in favor of the Ukrainians. Czernin had problems of his own, especially the prospect of hunger in his own country and the mutiny of the sailors on two Austrian warships on February 2.[34] For this reason the Ukrainian proposal became the backbone of the future agreement.

In the meantime the Austrian and German delegates left Brest for consultation with their respective governments. Even before Kühlmann's departure for Berlin he was already committed to the idea of signing a treaty with Ukraine, and he visualized an alliance of the two countries,

therefore Hoffmann considered the Rada's difficulties as only temporary.[35]
On February 1, he wrote to the Chancellor:

> I am inclined, in agreement with the Austrians and Turks, to pursue
> the plan of reaching a settlement with the Ukrainians in any case,
> even though the authority of the Rada is supposed to be greatly
> weakened at this moment. For the Austrians such a treaty is neces-
> sary, for us and the Turks advantageous. One should not, however,
> deceive oneself as to the real value of the proposed settlement be-
> cause of the shaky position of the Rada.[36]

Thus by February 1, Czernin was committed to signing a treaty soon, with
Ukraine or Russia.[37]

The Berlin conference took place on February 5, chaired by the Imperial Chancellor in the presence of Kühlmann, Czernin, Ludendorff and Hoffmann in addition to other officials representing the departments of the
Treasury, Commerce and the Office of War Food Supply. Just the presence of the representatives from the most important branches of the government was indicative of the seriousness of the situation at hand.

The agenda of the conference included three issues: (1) The German-
Austrian-Hungarian close cooperation and the question of procedural
aspect of negotiations. (2) The Polish question within the framework of
German-Austrian-Hungarian economic cooperation. (3) The status of the
negotiations in Brest-Litovsk and the future *modus procedenti*. Soon,
however, the Ukrainian issue rose dominantly, especially the claim of
Kholmland together with the demand for internal restructuring of the
Dual Monarchy. Czernin's expectation that Germany would support him
on the Kholm issue did not materialize, thus antagonizing Austria's pro-
Polish policy. Czernin was forced to make concessions on the Ukrainian
crownland and Kholmland, hoping to gain more economic advantages.
Should Ukraine ask for military assistance, it would have to be compensated with economic compensation providing that the supply of foodstuffs be equally distributed.[38]

In those days an optimistic mood prevailed within the Ukrainian delegation as to the chances of seeing their proposal accepted. Besides, work
on the preliminary draft of the treaty progressed to their satisfaction.[39]
Baron von Wiesner, the Austrian representative vigorously defended the

Polish interest in the Kholmland question and only at Hoffmann's insistence did Wiesner accept the ethnographic principle in drawing Ukraine's north-western border. This was a major setback for Austria's pro-Polish policy since Hoffmann's proposed line became a part of the treaty.

On Febraury 3, the Rada forces regained control of Kiev from the local Bolsheviks, a fact that enormously helped the delegation in Brest as it was able to communicate directly with the Rada. The news instantly was transmitted to the Austrians and Germans, making it harder, particularly for Czernin, to press for greater concessions, especially after the official confirmation of the Rada's presence in Kiev by their own lines of communication.

Another interesting episode deserves mention. In those crucial days Medvedev visited almost daily the official Ukrainian delegation and displayed great interest in its work and results.[40] Obviously, his "divided soul" entertained some sympathy for the Ukrainian national cause. Yet it also illustrated best the overall Ukranian tragedy of being divided at a crucial time.

The Central Rada, after consultation and acquaintance with the draft of the treaty, approved it and urged its officials to sign. Equally so, the Berlin conference ended with the determination of the Central Powers to conclude a treaty with Ukraine regardless of the outcome of the negotiation with Soviet Russia. Ludendorff's advice that the military assistance should be forthcoming only upon the Rada's request, found also general approval. On this occasion he introduced into the historical vocabulary a new term, "the Bolshevist poison" and the need to prevent its spread.[41]

On February 7, Kühlmann and Czernin returned to Brest. The draft of the treaty, including the Ukrainian demand in regard to the Ukrainian crownland were approved with only one provision stipulating, at Czernin's insistence, that the crownland issue be settled secretly in a separate agreement. Some minor issues affecting the German-Ukrainian relationship developed in the sessions of the judicial commission in regard to the exchange of prisoners of war. And here too, the argument about the financial reimbursement between Levytskyi and Krige had been resolved in the U-krainians' favor, i.e., no payments in the exchange process would be made regardless of the small number of German prisoners held in Ukraine and the very large number of Ukrainians in German prisoner of war camps.

Trotsky's last desperate attempts on February 7, to prevent the signing of the treaty by informing Czernin that the Rada already left Kiev, had little success. Both Czernin and Kühlmann unmistakably, and even in a threatening manner, expressed their determination to proceed with the signing. Germany's delegation was by then considering breaking the negotiations with Soviet Russia anyway, and proceeding with another military offensive.[42]

The last obstacles were removed on this same day, February 7. In a separate Protocol signed by the Dual Monarchy and the Ukrainain National Republic,[43] the Ukrainians obliged themselves to supply the Central Powers with one million tons of grain as a condition for the ratification of the Peace Treaty. As will be shown in the next chapter, Levytskyi having assured the availability of the foodstuffs in the proper quantity, placed his own government in a difficult position especially due to the Rada's ineffectiveness, its socialist policy, and the presence of the German and Austrian-Hungarian armies in Ukraine. Nonetheless, at that moment the price had to be paid.

The Ukrainians compensated this "payment deal" with a somewhat more satisfactory gain in a secret agreement between Austria-Hungary and Ukraine on the formation of a Ukrainian Crownland within the Dual Monarchy including East Galicia and Northern Bukovina.[44] The agreement also provided a Ukrainian guarantee to ensure the national and cultural development of the Polish, German and Jewish minorities living on the territory of the Republic. In fact, these rights had been earlier granted by the Rada, however, the Ukrainians in Austria were treated only as a "subject nationality," and obviously not as the Austrian Germans, Hungarians or even as the Poles were treated in Vienna. The agreement had been overshadowed by the paragraph that made ratification of the Peace Treaty and of the implementation of the "Secret Agreement" subject to Ukraine's fulfillment of the delivery of grain at specified periods.

In the closing days at Brest, Zalizniak secretly approached Czernin and Kühlmann inquiring about the possibility of financial aid in the amount of one billion Marks to rebuild the Ukrainian army, to utilize the Ukrainian prisoners of war and to transfer Ukrainian military units from Austria to Ukraine.[45] He argued that the loan was needed to continue the war against the Bolsheviks, to maintain law and order in the country, and to secure the deliveries of grain to the Central Powers. Both statesmen understood this need and expressed in principle their willingness to grant the Ukrainian government the loan in the amount asked at nominal interest. The loan was to be repaid in installments or with commodities. Czernin and Kühl-mann felt they could not act on it without official authorization of their respective governments. Whereupon Zalizniak informed the members of the delegation about the new possibility and despite stress on the impor-tance of the matter, the majority of the delegates refused to pursue this pos-sibility without prior approval of the government. "This view," Zalizniak ex-claimed, "seemed to be the top of political stupidity," and Holubovych, a member of the delegation, having been informed, "became very terrified" of the prospect of what would the "Russians and Jews say that he took money from the Germans."[46] He even prohibited Zalizniak from continu-ing the talks with the Germans and Austrians. He was, however, entrusted with negotiating with the Austrians about the possibility of releasing U-krainian prisoners of war and obtaining arms. Zalizniak approached Wiesner who had agreed to inform Czernin and to discuss the issue with the representative of the General Staff in Brest, Major Glesom, an intel-lectually rather stagnant personality. This "plainly stupid man" began to talk of a six months period needed for such transaction and other un-related details.[47] In desperation, Zalizniak and Sevriuk left for Vienna for a direct contact with the Austrian Military High Command, carrying with them an authorization signed by Levytskyi, Sevriuk and Liubyns'kyi. But once the mission became known to the Galician Ukrainian parlia-mentary representation, Zalizniak, realizing the impossibility of proceed-ing in secrecy with the mission left Vienna for Brest.[48] Here on the last day of the negotiations, Liubyns'kyi, at Hoffmann's urging, signed a pre-pared text of an appeal to the German people asking for military help to free Ukraine from the Soviet Russian invasion.[49]

With this action the flow of future events was irreversibly changed and became almost predictable. The treaty would be signed, the Ukrainian Republic, unable to free the country from the Bolsheviks, placed her future into the hands of the Central Powers. Moreover, lacking the needed financial resources in Ukraine the Rada's position would remain uncertain at best.

The ceremonial signing of the Peace Treaty between the Central Powers and Ukraine took place at 2 a.m. on February 9. A few hours later, a special courier informed the Ukrainian delegates that the Rada, unable to defend Kiev, left the city to the advancing Muraview army. Yet the Treaty of Brest-Litovsk, now an official international document, at least for the next several months, put its imprint on Ukraine and her immediate fate.

CHAPTER V

THE TREATY:
ITS NATURE AND IMMEDIATE IMPLICATIONS

The final session of the negotiations between representatives of the Central Powers and the Ukrainian National Republic began at 1:51 a.m. on February 9. Richard Kühlmann, Germany's Foreign Minister, opened the meeting with the statement:

> None of you could realize the historical significance of the presence in this room of the representatives of the Central Powers and of the young Ukrainian People's Republic gathered here for the signing of the first peace treaty of the World War. That this treaty will be signed by a young and promising state, which grew out of the storm of the war, gives the allied representatives special satisfaction. May this treaty be the first one to be followed by beneficial agreements for the Central Powers and the Ukrainian Republic as well.[1]

On his part, Oleksander Sevriuk, head of the Ukrainian delegation stated:

> We are pleased that as of today begins peace between the Central Powers and Ukraine. To be sure, we came here hoping that a general peace ending the murderous war will take place. . . . A new era of

reconstruction for our people will come about. . . . We did achieve democratic and for both sides honorable peace and it remains our responsibility to make it possible for Ukraine which brought the war at her frontiers to an end, to rise to a new life thanks to the signing of this historical act and as an independent state to enter into international relations. To this end our strength will have to be employed in order to bloom again.

Immediately thereafter the representatives of the five states placed their signatures on the document, containing ten articles and a separate "Final Regulations."[2] The issue of the Kholmland and an economic agreement were partly incorporated into the text of the treaty and partly directly linked to it.

The opening statements by Kühlmann and Sevriuk were certainly not an exercise in official political rhetoric, considering the overall satisfactory process of the negotiations and the contents of the treaty. Indeed, both sides were in need of peace. Only an immediate end to the war could provide all countries involved with the prospect of a better future. The treaty was not a dictate, but the result of hard-nosed negotiations and bargaining despite the unproportional political and military power of all countries involved. Even the much weaker Ukrainians had their hour of triumph and satisfaction by forcing Czernin into compromises he did not originally want. The more powerful Germany, while maintaining her dominant position, did not gain any territory at the expense of Ukraine. But because Germany's war aims coincided with basic Ukrainian interests it was possible for both countries to expect certain advantages—political, military or economic—especially in the case of Ukraine her ability to maintain her independence.

The text of the treaty did not include any punitive measures or indemnities, whereas economic obligations were made subject to payments or exchange of goods between the Central Powers and Ukraine. The demand by Friedrich Hans von Rosenberg, an official of the German Foreign Office, for a forty-year concession for the exploitation of Ukrainian coal and iron ore in exchange for Ukraine's right to incorporate Bessarabia was rejected outright by Sevriuk.[3]

Ukraine could live by and survive the terms of the treaty as formulated in ten articles determining:

1. The end of the war between the Central Powers and Ukraine;

2. That Ukraine's frontier with Austria-Hungary remain the same as the old Russian-Austrian-Hungarian border. Further to the north, the border was to be drawn along ethnographic principles with the Kholmland belonging to Ukraine. The final line dividing the Polish and Ukrainian territories was to be determined by a special commission.

3. Evacuation of the occupied territories was to begin immediately upon ratification of the treaty (mainly of Kholmland and Volhynia).

4. Diplomatic and consular relations among the states involved was to commence following the ratification of the treaty.

5. Renunciation of war indemnities.

6. Exchange of prisoners of war.

7. Immediate establishment of economic relations and the exchange of goods within a predetermined period payable in currency based on the gold standard with the corresponding details to be worked out in Kiev by a special commission.

8. Revival of public and private legal relations affecting the relationship in general.

9. All compatibilities agreed upon formed the whole.

10. A statement concerning the validity of the text of the treaty among the parties to the treaty.

A separate clause between Austria-Hungary and Ukraine affirmed the need for a speedy ratification of the treaty and for the exchange of the documents to take place in Vienna. The text of the treaty noticeably omitted mention of the already signed secret agreement between Austria-Hungary and Ukraine concerning the Ukrainian Crownland within the Dual Monarchy. The existence and the handling of that document revealed once again the deceptiveness of Vienna's diplomacy. According to Zalizniak's reports, Liubyns'kyi under Wiesner's instigation handed over to him the original text of the Agreement signed by Czernin and Ernst Seidler, the Austrian Prime Minister, for safe keeping by the German government. Liubyns'kyi had not the foresight of securing a copy for himself. The oversight was corrected by Zalizniak who obtained Wiesner's private notes and made a copy for Sevriuk. A few months later during Hetman Pavlo Skoropadskyi's rule in Ukraine a German official, at the insistence of Stephan von Rajecz, then Austrian Foreign Minister, destroyed the original document despite the protest of Viacheslav Lypyns'kyi, the Hetman's ambassador to Germany.[4]

The overall settlement as reported by Czernin to his government also contained a secret Protocol affirming Ukraine's ability to suppy one million tons of surplus grain to the Central Powers. The provision of transportation and other logistical assistance from the Central Powers would make deliveries possible. The deadline for delivery had been set for July 31, with the understanding that during the next six months trade would be carried out according to the provisions of the pre-1914 Russian-Austro-Hungarian Agreement. Within that period a new agreement was to be signed.

Another secret declaration assured cultural and national autonomy for the Polish, German and Jewish minorities in Ukraine, and for the Ukrainians in the Dual Monarchy. The Austrian government, no later than July 20, committed itself to passing a law concerning the creation of a Ukrainian crownland with the stipulation that this declaration would be nullified in case Ukraine failed to comply with one of the treaty's articles.[5]

Yet, Czernin's sense of accomplishment and confidence in his ability to use "secret diplomacy," was short-lived. While on the way to Bucharest to negotiate a treaty with defeated Romania, he learned that the secret agreement became public knowledge among the Poles in Galicia. One could speculate that Sevriuk on his way to Berlin revealed the text in order to force Vienna to act promptly on its implementation and not to relegate it to the archives. An outraged Czernin ordered Wiesner to go immediately to Berlin and to make certain that the copy was recovered from the Ukrainians and kept in the German Foreign Office. He also urged Wiesner to blackmail the Ukrainians with a possible Austrian and German refusal to support Ukraine.[6] Seidler, too, began to doubt the possibility of explaining the problem before the *Reichsrat*. A simple rebuff of the agreement would not satisfy the angry Poles who began to talk about "a fourth partition of Poland," referring to the Kholmland, and of the prospect of dividing Galicia into Polish and Ukrainian parts. Obviously, Vienna intended to have both—the Poles on her side and the assurance of obtaining the foodstuffs. The issue was finally resolved on March 3. Under pressure from Wiesner, and Rosenberg, an official member of the German delegation in Brest-Litovsk, Sevriuk and Levytskyi agreed to hand over their copy of the agreement. At that time it no longer mattered, for its contents were already known. The Poles were infuriated, adding to Vienna's desperation, and initiated on all levels political campaigns in the defense of

Kholmland, historically Ukrainian land.[7] The long-pursued Austrian pro-Polish policy began to crumble despite Czernin's desperate attempts to save it from the final collapse. His request, addressed to the German Foreign Office, to have in writing Berlin's willingness to nullify the treaty with Ukraine should she not comply with all the treaty's provisions, was nothing more than an oral commitment hardly binding the German government.[8] Germany ratified the treaty soon after, on February 22, proving only that her war aims did not coincide with the Dual Monarchy's interest.

As the pressure from the Poles intensified Czernin's blackmail increased commensurately. During Sevriuk's stay in Vienna on February 18, Wiesner forced him to accept modification of Article II, Paragraph 2, determining Ukraine's north-western border along a line of Tarnograd-Bilhorai-Prush-chany-Sarnaka-Melnyk-Pushchany. The new text provided instructions for the future Multilaterial Commission not to be bound by the aforementioned line, but it was free to draw a new border-line east from the originally designed, "considering ethnographic conditions and the wishes of the population." This change was subsequently accepted officially in a suplementary agreement signed at Brest by the representatives of the Central Powers and Ukraine.

But even this concession would not satisfy the Poles. The addition of a strong Polish position in the *Reichsrat* and in the Galician *Landtag,* and the role of the Council of Regents in Warsaw (an institution officially recognized by both powers) made the Poles a much stronger factor, especially in Vienna, than the Ukrainians. It is true that both Poles and Ukrainians had viewed Russia as their primary enemy, and consequently the Dual Monarchy was assured of their loyalties in peace and war alike. However, from Vienna's perspective the Poles were of greater value than the Ukrainians. Therefore, wherever Polish and Ukrainian interests collided, Vienna sided with the first, as Czernin's handling of the various problems proved.

The immediate reaction on the part of the Regents to the treaty, as reported by Stephan Ugron, the Austrian representative to the Council of Regents in Warsaw, was one of disbelief and anger. On February 10, Ugron reported to the Ministry of Foreign Affairs:

> The Regents' (Lubomirski and Ostrowski) reaction to my report (concerning the Brest-Litovsk Treaty with Ukraine) cannot be described. Both were dejected. Prince Lubomirski was physically

shaking and he could not find words to express his indignation. He spoke of the fourth partition of Poland, of which Austria was a part and he could not understand why Austria sold the Poles for a few railroad cars of grain. Ostrowski said that this treaty cannot prevail, for the Poles will protest to all neutral and Western countries.[9]

In addition to the official Polish protests in Warsaw there were strikes and demonstrations.[10] In its desperation the Polish government turned to Berlin to demand Polish-Ukrainian negotiations on the border issue and on February 12 sent a letter to the Ukrainian government via the German Embassy in Warsaw.[11]

A certain relaxation in Austrian-Polish tensions came about after the signing of Vienna's Protocol on February 18, modifying Article II. This was requested by the Polish Prime Minister Jan Kucharzewski in a note to the German military administration in Warsaw on February 12.[12]

On February 18 Wiesner hurriedly released the news about the Protocol to the Austrian embassies in Bern and Stockholm to be circulated among Polish circles and to the representatives at the Council of Regents. This informed them about the favorable solution of the Kholmland issue, "in the spirit of the Polish interest at the price of some Austrian concessions for Ukrainians, which, however, does not affect the state or national interests of the Poles."[13] He had in mind a revision of the border as determined by the treaty that would please the Poles since the new line would follow the ethnographic distribution of the population. Precisely for this reason he could not promise the Poles the return of the whole region of Kholmland. But even then this troublesome issue would not wither away.

Having exhausted all available means to please the Poles, Austrian diplomacy began spreading suspicion about Ukraine's ability to deliver 100,000 railroad cars of grain by July 1, which would provide an excuse for forcing Ukraine to conclude a new agreement accepting the Bug River as the Polish-Ukrainian border, with the Kholmland going to Poland. None of that happened and the Kholmland issue remained essentially unresolved until the collapse and disintegration of the Dual Monarchy in November 1918.

The events of the German-Ukrainian relationship proceeded differently during the immediate post-treaty period. Here implications as well as expectations differed considerably and so the requirements of formulating

German and Ukrainian priorities developed more smoothly than in the case of the Austrian-Ukrainian complexities. Certainly, even here differences and conflicts of interest remained, however, none of them became insoluble since both countries needed each other. Unlike the case of Austria-Hungary, an independent Ukraine had a place in Germany's *Ostpolitik*.

Whereas the Polish problem hung over Vienna and often paralyzed vital political and economic interests, Berlin on the other hand, considering the Polish issue basically as irresolvable, was free to conduct German-Ukrainian affairs at the expense of the Polish interest as has been the case with the Kholmland and Podlachia. Moreover, by February 5, it became obvious to the German delegation that an early agreement with Soviet Russia would not be forthcoming, leading the German Foreign Office and the Army High Command to the conclusion that Ukraine offered a real substitute for overall German war aims.[14] The treaty with Ukraine instantly transformed her into Germany's ally and Russia's foe. Given the conditions that existed, the Ukrainians could not afford to consider Germany's increased ability to fight on the Western Front. For that Vynnychenko apologized to the Allies, yet he had to admit that "German imperialism" was closer to the Ukrainian national interest than Russian Bolshevism. It is also true that the Central Rada having experienced only futility in dealing with the French and British representatives and after being attacked by the Soviet Russian army, resigned itself to negotiate and to collaborate with the Central Powers without the need for apology.

The immediate importance for Germany of the treaty with Ukraine centered around Article VII satisfying the *Wirtschaftsamt's* expectations. Accepting the gold standard as the means for the exchange of surplus goods, foodstuffs, and industrial products to be completed before July 31, seemed to satisfy the Rada's as well as Germany's expectations and requirements. The currency arrangement agreed upon determined the value of 1,000 Goldmarks for 462 Goldkarbovanets and 1,000 Goldkronen equal to 393 Goldkarbovanets. The exchange of goods would flow through specially designated centers set up by the governments. The commercial relationship was essentially based on the old German-Russian agreements of 1894-1904, which were quite favorable to Germany, but less satisfactory to Ukraine whose economic interest differed from that of the Tsarist Russian trade with Germany. This was especially true for Germany's favoring quotas (allocations) over the most favorable policy in the trade relationship. Other German advantages were ensured in Articles V and X, removing all restrictions in the transit of goods, although Germany could import Ukrainian iron without any quota restrictions. As observed by Borowsky,[16] this was obviously a one-sided advantage for German industry. Germany's expectation of dominating Ukraine economically had been further reinforced in a special clause making future custom agreements between Russia and Ukraine impossible. On the other hand, the Central Powers', and Germany's in particular, insistence that Soviet Russia conclude a peace treaty with Ukraine by the terms of the Treaty of March 3, 1918, gave Ukraine relative security and a real chance to remain an independent state. This provision, in the final analysis, seemed to keep Ukraine's "gains and losses" resulting from the Brest-Litovsk agreement in balance. Since the incorporation of Ukraine into the Russian Empire by Catherine II in 1781, Ukraine reappeared on Europe's maps as an independent state and officially entered the international arena. The price was perhaps too high but in the absence of any other alternative the Brest-Litovsk Treaty must be seen as a triumph for Ukrainian policies with the understanding that future events would relate and translate into the expectations anchored in the Treaty of February 9, 1918.

A similar optimism had to prevail in Berlin. Notwithstanding Germany's long-term goals at the "restoration of a civil Russia, politically and economically allied with Germany, with Ukraine being the center of such realization," as wishfully announced by Emperor William II on July 2, in Spa,[17] the treaty with Ukraine offered Germany a long list of advantages and gains. After almost four years of exhaustive war, and with still no end in sight, this first treaty had to have enormously uplifted the subdued spirit of the German people. Its psychological effect was no less than the promise of a brighter future. For this reason the treaty with Ukraine must be seen as more than just "Brotfrieden," as it has been regarded in Vienna.[18] Germany's enthusiasm was reflected best by Friedrich Naumann: "The first half of the war is behind us," and by Paul Rohrbach's celebration of Ukraine's independence as "a world-historic event, as history's verdict over the tatar-muscovite Russian inability to change."[19]

There is also a prevailing understanding among historians that the treaty hastened the conclusion of the treaties with Soviet Russia and Romania, thereby ending the war on the eastern fronts, and this was exactly what the Supreme Command of the German Army represented in the persons of Ludendorff and Hoffmann desired. The Foreign Office together with the Department of Commerce were equally entitled to share in Germany's successful policy in Brest-Litovsk. Therefore, the contemporary debate among German experts as to the existence of conflicting views prevailing within the Foreign Office, Army, and the *Wirtschaftsamt* amounts to a quarrel of no importance.[20] All three branches equally expected to share the advantages of the treaty. Moreover, the *Reichstag* on behalf of the German nation, ratified the treaty with a large majority with only a few representatives of the Poles and German independents opposing it. That outcome indeed represented a national consensus.

CHAPTER VI

THE CENTRAL RADA'S CALL FOR MILITARY ASSISTANCE AND THE LIBERATION OF UKRAINE

As could have been expected, the signing of the Ukrainian Peace Treaty initiated a new chain of events that in turn would determine not only its benefits but also its subsequent new consequences. From among these three immediate developments that determined the flow of events were: (1) Trotsky's declaration of February 10 terminating warfare on the eastern front without concluding a peace treaty, a formula known as "neither war nor peace" policy. (2) Germany's and Austria-Hungary's dilemma in the face of events in Ukraine that made their military intervention inevitable in order to secure the promised economic advantages. (3) The Central Rada's decision to request military assistance to liberate Ukraine from the Soviet Russian invasion, leading to still another agreement between the Central Powers and Ukraine of March 25, and the continuous presence of the foreign armies in Ukraine.

The Soviet Russian problem was to be resolved by Germany's decision to use military force once again and to dismantle the former Russian empire into a number of small independent states. In that line of reasoning the treaty should be "viewed as the beginning of an experiment, undertaken somewhat reluctantly by the Germans, aimed at extending the Reich's influence and power into the vast area of Eastern Europe."[1]

The immediate realization of Germany's aims had been discussed and decided on February 13 at the Homburg meeting of the Crown Council in the presence of Emperor William II.[2] There the hestiancy of Kühlmann, Hertling and Undersecretary Friedrich Payer concerning the renewal of the war was overcome by Ludendorff's formula[3] visualizing military assistance in response to calls for help from the Balts and Ukrainians against the Bolshevik invasion. The planned strategy was to comply with the principles of self-determination of the nations, an idea originally advanced by Bolshevik propaganda. The new term *"Polizeiaktion"* (police action), introduced at the Homburg meeting, became acceptable to both Kühlmann and Ludendorff, symbolizing unity in the implementation of the *Ostpolitik.* Appropriate messages had been dispatched to the respective representatives at Brest. At Hoffmann's urging, Liubyns'kyi had already on February 9 signed an appeal to the German nation[4] asking for military assistance. It was officially presented to the German government on February 15, and subsequently widely publicized in the German press. The appeal expressed satisfaction with the treaty and the establishment of friendly relations between Germany and Ukraine, continuing with a description of the extent of destruction in Ukraine by

> The bands of the Red Guard, the executions of the Ukrainian leaders and the heavy indemnities forced upon the people. That barbaric invasion from the north is aimed at the destruction of our independence, as was the case 254 years earlier, with fire and sword to subjugate the Ukrainian people . . . . In this difficult struggle for our existence we seek help. The German army has the power to help us secure our northern border against the further invasion of our enemy.[5]

On the Ukrainian side there was also the expectation that the Central Powers would send Ukrainian units organized from the prisoners of war, and to this end the Rada issued an appeal to all Ukrainian prisoners of war.[6] The German government expressed its willingness to comply with the Rada's wishes, though unconvinced that this would suffice and immediately issued an order to the Army to move into Ukraine. On February 16, the Ukrainian delegation sent a similar appeal to the Austro-Hungarian government, which in the given situation and after reevaluation of the consequences followed Germany's example. Thus the stage had been set for the next period. On February 16 Germany nullified the armistice with Soviet Russia and two days later the German army was again on the move on the Russian front and, as an invited friendly army, began to free U-kraine from the Russian troops together with the remnants of the Ukrainian army stationed in Volhynia.

On February 25 Hrushevskyi, on behalf of the Central Rada and the newly appointed chairman of the Council of the People's Ministers, Vsevolod Holubovych, issued a special appeal to the Ukrainian people explaining and justifying the German army's entry into Ukraine.[7]

Hrushevskyi on his part stressed Germany's previous interest in independent Ukraine, her benevolent treatment and education of Ukrainian prisoners of war, and her training of them for the future Ukrainian army. He was convinced that the liberation of Ukraine could not be achieved by peaceful means. In the past all Russian political parties had refused to recognize Ukraine's right of self-determination. The Bolsheviks had attempted to destroy the Central Rada and to subjugate again Ukraine to Russia and consequently had declared war on Ukraine. That chain of events forced Ukrainians to seek Germany's help because of her interest in an independent and strong Ukraine. Therefore, he believed the Ukrainians should welcome the German army as their friend.

Similarly, Holubovych's address to the Ukrainians justified the arrival of the German army as the consequence of the Soviet Russian war on U-kraine because Russian troops were

> Pillaging peasants and taking our bread, livestock and sugar to Russia. The destruction of our national wealth and the execution of the people by the thousands. The relationship between the German officers and our government is good and friendly, without any conflicts. The friendly German army does not interfere into the domestic affairs of the Ukrainian People's Republic, and requisition of foodstuffs is done not for export to Germany but only to supply the need of the army for which the Ukrainian government will compensate. I also feel strongly that the friendly relationship with Germany will be useful for our young Ukrainian Republic and it will help Ukraine to be placed on an equal base with other great powers.[8]

Indeed, there were ample reasons for the Ukrainians to meet the German army as the liberator from the oppressive Bolsheviks. They received the Germans without suspicion. In the cities, the middle class, being saved from the Bolshevik terror, welcomed the German army. The more nationally conscious Ukrainians anticipated the restoration of their national government.[9]

The Geman advance proceeded quickly. On February 24 Zhytomyr was taken and on March 1 Kiev was liberated from the Russian troops. To the great majority of Kievans the German troops arrived not as invaders and occupiers, as characterized by Soviet historiography,[10] but as sorely needed relief, even as their saviors. The three week-long terror in Kiev at the hands of Muraviev's murderous bands transformed the former war enemy into a friend in need. At the same time, the Austrian-Hungarian army moved into South Ukraine, taking Odessa on March 12. By the middle of April the entire Ukrainian territory was free from the Soviet Red Guards. The so-called "Ukrainian Soviet Socialist government" fled together with the Russian troops.

Along with the German army the Ukrainian division "*Syniozhupannykiv*" composed of former prisoners of war, entered the capital of Ukraine a day after Ukrainian units under the command of Symon Petliura took over Kiev, making the return of the Central Rada possible.

In the meantime, conflicts that arose between the German and Austrian armies as to the areas of operation were settled by an agreement of March 29, specifying their respective territories.[11] The larger and economically more important regions were assigned to the German army, including north-eastern Volhynia, Kiev, Chernyhiv, Poltava, Kharkiv, Novocherkask, Tavridia, and the Crimea. The Austrians had been assigned the rest of Volhynia, Podolia, Kherson, and Ekaterinoslav. Furthermore, dual military administration had been agreed upon for Nikolaev, Rostov, and Mariupol. The Black Sea ports Taganrog and Novorosiisk were put under German control. The industrial area of the Donets Basin, Melitopol and the Crimea were secured in May. All in all, Germany had 500,000 men stationed in Ukraine and Austria-Hungary 250,000.

Simultaneously, events of equal importance were taking place on the Russian front and in Brest-Litovsk that determined the immediate fate of Ukraine. The Russian army was in disarray and no match for the German offensive moving quickly into Russia toward Petrograd. Lenin, realizing the danger approaching the Bolshevist regime's survival and against the views of the "leftwing" within the party, insisted on an immediate conclusion of the treaty.[12] His strategy for saving the revolution prevailed within the Party's Central Committee and the Council of Commissars. Germany's terms had been accepted in the absence of any other available alternative. On March 1, 1918 negotiations were resumed in Brest-Litovsk. The Soviet delegation insisted on the immediate signing in order to prevent the German army from moving further. On March 3 the treaty was signed.

Not an inch of Russia's ethnic or historical territory had to be sacrificed for the peace treaty that indeed saved the Bolshevik regime. Articles III and IV made territories of Estonia, Curland, Lithuania, Lifland, and the greater part of Belorussia free from Russian domination. The German occupation of those territories became vitally important in the ensuing independence of the Baltic states, and for a short period, of Belorussia, which proclaimed independence on March 25, 1918, only to be overrun by the Soviet army in December of that same year. Turkey reclaimed the territories of Ardagan, Kars, and Batum. The two articles provided also for Russia's noninterference in the internal affairs of those territories.

Article VI dealt specifically with Ukraine. Accordingly, Soviet Russia recognized Ukraine's Peace Treaty with the Central Powers and was immediately evacuated by the Russian troops and the Russian Red Guard. Russia was also to cease all agitation or propaganda against the Government or public institutions of the Ukrainian People's Republic.

Of all the articles of the treaty the sixth was "the harshest one" for Russia, as admitted by Chubarian,[13] for "it cut deeply into Russia's economic potential, especially in regards to foodstuffs, coal and iron ore resources." The decolonization of the Russian empire and especially Ukraine's separation amounted to Russia's return to the pre-Petrinian period and made her into a borderland of Europe. In that case the Bolshevik regime, while surviving in Russia, could hardly become a menace to Europe. Within that context lies the meaning and importance of both the treaties concluded in Brest-Litovsk. It was, however, the Versailles Peace Treaty that once again reversed the flow of history to Soviet Russia's advantage and to Europe's decline in decades to come.

Considering the size of the territory in question, the number of people affected, the social and economic instability, as well as the powerful propaganda from Moscow, upholding the terms of both treaties should not have been left to Germany alone. Only the presence of the allies could measure up to the existing conditions. For all practical purposes this role could not have been entrusted to the aging and internally weakening Habsburg Empire. In that period only Ukraine could become the co-implementor of the emerging order in Eastern Europe since her interests coincided closely with Germany's aims. Hence, the events in Ukraine during the coming months were destined to shape the future and to ensure both treaties' prolonged duration.

The Central Rada returned to Kiev with the text of the Fourth universal of January 22 and with the Agrarian Law of January 31. Both binding documents, socialist in substance, were aimed at the revolutionary restructuring of the social-economic system in the young state. Accordingly, the Ukrainian revolution continued to be a socialist-nationalist experiment with emphasis on its socialist priority. On the other hand, the Rada's return was accompanied by the powerful German and Austrian armies, representing old capitalist regimes in pursuit of the economic and political interests of their respective governments. The prevention of a dangerous collision, which seemed bound to arise, was avertible but only if both sides would have been willing to exercise a maximum of good will, understanding each other's priorities and ability to compromise without jeopardizing their respective basic interests. Had both sides exercised pragmatism instead of doctrinism and exclusive reliance on military power it would have served them more advantageously. The task was not an easy one, but possible.

The Fourth universal once again reaffirmed the Rada's commitment to pacifism,

> not to support any war because the Ukrainian people desire peace, democratic peace to take place immediately. As soon as the war is over and peace agreements signed, the army shall be demobilized and replaced by a people's militia . . . . In regards to the agrarian question, the Rada's commission had prepared a law giving land to the working people without indemnity based on the principles of the abolishment of private property and of socialization of the land . . . .

Forests, water-ways, mineral deposits are the property of the people and shall be administered by the Ukrainian People's Republic. . . . The main branches of commercial trade and its profit will be utilized for the benefit of the people. . . . International trade will be the government's responsibility. . . . Also, laws will be promulgated monopolizing iron-ore, leather and tobacco industries and other product lines with huge profit margins. . . . The state's control will be extended over banks and credit unions. . . . All nationalities of the Ukrainian People's Republic enjoy the rights of national and personal autonomy, as has been granted by the law of January 9.[14]

The Agrarian Law of January 31, went even further with the policy of socialization and provided numerous additional specifics. The Commission entrusted to write the law reflected the views of the Ukrainian Social Revolutionaries, among them M. Shumskyi, who then turned Bolshevik and P. Khrystiuk, joined by the Russian S. R. Deshevoi and Pukhtinskii. The Law,[15] benefiting exclusively the poorest and landless peasantry would alienate landowning peasants with holdings of ten or more desiatyns, who constituted approximately fifty-five percent of the Ukrainian peasantry. On this point, the largest Ukrainian social class, the peasantry, representing over seventy percent of the population, was divided into two hostile groups symbolizing the priority of social revolution as opposed to national revolution. The Ukrainian S. D. and S. R., having embraced programs of the Russian radical parties, tried to transplant Russian models into Ukraine without any consideration of local distinctions, conditions, and national priorities. This meant that Ukrainian priorities would be ordered on the basis of Russian conditions. The two parties were unable to separate the Ukrainian revolution from events in Russia. Although their intentions were honest, the Ukrainian S. D. and S. R. did not exactly reflect the overall conditions in Ukraine. The British socialist Philips Price observed:

But the soldiers from the south-west front, instead of electing committees which declared their support for the Bolsheviks, as in the north, went over for the most part to the National movement, which was growing in the towns and villages of the Ukraine. This was largely explained by the fact that in the Ukraine the industrial proletariat formed a very small section of the population. On the other hand, there was a big, well-to-do peasant proprietor class, particularly in the regions east of the Dniester and the initiative in political movements had been very largely left to them and to the intellectuals of the provincial towns. Moreover, the owners of the sugar factories and the higher grades of the bureaucracy, were all either Poles or Great Russians from the northern provinces. This gave the popular movement a certain national tinge, which enabled the intellectuals to exploit the class antagonism of these regions in the interest of their petty bourgeois local movement. The revolutionary energy thus assumed her a national character, and its organ became the Ukrainian Rada, or Council.[16]

By competing for the sympathies and allegiances of the social groups, such as the "village proletariat," that were intensively targeted by the Russian and Ukrainian Bolsheviks, the Law, in effect, wrote off a large segment of the population from the Rada's potential supporters and defenders of Ukraine's independence. Also, it alienated the powerful class of landowners and industrialists who had lost their properties without indemnities. Many of them, including the Russians and especially the Poles could have become useful citizens of Ukraine in view of the Bolshevik rule in Russia.

And finally, the Law created chaos in the countryside and discouraged large and medium-sized landowners from planting crops on their estates in the coming Spring thereby depriving the Rada of the ability to deliver one million tons of the food supply promised to the Central Powers before July 31. Nor did it help the Rada to stop the Soviet Russian occupation of Ukraine but it created still another reason for the coming conflict between the German army and the Rada. The Rada's almost unanimous vote[17] on this radical Agrarian Law reflected both—commitment to doctrinism and underestimation of the elements needed for national statehood. As a consequence, "opposition to the Rada arose not only among the landowners but also among the wealthier peasants."[18]

An equally negative development had been taking place since mid-January within the Central Rada. The ideological conflict between the two leftist parties—S. D. and S. R., had further weakened the Rada's ability to govern. The left-wing of the S. R. demanded immediate reconciliation with the Bolsheviks by declaring Ukraine a Soviet Republic.[19] Unable to overcome the growing internal chaos and in order to protect the country from the foreign invasion, Vynnychenko and his Social Democratic cabinet resigned on January 30. The new Secretariat, composed predominantly of Social Revolutionaries chaired by Vsevolod Holubovych, initiated steps to embrace the Soviet system, only to be pushed out of Kiev by the Soviet Russian army. Muraviev, in his "Order no. 9" of February 4, ordered his army to "unmercifully eliminate all officers, cadets, haidamaks, monarchists and all enemies of the revolution."[20] His Red Guard did its best in executing the order by killing some 5000 people.[21] The People's Secretariat of the Ukrainian Workers' Peasants' Republic under the leadership of Evgeniia Bosh arrived from Kharkiv and began its short-lived rule in Kiev. Before its retreat from Kiev on March 1, the Red Guard ruthlessly plundered and looted everything in sight, food supplies, money from banks, weapons, furniture, anything that could be moved.[22]

Dmytro Doroshenko, one of the most prolific and renowned Ukrainian historians, describing the Rada's return to Kiev expressed the hope of many that:

> The government of the Central Rada cognizant of the harsh realities would position itself on realistic grounds and instead of the utopian projects and fantasies would begin with the practical work of rebuilding the national economy of the country, to put together an administrative apparatus so as to achieve order . . . to combat chaos and disarray brought about by the Rada's previous policy of social utopism and maximalism.[23]

Yet, except for a few personnel changes in the Secretariat, the Rada announced that all universals and laws remain in force,[24] assuring herewith the continuity of the former chaos. The difference however was that at this time two powerful armies stood on Ukrainian soil, together with the German and Austrian political representatives observing the worsening conditions which only could hamper the delivery of the promised goods. Lacking experience and knowledge in Ukrainian affairs, the German Foreign Office "tacitly accepted Ludendorff's overlordship and acquiesced in the German occupation of areas in the southeast that had not been encompassed in the original plan. It is not surprising, therefore, that the diplomatic representatives in Kiev were destined to play a secondary role in Germany's Ukrainian undertaking throughout the period of occupation."[25]

A harbinger of the coming conflict was the inability of the German or Austrian military and political officials to speak Ukrainian and their lack of any previous knowledge of the Ukrainian affairs prior to their arrival in Ukraine.[26] From among the German generals only Max Hoffmann was fluent in Russian, yet he did not stay in Ukraine for too long. Having found common ground at Brest-Litovsk, a few weeks later both sides began to look at each other more like strangers, instead of friends. Ukrainian ideologists could not understand German and Austrian conservative and pragmatical establishments and vice versa.

In absence of an effective administration directed from Kiev, both armies were forced to intervene in the various local affairs and conflicts, especially in cases affecting social order, their own security, and their countries' interest. This was especially true with the owners of the estates attempting to regain forcefully their land and properties with the tacit and often active support of the foreign armies, thereby contributing to the deepening of the social hostilities across the country. These "punitive detachments" had further detrimentally affected the relationship between the poor peasants and the occupational armies leading to the further decline of the Rada's power and prestige. This has been proved by the Odessa Russians' refusal to acknowledge its authority.[27]

In the given situation the Central Powers' benevolent neutrality could not last very long. The initial assurance of non-interference had their practical limits, too. Replying to Holubovych's telegram after the seizure of Kiev, Chancellor Hertling stated:

> I have received with the warmest satisfaction the news about Kiev's liberation. I salute you and the young Ukrainian army on the success and on behalf of the German nation I express my satisfaction that the German troops were destined to participate in the liberation of the Ukrainian people. . . . The German army is in your country, however, I am empowered to declare, that as soon as you will be convinced that its task is completed, the order will be given to leave.[28]

On the Austrian side, Count Johann Forgach, Vienna's representative in Kiev assured *Nova Rada's* correspondent that his government did not intend to annex any Ukrainian territory, to intervene in the internal affairs and is only interested in the restoration of normal economic conditions.

"The Austrian army came into Ukraine as a friend and not as an enemy. The army will be recalled as soon as order will be restored and upon the Ukrainian government's request."[29]

Against these politically motivated assurances, the German army's readiness to cooperate with the Central Rada to restore order and to secure deliveries as planned was based exactly on these priorities. Initially Ludendorff made this clear and General Hoffmann openly spelled out the army's role:

> The Central Powers having wanted peace with Ukraine to secure delivery of the bread had to get it themselves. Once having said A, we had to say B; we have legally recognized the Ukrainian government and we have therefore concluded a treaty. In order to see the treaty implemented we had to support the government which signed the treaty with us.[30]

It remains debatable how much the Central Rada was able to visualize its coexistence with the armies of the Central Powers considering emerging differences in regard to the implementation of the Brest-Litovsk treaty under very different conditions. In the meantime the two armies concluded an agreement on March 25 coordinating their military and logistic operations in Ukraine. This was aimed obviously at a more effective control of the territory and security for immediate deliveries badly needed in Germany, and acutely so in Vienna.

CHAPTER VII

FROM LIBERATION TO OCCUPATION

By the end of March 1918 the general situation in Ukraine presented the following picture: (1) The Rada's continued inability to pacify and to control the country and to achieve a national consensus resulting in the rise of internal opposition. (2) Rifts appearing in the policies of the Rada and the Central Powers. (3) The military occupation by the German and Austrian armies was completed. (4) The presence of the two armies necessitated a specific arrangement regarding their various responsibilities determined further by the policies and needs of their respective governments.

The Rada's social radicalism did not by any means reflect the interest and attitude of the entire nation. Itself the product of the "workers, soldiers, and peasants," the Central Rada and particularly its two main-stays—Social Democrats and Social Revolutionaries, was symptomatic of the revolutionary period dominated by elements committed to basic political, social and economic changes. In this regard the situation in U-kraine not only resembled prevailing conditions in Russia, but also exposed the "common revolutionary tradition" of nineteenth-century Russia. The difference, however, arose with the Bolshevik seizure of power in Russia and Lenin's primary reliance on the terror of the *Cheka* and the Red Army, which by January 1918 was estimated to have been 180,000-men strong. In Ukraine the Rada's concept of the use of terror and power was diametrically different. In contrast, the Rada having emerged organically from below remained inviolably committed to the "revolution from below." This did not impress Lenin and thus could not protect Ukraine from the Red Army.

Moreover, the Rada's domestic policy hardly had a chance to take hold considering its enemies on the extreme left, local Communists and their ally, Soviet Russia, and on the right, the conservatives and nationalists with the foreign armies in sympathy with them. Expelling the Soviet Russian troops from Ukraine only ended open warfare but not the subversive activities. The spreading of anarchy and propaganda impeded sorely needed normalization, without which the state apparatus could not function.[1]

Despite their exaggeration as to the importance and accomplishments of the Communists during 1918, the Bolsheviks never had a chance to seize power by themselves without the invasion of the Russian army. The real danger to the Rada's government in the ensuing period emanated from the right, from the landowners, well-to-do peasants, commercial and industrial establishments, and from the nationalistically-minded intelligentsia organized in such parties as the Social Federalists, the Ukrainian National Party (founded by M. Mikhnovs'kyi), the Ukrainian Democratic Agrarian Party, and the Ukrainian Party of Independent Socialists. The conservative camp found itself closer to the system represented by the two foreign armies.

Witnessing and disapproving of the Rada's socialist experiments, new groupings began to form, organizing themselves in the hope of reversing the trend through political activity. In Ukraine the historical memories had not faded as proven by the emergence of the Free Cossacks movement (*Vilne kozatstvo*). The movement grew strong not only among the owners of the large estates, but also among peasants. P. Khrystiuk, himself a Social Revolutionary and a noted historian of the Ukrainian revolution, explained it as:

> Voluntary, semi-military organizations of the peasants committed to defend villages against banditry and robberies which began to spread after the collapse of the former order, and by the need to forcefully defend economic class interest of the peasantry and

outgrowth of romantic historical traditions, and the memories of the Cassackdom of the past.[2]

The Rada's policy only inspired them to defend the principles of private ownership and to demand participation in the government. At the initiative of the Ukrainian Democratic Agrarian Party (*Khliboroby*) the first congress convened at Lubny on March 25. Two hundered delegates from the northern Poltava region in their resolution stated:

> The agrarian policy of the Central Rada is destructive for the state and for the national economy as well; the Congress demands the recognition of private property as the foundation of the national economy. The Congress demands that the right to own the land and living and material inventory be instantly restored. The Congress demands that landowners be granted ownership of a certain amount of land and be free to rent surplus land to peasants of smaller holdings. The Congress demands restoration of law and order in the Ukrainian state for socialists and non-socialists alike. The Congress demands that representatives of the land owners be included in the Central Rada.

The Congress had sent a special delegation to Kiev headed by Serhii Shemet. Since Hrushevskyi refused to have their case presented to the Rada, the delegates met with its representatives and Holubovych, but nothing was accomplished. Thus the existing rift was bound to widen resulting ultimately in a direct confrontation on April 28, 1918.

At that time the all-Ukrainian congress of peasants and landowners took place in Kiev, an event that not only coincided with but even gave some impetus to the fall of the Rada. After the occupation, the opposition from the extreme left within the country found itself in disarray so that during the months of March and April few activities took place on that side. The remnants of the communist establishment resided in Taganrog. There, only on April 19/20, 1918, came into existence the Communist Party (B) of Ukraine despite staunch opposition from the Russophiles. The first congress of the CPU, held in Moscow in July declared the party an autonomous organization of the Russian Communist Party (B). The party was obliged to comply with Lenin's policy of "respite" by abstaining from any military activity against the Central Powers. Some rather insignificant communist action that began only in July were limited mainly to organizing strikes and local terrorist acts. This partial "neutrality" of the left did not extend to new, rising challengers on the right—the conservatives and the nationalists. Yet the Rada's reluctance to compromise with them grew only more acute especially in view of its inability, or perhaps unwillingness, to meet the expectations of the occupying armies.

These armies came as invited allies but with a long list of "payments in kind." It is understandable that Berlin and even more so Vienna considered deliveries of grain as a ligitimate obligation to be forthcoming regardless of the Rada's fate, conditions, and any other factors that could be lifted by the armies already stationed in Ukraine.

Moreover, from the outset, the German and Austrian officers as well as political representatives, assessed realistically the prevailing situation and had no illusions about the Rada's weakness. Already on March 12, Hoffmann wrote:

> The difficulties in Ukraine lie in the fact that the Central Rada has no backing except for our military assistance. As soon as we withdraw our troops the whole splendor will fall apart, the reason being the land reform. On that the Ukrainian Social Democrats who control the Rada are as crazy as the Bolsheviks, while expropriating the land and giving it to the peasants, thereby destroying Ukrainian agriculture. . . . The peasants, having parcelled the landed estates, and facing uncertainty, do not cultivate the land.[4]

General Wilhelm Groener, the then commander-in-chief of the German army in Ukraine, wrote to his wife:

> Ukraine remains a socialist republic but for how long is difficult to say. The situation as it is right now cannot last for too long. Work must return to normalcy. Whether the present government is up to its responsibilities remains questionable. I am eager to meet the people of Kiev. An energetic and prominent head seems not to by among them.[5]

The German generals' assessment clearly reflected their understanding of order, discipline and of the actual situation. These differed considerably from the views of the Ukrainians in the Rada and the General Secretariat. Unfortunately, no attempts were made on either side to reconcile the differences and to bridge or revise their respective perceptions. At that time, however, it was up to the Rada to heed its stronger partners. For, neither Groener nor the Austrians were about to sacrifice the lives of their soldiers to defend the socialist Rada.

General Alfred Krauss, commander-in-chief of the Austrian forces in Ukraine, did not hide his low esteem of the Rada's ability to govern. In his view the Rada's ineffectiveness had already been revealed in Brest-Litovsk because "the Rada had no army to defend the country and to impose its rule." He blamed the Rada for its inability to control the countryside and to create conditions that would make delivery of food-stuffs possible.[6]

On March 23 the Austrian ambassador in Kiev, Count Johann Forgach, reported his first impression about conditions in Ukraine to Czernin:

> Based on my conversations with a large number of individuals I became convinced that in the nearest future we may export from Ukraine only one-half of the expected volume of foodstuffs by disregarding the present government which cannot be considered seriously either politically or economically due to constant changes in personnel, deliberations and prohibitive orders affecting the export by our organizations . . . . Should the export be hindered by the commissars our military authorities ought to be instructed by the Sumpreme Command to act definitely. This would release me from the fruitless interventions by the government in Kiev, which would be forced to acknowledge the real situation, i.e., the occupation of the country by our troops with all its conse-quences, including economic. Our military sacrifices of keeping the government in power are far reaching. While the government continues to ride on its theoretical hobby horses, we must be eco-nomically compensated wit the export of foodstuffs.[7]

On March 24 Forgach dispatched his report on the political and eco-nomic conditions, and the status of food reserves, the currency, and the relationship with the Rada's government.[8] The picture had already become stereotyped: the political vacuum brought about by the Rada's inability to govern, the agrarian chaos in the countryside making the delivery of grain doubtful, but huge reserves of foodstuffs were available provided the difficulties of collecting and shipping could be surmounted. His report, like previous ones, could only convince officials in Berlin and Vienna that there was no other way of obtaining foodstuffs except by use of military force and by disregarding policy, diplomacy and even the treaty itself.

A newly developing style had been initiated by the Military Agreement between Germany and Austria-Hungary of March 28, 1918.[9] The agreement, born primarily out of strategic-tactical considerations evolving from the occupation of Ukraine by two armies, underscored both countries' economic interest—attempting to minimize any rivalry and to divide the expected spoils. Its main point featured the territorial division, an arrangement of transportational facilities satisfying the needs of both countries, and above all, exploitation of the natural resources as determined in Article 5:

> The coal and iron ore regions east of Katerynoslav remain under joint administration and utilization at a ratio of 1 to 1. A special commission will prepare the draft of an agreement on the details. The distribution of iron ore will be regulated by the terms of an agreement to be signed in Berlin. The distribution of coal will be primarily determined by the needs of the railroad, commercial fleet and war ships, and needs of Turkey, will remain under the administration of the Central Railroad Bureau in Kiev in collaboration with the Black Sea Administration in Brail.

Articles 6, 7 and 8 regulated the stationing of Austrian troops in Kiev, in the various transportation centers and the stationing of the German nationals of the Austrian army in the German settlements in Ukraine. Article 9 provided for the common administration of communications equipment in Odessa. The agreement was immediately put in force.

Another important decision made on this same day led to the replacement of the rather independent General Alexander von Linsingen with

Fieldmarshal Herman von Eichhorn, thereby strengthening Groener's and the Army's position in Ukrainian affairs at the expense of the Foreign Office in Berlin.[10] Groener, a staunch enemy of the socialist Central Rada and the signer of the Military Agreement, reacted to the appointment by stating: "May God give that this historical act may result in Germany's welfare," and on the same day expressed his satisfaction with Eichhorn's nomination.[11]

The gap that began to develop between the Army and Wilhelm Street in Berlin over the growing influence of the army in Ukraine progressed rapidly. Groener's reaction to the Chancellor's telegram of March 28 to the Ambassador in Kiev, Adolf Mumm, illustrates this point.[12] Mumm was urged to exercise retraint in regard to Ukraine's internal affairs and to act only to uphold law and order. To that Groener wrote in his memoirs:

> People in the Foreign Office have not yet come to realize that we have to rule in Ukraine and the Ukrainian government has to dance to our music. The Foreign Office speaks about preservation of the *status quo* in the countryside, i.e., of plundering and robbery, and does so believing that the Ukrainian government exercises power in the country. . . . Count Forgach likewise holds little regard for the government. The officials pay lip service, but do not seriously think about the grain deliveries. They are incapable of acting on it anyway.[13]

From then on, Groener's letters to his wife almost daily contained reports about the hopeless situation in Ukraine, about the peasants' refusal to work the land expropriated from the landowners and about his determination to cooperate with the seventy-year-old General Fieldmarshal Eichhorn, making it possible "to freely act here."[14] This "freedom to act" meant to him supplying Germany with ample foodstuffs and to "exchange the horses by removing the Central Rada."[15]

Groener's understanding of Germany's interest in Ukraine, while not exactly reflective of the attitude of the Foreign Office, coincided completely with the views of the Office of Economics (RWA). Similarly to Vienna's original resolve, both branches of the German government began to consider exclusively Article VII of the Brest-Litovsk Treaty at the expense of all other provisions. This was underscored by dispatching a large economic delegation to Kiev. The German representatives of the RWA were instructed to concentrate on food supplies, the banking segment, railroad transportation and heavy industry. German investments in Ukraine and the fullfilment of Germany's economic obligations towards Ukraine were ignored. In a special memo addressed to the Foreign Office, the Office of Economics on February 23 stated:

> For the time being our interest lies in obtaining the promised amount of grain and other resources. The situation will change when our troops occupy Kiev, the Ukrainian Donets-basin, the ore mines of Krivoi-Rog and the Black Sea coast. Then, at the appropriate time, we have to obtain from the Ukrainian government assurances of further ore deliveries, the reinstatement of private property for our German landlords, as well as concessions in regard to our navigation on Ukrainian waterways. . . . It is important that this information is not released to the press at this time, and the press will get only some clues, to say nothing of our future demands resulting from the further penetration of our troops into Ukraine.[16]

The War Office stepped on the economic bandwagon by broadening significantly the formulation and pursuit of Germany's *Ostpolitik* in 1918. In a secret memo of March 1 to Chancellor Hertling, Hans Karl von Stein, on behalf of the War Ministry, articulated the Ministry's position on Ukraine:

> The German military aid to Ukraine and the northern peoples of Russia against the Bolsheviks justifies equivalent demands, at least compensation of either money or delivery of war material. In Ukraine, Germany should have a say in railway transportation in order to exercise greater influence on the economic conditions there to ensure a larger quantity of products for Germany. To this end additional agreements should consider: (1) The creation of a common administration of the railway system and binding tariffs which would counterbalance the American interst in Russia. (2) In regards to grain, Germany's claim for the Ukrainian surplus should be secured and an agreement reached in favor of Germany for years to come.[17]

This broad imposition of the economic-military establishment upon Germany's foreign policy and its determination of *Ostpolitik* priorities reflected the powerful influence Ludendorff had acquired since the nomination of Hertling as chancellor. Hertling himself "had an almost childish trust in the Supreme Command."[18] Probably under pressure of the military an important conference took place in Berlin on March 5, with Ukraine being the exclusive agenda item. Chaired by the State Minister Karl Helfferich, the conference included representatives of almost all governmental branches. The agenda centered on such essential issues as requesting financial compensation for the military assistance, economic demands as specified in the agreement with Ukraine and in specific delivery of surplus grain to Germany and the construction of silos, railroad transportation, the Black Sea coast and river transport, mines and assurances for the shipment of iron ore and manganese.[19]

The lengthy reports of all representatives and far-reaching discussions centered on the question of how to best protect Germany's economic interests. The only words of caution "to not demand too much from Ukraine in order not to contribute to the desire of Ukrainians for the reunification with Russia," came from the Foreign Office representative Johannes.[20] In that regard, as will be shown in the next chapter, the Foreign Office, and especially its representative in Kiev, Mumm, had preserved a balance between politics and economic considerations in regard to Ukraine even after the treaty was signed.

At the moment, however, Johannes, warning against excessive demands, found support from Stein who observed that the military assistance extended to the Rada was equally in Germany's interest. In contrast, the representatives of the Supreme Command, Major Windscheid and Vice Minister of the Treasury Jahn, insisted on certain material compensations. Finally it was agreed that to link the Ukrainian with the German railway system was in Germany's interest. Also, a consensus was reached on the utilization of Ukraine's sea and waterways transportation system, on intensive exploitation of its natural resources, especially of iron ore and manganese, on a future monetary compensation for military assistance, and on the need of some changes of economic agreements with Ukraine and their extension. The conference produced uniformity for all branches of government thereby strengthening the main direction of Germany's policy in Ukraine for months to come.

That meeting was held in complete secrecy, the Central Rada being neither consulted nor informed. The process of changing the German army's role from liberator to occupational force was thereby initiated. In the meantime other events and decisions indicated the coming changes.

As for Austria-Hungary's involvement in Ukrainian affairs and her motives in joining the military occupation of the southern Ukraine it should be remembered that the Austrian army moved into Ukraine on February 28 on Emperor Karl's order. This delay and a certain reluctance to act has been explained with reference to external conditions. "Austria had a genuine desire to refrain from doing anything that might destroy the chances for a general peace by agreement, which she rightly viewed as her only hope for survival as an empire."[21] It can also be argued that Vienna's fear of boosting Ukrainian preeminence within the Empire in relation to the Poles and other nationalities did not exactly contribute to the prospect of having a free and large Ukrainian state on her northern border. However, facing the dilemma of exclusive German domination of Ukraine while Austria was in dire need of grain from Ukraine became in intolerable prospect that forced the government to send the army into Ukraine. Having initially refused, Czernin now wanted to bargain by seeking the Rada's compromise on the Polish-Ukrainian border in the Kholmland region. This ploy was rejected by Ludendorff who preferred to play the Ukrainian card at the expense of the Poles, leaving the Austrians with no other choice but to join the German army. This exclusively opportunistic decision reflected Czernin's reference to the Brest-Litovsk Treaty as "Brotfrieden."[22]

Devoid of any longterm political ambition, Vienna's policy from the outset to the last days of the Empire's existence was limited to "getting foodstuffs and raw material, and to supporting the Ukrainian national-separatist conviction against the reunification with Russia in order to secure our economic interest in the future," as admitted by General Arthur Arz, Chief of the Supreme Command of the Austrian-Hungarian army, in the Summer of 1918.[23]

Vienna's lofty expectations were dimming with the first reports from the Austrian representatives in Ukraine. All of them described the situation in Ukraine in bleak colors, beginning with the Rada's inability to govern, the prevailing chaos in the countryside pointing to the poor prospects of obtaining foodstuffs. One report even suggested disregarding official channels and relying on forced requisition of grain.[24]

Forgach's secret report to Czernin on "The political and economic conditions in Ukraine," of March 23-26,[25] confirmed the dim prospects:

> The chairman of the Central Rada, a former professor of Ruthenian history at Lemberg (Lviv) university, is an idealistic theoretician, interested only in great designs not caring enough about the activities of the ministers and of the economy in particular. . . . The owners of large estates having delivered the imposed quotas of grain to the state, have lost their reserves to thieving peasants and are in no position to plant in the spring. . . . The peasants having taken the land from the landlords as they were promised by the Rada's universals, do not plant either, being uncertain about the future events and the chances to keep the land . . . . For this reason the optimistic expectations we hold back home, must be significantly reduced, i.e., in regards to the quantity of grain to be secured only modest figures can be expected. . . . Ukrainian ministers insist on state-controlled trade with Germany and Austria-Hungary, which obviously will be a complete fiasco considering the government's ineffectiveness.

Other parts of the report deal with currency and transportation matters, stressing the normal flow of goods as difficult.

This thoroughly bleak and adverse picture of Ukraine in March 1918, by an Austrian official of a very different social, economic, and political background, typified only the meeting of two quite contrasting realities and perceptions. By that time the Central Rada was only in the fourth week of its return to Kiev, hardly enough time to bring the country into normalcy following the Bolshevik disruption, ensuing terror and civil war. Of course, the inherent shortcomings of the Rada were not conducive to speedy restoration of law and order, especially in the presence of foreign armies. The Austrian-Hungarian army, more than the German, exhibited little respect for the Ukrainian government, thereby increasing the Rada's as well as its own difficulties. Therefore, Forgach's report, or plan of action, hardly can be seen as an objective evaluation of the Rada's qualifications to govern the country in a very difficult period of Ukraine's history.

Accordingly, Czernin responded immediately in a note of March 26:

The unsettled conditions in Ukraine and the Kievan government's irresolution do not permit waiting for negotiations. Therefore, acquisition and delivery of goods must begin without waiting for the conclusion of negotiations. The troops have been sent for the Rada's protection and securance of the goods to be received and therefore one must act accordingly. Resistance to the purchase and exchange of goods must be eliminated. Requisitions should not be used. . . . Purchase of provisions and supplies for the army must be done by commissars and cartel agents.[26]

The Austrian-Hungarian Supreme Command's reports to the Ministry of Foreign Affairs from the end of March throughout the month of April grew increasingly more pessimistic, citing ineffectiveness and deteriorating economic conditions and an alarming concern for the approaching Spring planting. In a report of March 30, much attention was given to the landlords' meeting in Kiev on March 15, which opposed the Rada's socialization policy, demanded the restoration of private ownership of land and that the government include representatives of the landlords.

Another army report of April 2, informed that:

The Rada and the government should not be seen as a popular representative body but as one arbitrarily composed. . . . The Council of Ministers headed by Holubovych is almost exclusively selected from the Social Revolutionaries and remains unpopular with the great majority of all segments of society and is kept in power solely by the power of the Central Powers. The moderate parties are not presented in the government. The members of the government as well as the civil servants, with only few exceptions, are inexperienced and young. They are capable of formulating and spreading slogans and utopian ideas, but lacking the ability to translate theories into realities.

The remainder of the reports were of a similar vein. Without detracting from any positive aspect or accomplishment, the reports left the impression that there existed not a state, but a huge vacuum of disorder, contradiction—a vastly rich land waiting to be exploited.

CHAPTER VIII

THE END OF THE PARTNERSHIP
AND THE DEMISE OF THE
CENTRAL RADA

It did not take long to test the "mismatched" partnership of Brest-Litovsk. While the partners shared some common goals such as the mutual desire for peace and Ukraine's independence, the underlying differences soon began to overshadow their initial premises. The problems arose equally from diverse philosophical, social and economic concepts that stifled reconciliation of common aims and mutually beneficial cooperation.

Like the Provisional Government in Russia, the Central Rada did not consider itself to be the Constitutional representative of all the people of Ukraine, but rather of a segment of certain social classes and groups. Lacking a constitutional base the Rada acted more like a provisional governing body during a chaotic period. Unlike the Bolshevik regime in Russia, the Rada did not use terror as a tool to obtain and to maintain political power. This quasi-democratic and quasi-revolutionary organ could have eventually survived had it not been attacked by Soviet Russia. Yet having failed to realize the importance of a national army, the Rada thoroughly disarmed itself and so weakened its chances of leading and completing the national revolution. Thus, its own social and economic programs, which necessitated creation of a national state before the implementation of social experiments, had no chance to succeed.

76

In the meantime the prevailing disorder began to involve the German army, which was sporadically attacked in the countryside forcing some commanders to use drastic measures.[1] The Minister of Justice, Mykhailo Tkachenko, while having failed to pacify the country, on March 23 issued a circular denying German and Austrian military courts the right to take any action against the civilian population as such action would amount to interference in Ukraine's domestic affairs. The German reply expressed dissatisfaction with the wording of the announcement and publication of the circular without prior consultation.[2] Adding further to the growing suspicion and alienation this affair resulted in the controversial order of April 6 by Fieldmarshal Eichhorn.[3] In tough and unmistakable terms the order, issued without the Rada's knowledge, stated among other points:

> The harvest will belong to those who will sow the land and they will be paid. The peasant who takes more land than he can plant harms the Ukrainian state, and he will be punished accordingly. Where the peasants cannot themselves cultivate all land and where landlords are present, the latter are obliged to proceed with the planting without interference into the legally distributed land. Peasant resistance is prohibited, pilfering grain and destruction of crops in the fields will be severely punished.[4]

The Order took the Rada by surprise, but rendered helpless the ministers' reactions to verbal protests. Kovalevskyi, the Minister of Agriculture, denounced the order as "the product of the influence of certain circles with the large landowners playing a decisive role."[5] The Little Rada had passed a resolution stating:

> The German army has been invited by the government for purposes determined by the Ukrainian government. Any interference of the German and Austrian-Hungarian army into Ukrainian social and economic affairs is inadmissible. Any interference makes the Ukrainian government's compliance with the provisions of the agreement impossible.

Thereupon, Kovalevskyi instructed the Ukrainian people to disregard Eichhorn's order and the Minister of Foreign Affairs, M. Liubyns'kyi, was instructed to intervene in Berlin.[6]

On April 18, Prime Minister Holubovych conferred with Mumm in regard to these matters.[7] He later admitted that the order reflected the
policy of his government. The issue was somewhat diffused but not forgotten. Mumm reported to the Foreign Office in Berlin:

> Today we discussed the urgency of the Spring planting. Apparently
> Holubovych will not yield to the demand of the landowners and
> peasants to delay implementation of the land expropriation law, but
> only to determine valuation, creating sort of a monopoly. Hence,
> cultivation of the land remains uncertain. . . . Since we went along
> with the present government and did not take over the country's
> administration, we are not able to prevent their theoretical ideas.
> Therefore, our situation here remains extremely difficult.[8]

In this same telegram Mumm also reported about his meeting with the
Austrian Fieldmarshal Langer who suggested requisition as the only means
of obtaining grain. Not surprisingly, this proposal appeared "unobjection-
able" to Mumm.

Vienna's positive reaction to Langer's suggestions came in a Foreign
Ministry's telegram of April 3 to Forgach:[9]

> Fieldmarshal Langer tells me about his conviction that a larger quan-
> tity of foodstuffs from Ukraine can be obtained by replacing the
> present Ukrainian government with another one which would not
> passively resist, by sending more troops to Ukraine, using appropriate
> energy and recklessness. . . . In regard to the first point, I request
> your opinion and personally I would not object to have this totally
> isolated government replaced. Of course, we should try to win over
> Germany to our point of view and to have Ambassador Mumm's sup-
> port. Immediate steps are being taken to send four to five divisions
> to Ukraine. . . . The supply of foodstuffs could possibly prevent
> Austria's collapse. Austria is in no position to prevent the catastrophe
> unless 50,000 carloads can be delivered before the harvest. Please
> hurry and do whatever must be done.

The end of the Empire near, Vienna's desperation to save the Monarchy at any price meant that Ukraine's interest would be a low priority. The intention to remove the Central Rada would begin slowly to be translated into action whenever appropriate conditions would permit.

Similarly on the German side during the first two weeks of April, there began to emerge the conviction of the uselessness of the Rada and the search for a new alternative. Officials in Berlin, some German political representatives in Kiev and military leaders continued to support an independent Ukraine. The problem to be dealt with was the government of the Central Rada, which began to be seen as basically incapable of governing and of meeting Germany's expectations.

Most of the documents available together with some recently published monographs suggest that beginning in early April the German Army leadership (Ludendorff, Hoffmann, Groener, Eichhorn) emerged as the most influential interpreter and implementer of Germany's *Ostpolitik*.[10] It was Groener who in his diary and letters to his wife sarcastically described the Central Rada as *"Regierungskasper"* (governing puppets) and as "adolescents occupying miniature cabinet posts," and as "useless," and the Ukrainian state as a "chaos."[11]

On April 3, Groener handed Holubovych a sharp protest about the delay of negotiating an agreement on grain delivery. To his wife he wrote: "The so-called government leads us around by the nose . . . . Should it continue to do so nothing else will be left for us but to put another government in its place."[12]

Mumm, reporting about the meeting to the Chancellor, had noticed Holubovych's willingness to proceed with negotiations and abstained from derogatory comments.[13] To the progress of negotiations Forgach revealed in his report that the Ukrainian government immediately secured for the Central Powers twenty-five million puds of grain and that 210 loaded railway cars left for the border.[14] Obviously, the Ukrainian government was able to function under difficult conditions, contradicting Groener's low opinion of it. Indeed, the agreement on grain was progressing well, which according to Mumm, held promise especially in view of deliveries of one million tons of grain and of forage for livestock before July 31.[15] Much attention was paid during subsequent deliberations with the representatives of the Ukrainian government to payment procedures and compensations for large landowners. Both Mumm and Forgach had seen the issue as closely related to Ukraine's ability to supply the promised foodstuffs.

On the other side, the Rada's unwillingness to reverse its socialist policy led to an alliance of the Ukrainian conservative-nationalist groups and the German Military High Command in Kiev. By the middle of April even Holubovych became aware of the growing difficulties. In the presence of the German representatives he exclaimed, "it is high time to chase the Rada to the devil."[16] Perhaps, while unaware of the coming events, Holubovych was proven right by history. Even at that late hour the coming confrontation could have been averted had the Rada become more pragmatic and willing to view the entire situation in Ukraine in a realistic light. Yet this did not happen. Hrushevskyi was not Lenin, nor Josef Pilsudski and certainly not the Finnish General Carl G. E. Mannerheim, all three of whom differently perceived the road to statehood.

In the meantime, on April 9 an agreement was concluded regarding Ukraine's grain delivery.[17] The final wording of the text lowered the amount of grain, forage, fruits, and oil seeds to sixty million puds to be delivered before July 31, 1918. The first shipment consisting of six million puds went to Austria-Hungary before April 30, to be followed by twenty-one million before May 31, and forty-one million before June 30, and sixty million puds by July 31. The agreement provided details on pricing, terms of payments, and modes of transportation. Two supplementary arrangements of April 11 and 13 specified additional deliveries to the Central Powers: a total of one million puds of grain, forage for livestock and legumes, 400 million eggs, and 45,045 tons of beef, in addition to potatoes and vegetables.[18]

This most favorable agreement for the Central Powers should have convinced the Germans and Austrians of the Ukrainian government's good will. Indeed, Mumm was willing to postpone the overthrow of the Rada "until our negotiations on grain are safe under the roof."[19] However, Ukraine had more reasons to be suspicious of the Central Powers' plans and intentions when it came to their economic obligations. By April 3 it was clear that the Central Powers were in no position to supply the promised industrial machinery and the Ukrainians had to be satisfied only with some railroad equipment and with a small number of plows and harrows.[20] Obviously, not only the Rada but equally so the Central Powers could not always meet their agreed upon deliveries.

Despite some visible progress, Mumm remained suspicious of the Rada's chances of staying in power. On April 11 in a report that was very much in line with Kühlmann's thinking, he urged continuing support of the Rada or any other Ukrainian government that recognizes the Brest-Litovsk Treaty. "Recognition and the separation of Ukraine from Russia will be assured once her state-system will significantly differ from that of the Bolsheviks in Russia."[21] In other words, the door was left open for the replacement of the Rada with a regime acceptable to the Central Powers, provided it was anti-Bolshevik and possibly conservative. By then, as will be shown in the following pages, the change was already in the making. It would, however, have been premature to assume that the German Foreign Office at that time aimed at a future restoration of the Russian Empire at the expense of Ukraine's independence, as suggested by the German historian Peter Borowsky.[22] No such clear-cut evidence is available, not even in Groener's memoirs. On the contrary, on April 23 in a telegram to the Supreme Eastern Command he disapproved of Colonel M. Stolzenberg's[23] foolish suggestion "to arrest the Ukrainian government." Instead he felt that, "in regard to internal as well as external reasons, I feel, that changing the government should be left to Ukrainian individuals, provided that the Ukrainian state be maintained."[24]

The Central Powers' growing dissatisfaction with the Rada's policy expressed by Forgach, Mumm and Groener, never reached the level of the decision to destroy the Ukrainian state. Even on the eve of the Rada's downfall the joint Austrian-German conference of April 23 and 24 had not alluded to such an intention. On the contrary, they explored ways and means of replacing the government. While no names were officially mentioned, it can be assumed that the right person would have to be General Pavlo Skoropadskyi with whom both the Austrian and German officials had been in contact since early April.[25]

The conference of April 24 including Groener, Mumm, Forgach, Colonel Stoltzenberg, the Austrian Major Fleischmann, and Walter Princig, a member of the Austrian Representation in Kiev, conspired to reach an agreement on the following points:

(1) Cooperation with the Rada was no longer possible.

(2) The creation of a "Governor-Generalship" should not be considered.

(3) A Ukrainian government was to be maintained as long as possible, but subject to the dictates of the German and Austrian military commands; it also had to abstain from interfering in the Central Powers' military and economic measures. The following additional restrictions were to

be imposed on the new Ukrainian government: a) A Ukrainian army must not be organized as long as the German and Austrian troops remained in the country; the size of the Ukrainian police force was also subject to regulation by the occupying powers. b) The German and Austro-Hungarian military courts were to adjudicate all offenses committed against the Central Powers' military personnel in the country. c) The Ukrainian state administration was to be purged of all "unclean elements." Land committees and other similar bodies were to be dissolved. d) Since Ukrainian war production laws were not in existence, German, Austrian and Hungarian laws were applicable. e) Restrictions imposed by the Rada government regarding trade of foodstuffs and raw materials were to be declared null and void. Free trade was to be allowed. f) The agrarian question was to be solved through the restoration of the principle of private property. Peasants had to pay for land which came into their possession. Large estates were to be maintained until legal limitations on their size were promulgated. g) Financial and monetary problems were to be solved along similar lines. Other conditions and limitations were reserved for military and economic agreements to be concluded in the near future.[26]

This program, agreed upon *de facto,* aimed at making Ukraine an "occupied territory." The projected new "government" would be allowed merely to act as an organ controlled by the occupation armies. The former partnership was to be replaced with a system of dependence encompassing all political, social and economic spheres. Borowsky and Fedyshyn generally agree that the decision to remove the Rada came as a direct response to the Rada's memorandum of April 13 defying Eichhorn's order. This is further confirmed by numerous anti-Rada references by Groener as well as by Mumm's reports, especially the one of April 14 to Secretary of State Stein asserting that Germany could no longer go along with the Central Rada, which was to be tolerated only until all pending economic agreements were completed.[27] The sequence of events fueled Germany's and Austria-Hungary's determination to proceed with their plans.[28]

The economic agreements with Ukraine of April 9, 11 and 13, had been finalized and signed on April 23. With this signature "the Rada signed its own death warrant," in view of the plans in the making.[29] It was signed by Mumm, Forgach and Mykola Porsh.[30]

Now the stage had been set for the final act, which culminated in the ongoing conferences of internal opposition to the Rada and the representatives of the Central Powers. By early April, the internal opposition was no longer limited to the aforementioned Ukrainian Democratic Agrarian Party. Another influential group consisting of landowners, industrialists, and businessmen, known as "Protofis," at their meeting in Kharkiv on April 17 rejected the Rada's policy and demanded its replacement, insisting on restitution of thè land to former owners, support for industry, and an effective monetary policy. Those segments, representing Ukrainian nationalistic views within the Socialist-Federalist party who were not represented in the Rada government had little sympathy for the policy of the Social Revolutionaries and Social Democrats. The situation grew more acute for the Rada with the appearance on the political scene of General Pavlo Skoropadskyi in whom the opposition, as well as the Austro-German political and military leadership in Ukraine, found the right man for the right time and purpose.

Pavlo Skoropadskyi,[31] (1873-1945), was a scion of an illustrious Ukrainian Cossack family that included Hetman Ivan Skoropadskyi (1708-1722). While serving in the Russian army, Skoropadskyi, having participated in the Russo-Japanese war, was promoted in 1912 to the rank of Major General and was commander of the 34th Army Corps during the First World War. This made him the most visible Ukrainian in the tsarist army. Remaining nationally conscious, Skoropadskyi entered the pages of Ukrainian history in the summer of 1917 with his successful Ukrainization of his corps. He transformed it into the First Ukrainian corps, establishing a solid foundation for a future Ukrainian national army. In the following months he was recognized as the leader (*Otaman*) of the Ukrainian Free Cossacks, a new movement simultaneously arising. The socialist Central Rada, however, had no use for his talent or for a Ukrainian national army. This forced him to remain in the background even after the Rada's return to Kiev, though neither the domestic nor external foes wrote him off. Basically apolitical yet interested in Ukrainian affairs, Skoropadskyi, like many other officers and victimized landowners, grew disenchanted with the prevailing chaos and the policy of the socialists, making a novel alliance possible.

The first contact with Skoropadskyi was made by the Austrian representative in Ukraine, Major Fleischmann, who reported to the Supreme Military Command in Baden that Skoropadskyi was in the process of preparing for him a special memorandum. He then suggested that Skoropadskyi could become useful for Vienna.[33] There is no evidence available in Austrian documents on the outcome of this initial contact, which seemed to have been of no immediate consequence.[34] Another initiative and further contacts came from the German side. Sometime during the middle of April, *Hromada,* an umbrella organization representing the Democrat Agriculturalists and an association of large landowners, made contact with the German army. On April 24 a *Hromada* representative submitted Groener a list of names of ministers for a future government and budget proposal of expected expenditures of a planned *coup d'etat.* The overall cost had been estimated between 13.4 and 22.9 million rubles on the basis of a loan to be repaid shortly after the *coup.*[35] Aware of the plan's consequences, Groener thought that Austria-Hungary should equally share in the conspiracy "to suppress revolutionary accomplishments."[36]

Moreover, he disapproved of the Supreme Command's instructions to take military steps against the Central Rada, being convinced that the situation in Ukraine did not yet warrant such a step, and that only future events would justify it.[37] Besides, the plans were elaborated at the conference of April 24 and kept on hold.

The unexpected turn of events began to proceed on April 25 with the arrest of the Russian-Jewish banker Abraham Dobri. He was suspected of collaboration with the Germans by the radical group "Committee for the Rescue of Ukraine." The Dobri affair,[38] primarily an internal issue, nonetheless became an international problem, thereby calling for action. Since the order to arrest Dobri was issued by the Minister of Internal Affairs, Mykhailo Tkachenko, dramatic consequences were set in motion. To Eichhorn the arrest meant a hostile act by the Rada against the German interest, for Dobri, a former member of the Cadet Party, frequently criticized the Rada policy and favored restoration of private property, especially for industry. Among German circles he was favorably looked upon, therefore his arrest turned into a quasi *casus belli.* On April 25, Eichhorn, with Mumm's and Groener's consent, promulgated an order regarding the enforcement of German military court jurisdiction in Ukraine.[39] Even upon Mumm's intervention with Prime Minister Holubovych in conjunction with an eighteen-hour ultimatum demanding Dobri's release, nothing changed.

The German military law in Ukraine provided for court martial for acts of civic disorder and acts against the Central Powers' armies, and the German authorities began to investigate the case. The German army disarmed the Ukrainian Blue Division stationed in Kiev and composed of former prisoners of war during the night of April 26-27.

Panic-stricken, the Little Rada was called into session on April 27, without protection by the army or police force, to be informed by the Minister of Defense O. Zhukovskyi that a few hours earlier he ordered the disarming of the second Blue Division stationed in Kovel and marching toward Kiev. The disarming of the first division was explained by Colonel Stolzenberg as a mistake and a measure to save military equipment. Zhukovskyi's order to disarm the second division had been explained to the former Secretary of the Central Rada, V. Postolovskyi as caused by the division's unreliability with its anti-Rada attitudes among the officers under German influence.[40] However, on the German side, Ludendorff defended the disarmament as the result of the radicalization of the soldiers rendering the units militarily useless.[41] While motives seemingly differed, in reality neither the Central Rada nor the German army had any need for their continued existence.

At the meeting of the Little Rada Holubovych discussed in detail the draft of a new constitution and the business of pending bills about the Polish and Jewish organizations in Ukraine. He also reported on the debate in the German Reichstag concerning Eichhorn's order and told the Rada that the Socialist representatives of the Reichstag demanded the recall of Eichhorn and other high-ranking German officers from Ukraine.[42]

At that time other events were rolling along almost on schedule. On April 26, Groener received Pavlo Skoropadskyi to discuss procedural details of the change of government.[43] By then Groener was already well informed about his guest through Major Hasse who had met Skoropadskyi on April 13 and 15. Thus Groener's search for a new government was about to be concluded with only minor details to be finalized in favor of the German army terms of course, as proven by the nature of the condition imposed upon Skoropadskyi.[44] The stipulations were harsh and unequivocal as previously formulated in the German-Austrian agreement of April 24. Skoropadskyi, having acknowledged this situation, told Groener: "I declare my government's readiness to comply with the above points and expect in return reciprocal German economic and military assistance."[45] He agreed to recognize the peace treaty of Brest-Litovsk, the dissolution of the Rada, to hold elections in consultation with the German Command, to compensate the Central Powers for their military assistance and to sign additional economic agreements. In his memoirs, however, Skoropadskyi expressed some reservations concerning the monetary settlement and compensation, issues already favorably dealt with by Groener.[46]

With the Central Rada in session on April 28 to hear Holubovych's expose on the current events, followed by criticism of the action of the German army in Ukraine, the session was interrupted by intruding German soldiers. A young German officer announced in Russian: "In the name of the German government I am ordering you to raise up your hands." All but Hrushevskyi complied with this demeaning demand, followed by his call to identify Tkacheno, Minister of Internal Affairs, Liubyns'kyi, acting Minister of Foreign Affairs, Zhukovskyi, Minister of Military Affairs, Kovalevskyi, Minister of Agriculture and Haievskyi, Director of the Ministry of Internal Affairs. From among the identified persons, only Liubyns'kyi and Haievskyi were in attendance and were promptly arrested. After a body search for hidden weapons and the arrest of a few representatives, the remaining Rada members were dismissed. The arrest of Zhukovskyi, Tkachenko's wife, and the Chief of the city militia, P. Bohatskyi, followed later. Tkachenko went into hiding. A few days later, his wife and Liubyns'kyi were released. Prime Minister Holubovych was arrested the next day while returning from Mumm's residence after submitting his official protest against the unnecessary treatment of the German soldiers. The Central Rada was still in session and demanding action.[47]

The chapter was closed; the former ally, the Ukrainian Central Rada, became an enemy to be treated harshly. Germany's prestige and her *Ostpolitik* sank to the level of a lawless gang. Mumm criticized this ruthless practice on the evening of April 28. In the presence of Eichhorn, Groener and Stolzenberg he spoke of "elephants in the china shop" and of "boundless stupidity," yet he failed to apologize on behalf of the German government and to disassociate himself from the "storming of the Rada."[48] Chancellor Hertling's lukewarm personal indignation and his urging Emperor William II to investigate the military-civilian competence in Kiev aroused only the Emperor's displeasure, but no action.[49] In Berlin the Ukrainian "Palm Sunday case" in spite of Hertling's realization of its damage to Germany's eastern policy, was overshadowed by the events in Kiev of April 29.

On that day in 1918, disregarding Eichhorn's order of April 25 prohibiting unauthorized gatherings, the previously announced congress of the agriculturalists took place in Kiev's circus building.[50] The congress, called together by the League of Landowners (*Soiuz zemelnykh zemlovlasnykiv*) attracting 6,432 delegates representing eight gubernias, submitted an agenda aimed at the restoration of private land ownership and demanded dissolution of the Rada. General Pavlo Skoropadskyi, popular among the delegates, was welcomed with an ovation. Michael M. Voronych, president of the congress and former tsarist governor of Bessarabia, proposed to elect Skoropadskyi to "Hetman of all Ukraine." This old Ukrainian title from the time of the Cossack period, implied a strong monarchical form of government that was on the mind of the social class represented at the congress.

Whether prearranged or not, the enthusiasm was real and reflected the mood of those present. In his acceptance speech Skoropadskyi thanked the assembly for entrusting to him the leadership, and assured the delegates of his desire to restore order and thereby save Ukraine. Elected by acclamation in the city without a Ukrainian army and in a country controlled by foreign armies, Skoropadskyi began to act as the new ruler while the Central Rada was still in session. A detachment of the Hetman's soldiers dispatched to take the Rada's building suffered three casualties. The members of the Rada, when being informed about the events, dispersed never to convene again. They did not officially resign or transfer their mandates as the representatives of the Ukrainian people as they claimed to have been. On the contrary, the Rada in its last session adopted the constitution of the Ukrainian National Republic and elected Mykhailo Hrushevskyi as the first president of the Republic.[51] It is to the credit of the Central Rada that the first parliamentary national democratic system originated in Ukraine and not in Russia. From the ashes of the revolution, Ukraine with her democratic Cossack tradition of the seventeenth century was about to emerge as the carrier of democracy in Eastern Europe at a time when Russia was sinking deeper into a totalitarian state. Within that context of history, the Brest-Litovsk Treaty, enabling the return of the Rada to Kiev, enhanced the history of the Ukrainian people. Yet, this same treaty became equally responsible for the interruption of the Ukrainian march toward democracy. Skoropadskyi's regime proved to be more an anti-climax than a continuance of the reestablished tradition.

The League of Landowners, though well organized had hardly represented a significant segment of the population, perhaps no more than ten percent. This made Skoropadskyi's mandate even less representative than that of the Rada, which was elected by various social and professional councils, who chose to support the Hetman hoping to serve best the U-krainian national cause at that uncertain time of history supported him.

The overthrow of the Rada's government had been received by the leadership of the Austrian and German armies, as well as by the governments in Berlin and Vienna with mixed reaction. There were no signs of regret but equally so their expectations remained unclear. At that time, in Vienna's military and civilian circles the whole "Ukrainian issue" boiled down to a single concern, "to squeeze out from Ukraine as much food-stuffs as possible."[53] Their concern was statistics and the maintenance of order in Ukraine, but not the fate and interest of the Ukrainian people.

With Skoropadskyi in power, the Germans were assured of their interest in general and in controlling the government in particular. However, "the problem facing the German army did not change at all."[54] The Hetman's political base proved to be too narrow to bring about a national concensus. Compliance and sorely needed allegiance, especially among the agitated poorer peasantry who were either forced to hand over land they parcelled or to work the lands still owned by large landowners did not come about. From General Hoffmann's distant perspective at Kovno it appeared that:

> The man [Skoropadskyi] recognizing the Brest-Litovsk Treaty together with all additional economic arrangements, is acceptable to us. The change of the government may minimize Eichhorn's not too skillful act in regard to the former Ukrainian government. . . . I am afraid that the trouble created in Ukraine might bring her down. The Supreme Army Command and Eichhorn unconsciously strive to unite Ukraine with Russia. As of now it does not matter, but for the future I would rather see Ukraine remaining independent.[55]

This potential danger had also been recognized by Paul Rohrbach during his travel through Ukraine in May 1918.[56] So had Ludendorff, one of the earliest supporters of a free Ukraine for Germany's national interest. At the Spa conference on July 2, he expressed doubt as to the presence of Ukrainian national determination and consequently he thought that it would be impossible for Germany to prevent unification.[57] Groener, the man most involved with the overthrow of the Rada and Skoropadskyi's seizure of power, though not directly involved in the actual execution of the *coup d'état*,[58] welcomed the change of government. However, he remained committed to the preservation of the Ukrainian *"Kulisse"* (background), i.e., government subservient to Germany. In fact, Groener considered himself to be the real power behind Skoropadskyi. The meeting to discuss a list of ministers of the government took place in his office in the presence of both ambassadors on May 1.[59] Reporting to his wife on May 4, he wrote:

> Our successful revolution here is past us, the people in the street talk about that the German Supreme Command staged this revolution and certainly they are not very wrong in saying so. It could not go on with the old government. . . . The only inheritance of the old government is the complete destruction of economic life. . . . The new government is completed. Yesterday the new Prime Minister [Mykola P. Vasylenko] reported to me and found my approval. . . . Whoever will not be approved by Supreme Command, cannot become a minister. This way we hold the government strongly in our hands.[60]

A few days later on May 7, Groener went still further, as reported by the Austrian official Princig:

> General Groener during my visit talked favorably about the Hetman's surroundings. He thinks that as of now one should wait and see how the new regime functions and how it will be accepted in the country. . . . Should it not happen, from the German side an attempt will be made in cooperation with other parties, to provoke the military occupation of the country, with the removal of the Hetman to follow.[61]

Two months after the Rada's return to Kiev with the help of the Central Powers' armies, Ukrainian sovereignty had been reduced to the status of formality, a state government in form, but hardly in substance, a geographic entity under Ukrainian administration. By the end of November

1918, Germany's *Ostpolitik* came to an inglorious end, followed within a few months by the second Soviet Russian invasion of Ukraine in 1919. The Brest-Litovsk document merely became a page, albeit an important one, in Ukrainian history to be remembered by many for many different reasons.

CHAPTER IX

RATIFICATION OF THE BREST-LITOVSK TREATY BY THE GERMAN REICHSTAG

The signing of the Brest-Litovsk Treaty between the Central Powers and Ukraine on February 9, 1918, had at that particular stage of the war the potential to influence significantly the final outcome of the war. After all, it brought peace to one-third of the eastern front together with the prospect that peace could be extended to the northern portion of the front by concluding a peace treaty with Soviet Russia. In fact it meant and even justified hopes for ending the war for the Central Powers. It uplifted enormously the spirit of the German people and certainly of the government and of the army. And last but not least, Ukraine, "the bread-basket of Europe," meant plenty of foodstuffs and raw materials so desperately needed in Austria-Hungary and Germany. The British blockade was to be breached by the railroads leading to the rich Ukraine—a prospect shared by all Germans. Still another rising vision blinded the minds of individuals in the Foreign Affairs and Defense ministries and especially in the Supreme Command of the Army—the realization of the *Ostpolitik* that would make the whole of Eastern Europe a sphere of German influence eliminating thereby the danger of a two-front war in the future, and opening a huge market for the German industry. Such a prospect found sympathetic support with the majority of the German people.[1]

Indeed, the flow of history seemed to be redirected toward another major revision of the political map of Europe. To the historian the Brest-Litovsk Treaty with Ukraine remains of special interest as the first example of Germany's intention regarding post-war settlements in case of victory and indicative of the Reichstag's handling of its responsibilities.[2]

The German Reichstag elected in 1912 can be seen as a representative body of the German people and of the prevailing public opinion. Over twelve political parties, ranging from the Left to the Center to the Right[3] enjoyed freedom of expression, even during wartime. This makes it possible to reflect upon their mood and political orientations, even while the Reichstag was not constitutionally a governing body and especially during the war "was not in a position to assert itself against the dictatorship of the Supreme Command."[4]

Except for a few experts and supporters such as Paul Rohrbach, Albrecht Penck and Axel Schmidt who were well informed, the majority of the German public as well as the politicians knew very little about Ukraine prior to 1918. Nonetheless, the debate in the Reichstag, in certain aspects, revealed the presence of sufficient knowledge of the situation in Eastern Europe and of the Ukrainian case in particular. The speedy ratification of the treaty, however, can only be explained by Germany's immediate concerns: prospects of obtaining foodstuffs and liquidation of the eastern front. Thus, Ukraine became the first country to be debated in the Reichstag as a partner in the *Mustervertrag* approved by the Bundesrat on February 19. The ratification debate in the Reichstag began already on February 19 and lasted until February 22, i.e., at a time when two-thirds of Ukraine was still under Soviet Russian occupation.

Nonetheless, Dr. Paasche, Vicepresident of the Reichstag, in his opening speech expressed confidence in the advantages for Germany stipulated in the text of the treaty:

> The treaty represents an important step forward to be welcomed by the German people and its allies. The immediate future will show significant economic importance of that rich country for our economic development. The treaty had proved that we and our allies take seriously the Emperor's words: 'We are not engaged in a war of conquest. Without indemnity and without territorial annexation we have signed with the newly emerged Ukrainian Republic a peace

treaty honorable for both sides, with the intent to bring about friendly relations and advantages to both sides.'

He blamed Soviet Russia for refusing to sign a peace treaty with the Central Powers, condemned the Bolsheviks' terror and spoke warmly of the
national struggle of the Baltic peoples and of Finland.

The debate continued the next day with Secretary of State Richard
Kühlmann's report about the negotiations in Brest-Litovsk, the emergence
of a free Ukraine, the Ukrainian willingness to fight for independence and
the difficulties in negotiating with the Soviet Russian delegation. Kühlmann elaborated on the difficulties encountered in the negotiatins with
the young Ukrainian representatives concerning the Kholmland issue,
Ukraine's border with Austria-Hungary and Vienna's unwillingness to meet
the demands for the establishment of the Ukrainian Crownland within the
Empire. He disavowed himself from the Austrian stubborness which could
have led to the collapse of the negotiations. Austrian recalcitrance met
with the disapproval of the majority of the German people, as confirmed
by the applause of the representatives. Germany's support of the Ukrainian position on Kholmland had been explained by Kühlmann's reference
to large reserves available in Ukraine. As to the legal and economic provisions of the treaty, he noticed that the treaty had been viewed as the basis
for the future diplomatic and economic arrangements in that part of the
former tsarist empire. Replying to critics of the treaty, he assured the
House that the treaty with Ukraine would only speed up an agreement
with the Trotsky regime. Finally, by recommending ratification, Kühlmann pointed to the general approval of the treaty by the German public.
In that he was correct as will be shown.

The representative of the Centrum, Adolf Gröber, was the first to welcome the signing of the first peace treaty submitted to the Reichstag for
ratification. On behalf of his party he offered strong support:

> The treaty with Ukraine provides a real supposition, the founda-
> tion for other agreements to follow. The treaty's most important asset
> is the breaking of the iron blockade imposed by Germany's enemies.
> The treaty with Ukraine means an agreement with the richest part of
> Russia and justifies the hope for obtaining foodstuffs in satisfactory
> quantities.

He also criticized General Hoffmann's signature under the text of the treaty and questioned his authority to be part of a political settlement. He justified the compromise on the Kholmland issue as necessary to conclude negotiations in the interest of the German nation and because the conflict needed to be resolved on an ethnographic base as reflected by statistical data. This had been taken care of by a supplementary agreement and by Article 2 of the treaty providing for a plebiscite in the disputed area. Additionally, he asked for the maintenance of the present occupational lines until Ukraine solidified itself and was in a position to secure for her national minorities life, health, and private property.

The next speaker, Social Democrat Eduard David, having voiced his objection to the government's "militaristic policy" used against Soviet Russia, argued that the government come to terms with Lenin's regime. As for Ukraine he reminded the House that:

> In Ukraine the large majority of the people supports the present socialist government, which in contrast to the Bolsheviks is moderate socialist-democratic and the Bolsheviks in recent elections to the Constituent Assembly emerged as a miserable minority . . . . In case of need for our intervention in Ukraine we should restrict ourselves and abstain from any action outside of necessity . . . . Our intervention into the internal affairs can only contribute to the worsening of the situation. In Ukraine our interest in peace should produce the results we desire, namely obtaining grain and other agricultural products, yet abstaining from the political conditions.

David also stressed the need for resolving the Kholmland issue on ethnographic principles without damaging German-Polish relations. He spoke against implementation of a military policy in Eastern Europe. Furthermore, he declared his party's support for the ratification of the treaty with Ukraine.

Since the two largest German parties, the Center with ninety-one representatives and the Social Democrats with 110, approved the treaty, ratification was secured. The first rejection came, as could have been expected, from Marian Seyda, representative of the Poles. In a lengthy speech Seyda spoke of a "fourth Polish partition" brought about by the treaty's provision concerning the Kholmland. He claimed this region for Poland on historical grounds. "The treaty is cutting off a piece of Polish land and giving it to Ukrainians. This land contains a majority of Poles and Catholics . . .We shall not recognize diminution of our fatherland." Having condemned the treaty as unjust he refused its ratification. Seyda's speech found applause and approval only from the seventeen Polish representatives and from a half-dozen German representatives of the extreme left.

On behalf of the Progressives (Fortschrittler Volkspartei), with forty-two representatives, spoke Heinrich Dove. He rebutted Seyda's argument claiming that Germany's national interest would be damaged and he rejected David's request imposing restrictions upon Germany's policy in regard to Soviet Russia. After approving Kühlmann's handling of the negotiations, Dove stressed the presence of the ability of the young Ukrainian Republic to build a state:

> There exists an essential prerequisite for the foundation of the state. On one hand there is a national consciousness which has been suppressed by the powerful tsarism of the multinational Russian Empire, and on the other hand a natural premise for a revival of economic life, fertile soil and land not available in other parts of the world. And exactly the exchange of products between that agricultural land and our industrial country offers the best prospects for our normal relationship. Especially the treaty's articles on economic aspects are very useful and appreciable.

He rejected Polish accusations about "Poland's fourth partition" and strongly objected to the Supreme Command's involvement in political affairs, warning that this might create repercussions. "In Ukraine Bolshevism is not the result of internal developments but has been brought exclusively from abroad."

The most elaborate and most knowledgeable presentation in favor of the ratification came from Gustav Stresemann, on behalf of the National Liberal Party and its forty-five representatives. He complimented Kühlmann for successfully conducting the negotiations with Ukraine and for protecting Germany's interest. Turning to Soviet Russia, he demanded the release from prison of thousands of innocent people, the recognition of the independence of other nations and the withdrawal of troops from Finland and Ukraine. He criticized David's softness on Bolshevism and especially the journal *Sozialistische Monatshefte* for its disapproval of the treaty with Ukraine and its insistence on the preservation of Russia's integrity. He concluded that "the old Russia is a thing of the past, and events are moving towards the self-determination of the nations." Replying to the Polish faction's stand on the Kholmland question he accused them of insisting on the restoration of the "grand Poland" without any regard to the ethnographic borders and of desiring to recreate Poland on her former territories with access to the sea. "In a war in which thousands of Germans have been bled against Russia, the Poles dream of nothing but how to take away the German territory, a fact which finds no sympathy with the German people . . . the Poles are conspiring with the Bolsheviks to march against Ukraine, our ally." Defending the treaty with Ukraine, Stresemann cited these statistics:

> Ukraine exported 39 percent of Russia's total export of grain; 80 percent of its sugar; 1,300,000 puds* of coal of 1,900,000; 325 million puds of iron out of 500 million. This makes Ukraine a very important economic factor, and Russia without Ukraine can hardly survive. The treaty with its economic importance can be seen as a model agreement for the restoration of our economic relations to compensate for our losses in that war.

The position of the Conservatives (43 representatives in the Reichstag) was put forward by Kuno Westarp who spoke in support of the government's policy and of the Brest-Litovsk Treaty. He stressed its chances of breaking the Anglo-American blockade and the prospects for the establishment of good relations with Russia in the future. "In view of all advantages offered by that treaty we don't support its criticism for giving to Ukraine Kholmland, for the statistical data for that region is very unclear." Westarp approved of Kühlmann's and Czernin's compromises without which an agreement with the Ukrainians would have been impossible. "From the vantage of Germany's interest it does not make sense to support the Polish claims at the expense of good relations with Ukraine."

Opposition to the treaty was expressed by Georg Lebedour, a representative of a minor radical left party, the Independent Social Democrats,

---

* 1 pud (pood) = 36.07 lbs.; 16.36 kg.

which in 1919 joined the Communists in the Berlin uprising. His hostility towards national movements, including the Ukrainian, made him compare Ukraine with Bavaria. He rejected the socialist Central Rada's claim to be the sole representative of the Ukrainian people and therefore entitled to proclaim the independence of Ukraine. Painting the worst possible scenario about the Rada's future and extolling the Bolshevik successes in Ukraine, he predicted the fall of the Rada. "Her only chances to survive rests with a military intervention by the Central Powers." He urged strongly against interfering "into Russia's internal affairs," to withdraw the German army from Ukraine and to leave the Rada to her fate. He also rejected the Rada's claim to territories with a mixed population such as Kholmland, concluding that "not the governments but the proletariat will deliver peace in the whole world."

The first day of the Reichstag debate ended with Kühlmann's additional information and comments, noticeably about Hoffmann's signature. This had been explained by the nature of the treaty which included both an armistice and a peace treaty signed during a war. On Paasche's recommendation the Reichstag agreed to proceed with the second and third readings of the text of the treaty required for ratification.

The debate over ratification proceeded on February 22 along parliamentary procedures. Submitted were the texts of the Peace Treaty and the German-Ukrainian Supplementary Agreement. The reader, Prince zu Schönnaich-Carolath, a Liberal Democrat, proposed to discuss the documents by articles and within the following areas: (1) political aspects; (2) economic problems, and (3) judicial issues. He also noted that Ukraine had decided to remain a neutral country, not allying with Germany and, quoting Kühlmann, he informed the representatives that measures would be taken to protect the rights of the 60,000 Catholics in Kholmland. The economic part of the treaty had been previously discussed by the special Commission in the presence of Professor Penck, who provided the Commission with information on Ukraine's economic and ethnographic conditions and those of Kholmland. It was agreed that the old economic treaty with Russia would remain valid for the Ukraine until a new agreement could be made. There was no objection by the Commission as to the legality of the treaty, making approval possible with only two negative votes.

Representative Dove continued with the reading of the articles. Brief comments and questions followed. The representative of the Centrum,

National Liberal, Conservative, and Progressive parties, though in general agreement with the economic provisions, expressed deep concern about the Central Rada's policy of land socialization and difficulties in getting the promised quantity of foodstuffs, especially due to transportation problems. Yet, the hopes of seeing Article VII of the treaty translated into economic realities, i.e., foodstuffs and raw materials, overshadowed any reservation. Centrum representative Mayer voiced a warning to the Rada not to implement the policy of expropriation of the land estates without indemnities. In the case of German citizens such measures would constitute a violation of international law. It would also present a great problem for some 400,000 German colonists in Ukraine. Therefore, "when our army will liberate Ukraine from the Bolsheviks, it should be hoped that the Ukrainian government in appreciation will treat the German colonists like German citizens."

Additional information concerning Article XII of the old Russian-German Trade and Navigation Treaty of 1894/1904, to be applied in the Ukrainian case, was provided by Johannes Kriege, chief of the Legal Division of the Foreign Office. Articles XII and XIII of that treaty provided for the reimbursement of the owners of expropriated land. All German nationals in Ukraine would be affected by these provisions and the Ukrainian delegation had been informed about Germany's position on that point.

During the third reading Schneidemann, and especially the Polish representative Stychel, once again objected to the handling of the Kholmland problem and to the refusal to admit the Poles to the negotiating table at Brest-Litovsk. Their objections were rebutted by Count Westarp who pointed out the vital importance of the treaty. This was acknowledged also by the explicit refusal of Great Britain to recognize the treaty. Stresemann accused the Poles of being "priests of hatred" and expressed the wish to maintain "the best and friendly relations with the young Ukrainian state." The treaty was approved by an overwhelming majority with long and vigorous applause.

The motives for the representatives' enthusiasm were several and convincing: A partial peace at the front with the prospect of its extension to the rest of the eastern front, expectation that much needed foodstuffs would be obtained despite the British blockade, and the chance to uplift the morale of the army and the German public after almost four years of unrelenting war. Given these factors and under these conditions Ukraine became a vital partner and contributor to Germany's *Ostpolitik*. The two countries met in 1918 without any previous intention and planning, making their "partnership" accidental rather than an spontaneously desired political alliance, despite the presence of the "common enemies"—the Poles and the Russians. Still another unexpected, yet no less significant reality to the German-Ukrainian relationship was the newness of the Ukrainian state and the absence of political experience in contrast to the well established and functioning German Reich at the peak of its power. The meeting of "revolutionary enthusiasts" wtih the conservative-militaristic establishment was bound to produce conflicts after expectations rapidly passed away.

It is to the credit of some of the Reichstag's representatives, especially to the Social Democrats and members of the Centrum that they voiced objections against the active involvement of the army in delicate political processes at Brest-Litovsk and then in Ukraine. Some of them exhibited sufficient knowledge of the prevailing conditions in Ukraine and Bolshevist Russia. Their German patriotism and concern for their country did not blind them in the face of rather confusing issues related to the Ukrainian case, including national self-determination linked closely to the socialism of the Central Rada. It is only unfortunate that in the months to come the Reichstag had little input and control over the events in Ukraine, a fact which could either correct or initiate a different stage in the Ukrainian-German meeting.

CHAPTER X

ECONOMICS OF THE BREST-LITOVSK TREATY:
A SUMMARY

Economic conditions were the underlying motives of the Brest-Litovsk Treaty. This was an overriding factor with Austria-Hungary. Faced with a most serious food shortage by the end of 1917 domestic riots threatened the country. In the case of Germany the economic aspect was interwoven with political and military considerations that were the aggregate of the concept *Ostpolitik,* although sometimes confused with *Kriegsziele* (war aims). Two other partners in the Brest-Litovsk treaty, Bulgaria and especially Turkey shared only some goals of the first two powers. The prospect of victory and the end of the war was present there, too. Turkey welcomed Russia's military disappearance from the Black Sea assuring security of the Straits.

The Ukrainian situation, on the other hand, being entirely determined by political conditions, had to be resolved on two levels: the Central Powers' expectations and Ukraine's chance to survive as an independent nation. While pursuing the political end, the Central Rada's delegation was compelled to comply with the economic needs of the Central Powers, which it tried to exploit effectively in securing two political goals: recognition of the Kholmland as a Ukrainian province and getting Vienna to promise political autonomy to Galicia and Bukovyna in the form of a separate Crownland. The price for this political accommodation was spelled out in Article VII, Paragraph I of the Treaty: one million tons of food products to be made available to the Central Powers before July 31, 1918, at an agreed upon price.

There is no argument as to Ukraine's ability to deliver one million tons of agricultural surplus as shown here:

TABLE 1

World Grain Production, 1909-1913*
(in million tons)

	Wheat	Rye	Barley	Oats	Total	%
Ukraine	4,300	600	2,700	300	8,600	21
Argentina	2,600	--	--	620	6,100	15
United States	2,960	10	160	60	4,100	10
Romania	1,430	100	350	150	3,100	7
Russia (without						
Ukraine)	100	200	1,000	800	2,200	5

*Source: R. Dyminskyi, ed. *Handbuch der Ukraine* (Leipzig, 1941), pp. 204-5.

Ukraine's share of grain export during that period amounted to 7.9 million tons, or one-fifth of the entire world export of grain. Ukraine's requirement for its domestic consumption had been estimated at sixty-eight percent, with thirty-two percent of the production left available for export.[1] Despite the lack of precise data available for 1918, it can reasonably be assumed that one million tons of grain were available for export, therefore, the Ukrainian delegation acted in good faith in Brest-Litovsk. The problem, however, rested with logistic factors, such as the disruptions created by war and civil unrest, the Rada's untimely legislative acts socializing the land, and finally the deadline itself making it technically impossible to supply such an amount of foodstuffs within a six-month period. This should have been understood by the Austro-Hungarian government. They should not have used it as an ill-founded excuse to refuse to comply with other provisions of the agreement and its component parts. Vienna's failure to export to Ukraine the agreed upon volume of industrial products, together with the feeding of the 250,000 man army stationed in Ukraine counterbalanced Ukraine's flawed action. On the whole, however, Ukraine's obligations and export of goods to the Central Powers was significant, despite all the obstacles present, as recorded in numerous agreements and statistics.

On April 9 an agreement was signed to deliver one million tons of grain, fodder and legumes, followed by an agreement of April 11 for 400 million eggs and two days later by an agreement to ship 45,045 tons of beef.[2] On April 19 Germany agreed to deliver to Ukraine 315,000 tons of coal before July 31, 1918. In a Protocol of April 21, Ukraine obliged herself to export 37.5 million tons of iron ore. One day earlier, Ukraine had agreed to deliver 300 railway box cars of lumber. A comprehensive economic agreement reached on April 23, between Ukraine and the Central Powers' Economic Office in Kiev dealt with foodstuffs, horned livestock and financial arrangements. From now on all economic activities and the supervision of trade was directed and controlled by the Economic Office, which soon established its own branch offices in various provinces of Ukraine and acted as the official agent for Vienna and Berlin. The Office was also charged with regulating the quantities of export destined for Austria-Hungary and Germany. Much of the transactions were carried out without the knowledge of the Ukrainian government and not always reported to the government. On May 22 the Council for Food Supply was created by the Ukrainian government to oversee the economic transactions with the Central Powers and to control unauthorized military requisitions of the occupying armies as well as check purchases by private Austrian and German companies.

On September 10 Germany and Austria-Hungary concluded with the Hetman government an Economic Agreement for the fiscal year 1918-1919 regulating production, export, payments, transportation, customs and organizational matters. Operating on the assumption of normalization of social and economic conditions in Ukraine, the agreement projected grain production for the period of September 1918 through August 1919 at 5.125 million tons, reserving sixty-five percent for Ukraine's domestic consumption and thirty-five percent, or 1.75 million tons for export. Considering Ukraine's agricultural potential, the numbers appear reasonable, confirming her ability to comply with the Treaty's provisions. Equally so, the pricing of the products involved was acceptable to the Ukrainian interest,[3] as prices were set above the then prevailing world market prices, reflecting the growing independence of the Hetman regime. In case the projected quantity of grain would prove insufficient Ukraine would have to compensate the Central Powers with an increase in export of sugar of up to 50,000 tons and of alcohol spirits of twenty percent.

The Agreement provided for Ukraine's additional export of the following items before June 30, 1919: 350 million eggs (4,000 boxcar loads), 11 million puds (1 pud = 36.07 lbs.) beef, 300,000 head of sheep, 2 million live chickens, 200,000 puds of meat and sausages, 2.5 million puds of sugar, 400,000 puds of butter, cheese and bacon, an unspecified amount of potatoes, fruits and vegetables. Also included in the agreement was unlimited free export of raw materials such as flax, hemp, and scrap iron.[4]

While the September Agreement in many aspects can be seen as a compromise reflecting the stronger position of the Hetman government, it nevertheless gave Germany in particular certain control of the country's economy and provided good prospects for future advantages. Germany's failure to achieve maximal gains reflected not only the worsening situation on the Western front and in Soviet Russia, as suggested by Borowsky,[5] but also the political skill of Ukrainian government officials, especially those of Prime Minister Lyzohub and his Foreign Minister, Doroshenko, who were determined to defend the Ukrainian national interest.[6]

Czernin's accusation of Ukraine is not providing for the starving Viennese,[7] illustrated by his data, has been answered by Doroshenko's realization of the onesidedness of the economic trade relationship. Accordingly, Ukraine delivered to the Central Powers 890,000 tons of goods of all types and received from them only 490,960 tons in return.[8] Not included in Doroshenko's figure is the amount of food and other articles used to support the 500,000 men of the German and 250,000 men strong Austrian armies, estimated at 300 freightcar loads daily in addition to that the soldiers sent privately to their families back home. Czernin, on his part, estimated the export from Ukraine at 129,310 tons, of which Germany received 61,349 tons, Austria-Hungary 57,965 tons, and Turkey and Bulgaria 4,799 tons.

Somewhat different statistical data for Ukraine's export had been provided by the Kiev-based Railroad Central Office on November 4, 1918 for the whole period of the occupation, i.e., up to October 26.[9]

TABLE 2

By product:

General Foodstuffs	22,148 boxcar loads
Grain	9,132 boxcar loads
Raw Materials	3,456 boxcar loads

By country:

Germany	14,162 boxcar loads
Austria-Hungary	19,898 boxcar loads
Bulgaria	130 boxcar loads
Turkey	195 boxcar loads

Doroshenko's data on export and import illustrate clearly the inequities of the trade and economic relations in general.[10]

TABLE 3

	Export		Import	
Product	No. of boxcars		Product	boxcars
Grain	6,326		Coal	21,428
Straw and Hay	1,406		Machine Oil	804
Sugar	3,458		Agric. machinery	1,651
Eggs	2,009		Other	665
Cattle	5,500			
Horses	7,000		Total	24,548
Cheese, Butter	330			
Leather	158			
Flax	200			
Resins	231			
Manufactured goods	264			
Military equipment	3,445			
Other	14,131			
Total	44,458			

In addition to officially reported exported goods from Ukraine, Doroshenko provides data on the so-called contraband trade from Ukraine for the period April-October 1918, compiled by the Ukrainian Ministry of Trade and Industry:

TABLE 4

By product	Quantity in pud	boxcar load (incomplete)
Grain	351,269	36
Flour	102,746	not given
Fiber materials	253,848	not given
Horses	12,095	30
Cattle	300	63
Leather	86,142	not given
Metals	38,984	19
Minerals	71,928	not given
Rubber	82,695	not given
Medicine, perfume	18,701	not given
Chemical products	13,286	not given
Forage	71,039	1,120
Sugar	734	not given
Vegetables	6,423	734
Cannery products	36,430	not given
Colonial goods	53	not given
Military equipment	27, 944	not given
Total	1,174,617	2,002

The balance sheet of Ukrainian trade with the Central Powers in number of boxcar loads according to Doroshenko's data on both official and contraband transactions, shows 45,783 for export and for import only 24,548 car loads. This lopsided picture of economic relations is even more evident in the various product categories with 21,428 boxcar loads of coal imported to Ukraine, whereas Ukrainian consumer goods were estimated at 40,000 car loads.

The disparity in trade coupled with the enormous advantages in favor of the Central Powers has been properly acknowledged, at least by some individuals. Czernin himself had to admit that "millions of people were herewith saved from starvation and this should be acknowledged by those who condemn the treaty."[11] Karl Nowak concluded: "Each person in Austria-Hungary received during eight months one and one-half loaves of Ukrainian bread in addition to two kilograms of foodstuffs. By the Spring of 1918 the hunger was over."[12] And Glaise-Horsetenau wrote: "Before the collapse there arrived from Ukraine altogether 42,000 car loads to Austria-Hungary, an amount which made a difference in a country of fifty million people."[13] The German historian of the Brest-Litovsk agreements, Volkwart John, argued that the "economic regulations of the Brest-Litovsk treaty with Ukraine were based on reciprocity," therefore, "the Brest Peace was more balanced than the Versailles Peace Treaty."[14] The truth, however, remains indisputable—both settlements failed even if for very different reasons. Only the Brest-Litovsk Treaty with Ukraine in its intention had the real potential of becoming a just settlement. This appears especially appropriate for the Eastern Europe of which Ukraine is an important part, particularly when measured against the events of the Brest-Litovsk era to the present.

CHAPTER XI

EPILOGUE

The overthrow of the Central Rada on April 29, 1918 did not legally terminate the Brest-Litovsk Treaty and did not end the Central Powers' involvement in Ukrainian affairs. The new regime of Hetman Pavlo Skoropadskyi had recognized the treaty and assured General Groener of his willingness to comply with its provisions. This made it possible for Berlin and Vienna to extend their *de jure* recognition of his government and to preserve the outward continuity of Ukraine's legal status and her foreign policy.

While these procedural formalities ensured Ukraine's existence as a state, at least for those in authority on both sides of the new partnership, actual conditions remained less convincing. The Central Powers signed the treaty with a government that had its beginning and legitimacy as a revolutionary organ representing a sizable percentage of the population. However, Skoropadskyi's *coup* with the active role and support of foreign powers against the organically emerged Rada, in fact, removed the existing base of power in Ukraine. Moreover, the organized opposition represented only a minority of the population, diminishing even further the base of popular representation and of support. For this essential reason and within this line of arguments Ukraine's position after April 29 can best be described as a state with only limited sovereignty making Skoropadskyi's regime more a recipient than a holder of political power.[1]

Although the fall of the Rada and Skorpadskyi's seizure of power did not surprise officials in Vienna and Berlin, serious attempts were made on the German side to minimize the negative impact of these events. Critical interpellating by the German Socialist Party in the Reichstag as well as disapproval of the actions of the German military in Ukraine by German liberal and socialist newspapers served as a warning to both the policy makers and the military establishment. On their behalf Ambassador Mumm and Fieldmarshal Eichhorn made public their commitments to the preservation of the Ukrainian character of the state. Both were equally interested in the preservation of social peace and stability in Ukraine so that the supply of foodstuffs would not be jeopardized.

Eichhorn, unsure of Berlin's position as to Ukraine's future and the consequences of the overthrow of the Rada, declared:

> Any fluctuation in our policy would be damaging, since it might result in weakening the confidence which is being placed upon us. The more taste the Hetman develops for power, the more likely he is to promote the strengthening of the idea of a national Ukrainian state and turn his inner eye away from Great Russia.[2]

Eichhorn was officially committed to the preservation of Ukraine, at least as a functioning entity, and he encouraged the Hetman in that direction. Even before Germany's *de jure* recognition of the new government on May 26, at a dinner in honor of the Hetman, he said:

> As a soldier I can tell you that we came here willingly to help the people striving to liberate themselves from their oppressor. We were destined with the noble assignment to become the first pillar of the young state in its first stage of construction. Despite some unfriendly and even hostile reaction we encounter in this country I believe nonetheless that as soon as Ukraine will become strong as an independent state the people will remember gratefully the German soldiers. I am certain that such a time will come . . . . Long live Ukraine and her Hetman.[3]

Yet, Eichhorn's real perception of the role of the Ukrainian government in relationship to the Central Powers and the German army in Ukraine differed greatly from the polite dinner remarks, as documented in his instruction of May 22 to the German officers.[4] It began with the assurance that the Hetman confirmed in writing the acceptance of all of the army's demands in return for German support. Any agitation in the countryside against the government, especially by the Social Revolutionaries leading to riots and undermining the new government's authority was to be suppressed by force. Peasants were reminded of the Fieldmarshal's order promising them the right to harvest the crops from the land they had planted. Additionally, the document informed:

(1)   The Hetman considers it to be his responsibility to comply with the terms of the Brest-Litovsk treaty. . . . The date for the election to a new constituent assembly will be determined in consultation with the Army Command.

(2)   The size and the activity of the future Ukrainian army will be determined by an agreement with the Army Command.

(3)   All land councils will be dissolved and replaced by the government's administration. All unreliable individuals will be removed from the government.

(4)   All obstacles in the supply of foodstuffs will be eliminated and no new restrictions will be imposed.

(5)   An agreement must soon be reached to compensate Germany for her assistance. Also, a special military convention shall regulate all military affairs.

Obviously, not much freedom was left for the hetman to govern the country. The former minister of foreign affairs, D. Doroshenko, in light of the existing conditions in Ukraine wrote:

> The German military and political representatives exploited the presence of the German army in their treatment of the Ukrainian government. They objected to the formation of the Ukrainian army, interfered into Ukraine's internal affairs and even objected to the nomination of ministers to the government, as happened with my own case. To fight against this situation was only possible by moving the German-Ukrainian relations from Kiev to Berlin.[5]

By that time, however, Berlin was preoccupied with the Soviet Russian relationship, with political strikes in Germany, and especially with the situation on the Western front where Ludendorff's Spring offensive had failed to break through due to 140,000 fresh American troops. The status of Ukraine was once again of secondary importance, seen merely as the main source for foodstuffs.

Even Ambassador Mumm's reports to Chancellor Hertling[6] could not reverse the growing trend within the Foreign Office toward a closer cooperation with Soviet Russia.[7] Not hiding his sympathy for the Ukrainian cause, Mumm urged Berlin seriously to consider two alternatives in regard to German Ukrainian policy:

> There are two possible approaches that we can follow in our policy toward the Ukraine. One of them is a ruthless exploitation of the country, regardless of ultimate consequences. The other approach is the creation of a viable political organism which, in close association with Germany, would become an important, military, and economic factor in our eastern policy in the future.[8]

Mumm's argument, reasonable by any standard of successful international diplomacy, seemed to fall on deaf ears within the Foreign Office. The center for German decision making remained in Kiev, i.e., it was entrusted to the German Command, a fact that pleased the Austrian general Alfred Kraus and Vienna, who were never sincerely committed to a pro-Ukrainian policy. The non-ratification of the Brest-Litovsk treaty by the Austrian Reichsrat, opposition to the Kholmland settlement and non-compliance with the secret agreement concerning the Ukrainian crownland characterized Vienna's policy toward Ukraine during the last months of the Empire's existence. While extending offical recognition to the Hetman regime together with the other three powers on June 2, the Austrian government continued its anti-Ukrainian intrigue. Baron Stephen Burian, Czernin's successor, urged the governments of Germany, Bulgaria, and Turkey against exchanging ratification notes unless the Ukrainian government agreed to the revision of Ukraine's western border in the Kholmland area in favor of the Poles. The Austrian plot failed and the exchange of ratification documents took place in Vienna on July 15 and 24, respectively. But this did not end Vienna's obstructionism, especially in regard to the nullification of the secret agreement. The Austrian envoy in Kiev, Forgach, taking advantage of the

situation, pressured the Hetman to nullify officially the agreement whereupon the original copy was burned in Berlin on July 16 at Vienna's insistence. In the notes of July 24 and 28 the Ukrainian government pro-
tested in vain this *fait accompli* symbolizing a new relationship between
the Hetman's administration and the Central Powers as the powerless
partner in the treaty of Brest-Litovsk. Berlin, on its part, satisfied with
the control over the Hetman regime, continued its formal pro-Ukrainian
policy. On November 9 Germany agreed to dispatch two divisions into
Kholmland to facilitate the establishment of the Ukrainian administration. This, however, did not prevent the Poles from occupying the area
a few days later as a result of the armistice of November 11 and the fall
of the Hetman's regime in Ukraine.

Similar differences underscoring Germany's and Austria-Hungary's
divergent Ukrainian policies hampered the negotiations between Soviet
Russia and Ukraine as stipulated by the terms of the March 3, 1918
treaty with the Bolsheviks. While both countries had an economic interest in the prolonged Russo-Ukrainian negotiations, the Germans consistently maintained a pro-Ukrainian stance, especially in redrawing
Ukraine's northern frontiers, whereas Austrian participants concerned
themselves totally with the protection of their opportunity to exploit
Ukraine's economic resources.

Yet, Germany's stand was not entirely consistent. It reflected a lack
of consensus on specific issues in regard to Soviet Russia and Ukraine.
Opposing views on the direction and substance of the German *Ostpolitik*
held by William II, Ludendorff, and the Foreign Office,[10] prevailing
during the Summer and early Fall, had weakened Berlin's ability to act
more forcefully. This resulted in Moscow's reluctance to conclude a peace
treaty with Ukraine. The Bolshevik tactics of dalays, wait and see, while
at the same time building an effective army, once again confirmed Lenin's
political skill. To the Russian Bolsheviks Ukraine, too, meant bread and
natural resources for the sheer survival of their regime. Yet the chances
for continuous Ukrainian independence were not only in the hands of the
Hetman's uncertain government, but were also deeply dependent on
Berlin's moves. That combination of factors and circumstances left Ukraine
completely unprepared and alone. Her future was uncertain and she
remained dangerously divided internally and without the prospect of
aid from the victorious Allied Powers who were willing to forget Ukraine's
treaty with the Central Powers.

In fact, the ties with the Entente were preserved since the Central Rada as well as the Hetman agreed to the presence of French and British representatives in Ukraine despite of Austrian and German objections. After all, Ukraine remained a neutral country and did not join the Central Powers' war against the Entente. By October 1918 Germany finally agreed with the Herman's insistence on establishing formal diplomatic relations with the Allies.

On the other hand, the Central Powers never objected to Ukraine's relations with neutral states, especially with Spain, Holland, Switzerland, Denmark, Persia, Greece, Estonia and even with Italy. Nor did the Central Powers object to Ukraine's relations with the newly emerged free national states on the territory of the former tsarist Russia such as the Cossack State of Don, Belorussia, and the Caucasus states.[11] "On balance, all these ties provided little advantage to Kiev but had a potential value for the development of Ukrainian statehood in the future."[12]

Much of the credit for the Hetman government's limited political accomplishments under the prevailing restrictive conditions must go to Foreign Minister Doroshenko. Hampered by the frequently antagonistic German representatives in Kiev, Doroshenko was foremost committed to serving the Ukrainian interest.

> His cardinal objective was to terminate the German guardianship in the shortest possible period of time to use it in the interim for the reunion of what he regarded as Ukrainian irredentas in Kholm, Bessarabia, the Kuban, and the Crimea. The second foreign policy objective was the obtaining of recognition from neutral countries and, if possible, from the Entente Powers. The third aim was the conclusion of peace and the delineation of the frontier with Soviet Russia.[13]

While he succeeded in some of his objectives, Doroshenko's vision of a future independent Ukraine was about to be swept away by newly unfolding events beyond his control. Among the most decisive of these were the Central Powers' defeat, Skoropadskyi's proclamation of November 14 of a federation with a yet to be "restored great Russia," followed by the uprising of the Ukrainian opposition led by the Directory that tempted Soviet Russia to again attack Ukraine, and, finally, the Allies' failure to support the Ukrainian national movement instead of the remnants of the tsarist regime's "White Russian generals."

A closer examination of the causes and consequences determining the fate of Ukraine reveals that some factors playing a part in the Ukrainian drama, or in the debacle, to use Reshetar's term, were internally nourished during the eight months reign of the Hetmanate. The overthrow of the socialist dominated Central Rada government caused a sharp ideological rift within the society, never to be reconciled. The socialist parties' categorical refusal to accept the Hetman's invitation to participate in his government while ideologically understandable, proved nontheless shortsighted from the perspective of the overall national interest exactly at that stage of history and national interest. Consequently, the Hetman regime became the exclusive vehicle for the predominantly conservative and even extreme right-wing elements, some of whom were espousing strong pro-Russian sympathies and showing little understanding for Ukraine's national and social aspirations. Subsequently, instead of narrowing the internal divisions, the conflict worsened, leading to the formation of the Ukrainian National Union comprising socialists as well as nationalist elements, and finally to the uprising by the Directory.[14] Though the Directory's patriotic intentions and reasonings may have had some validity, the very timing of the uprising proved to be ill-chosen, considering all the prevailing negative conditions. A particularly acute threat was Soviet Russia's eagerness to invade Ukraine. To overthrow an unpopular hetman proved to be an easy undertaking, yet the Directory's inability to restore and to protect Ukraine's independence remains to the final verdict of history as an exercise in futility and complete failure. Through Vynnychenko, Lenin was well informed about the uprising's preparation. He was waiting for the chance to harness the riches of Ukraine for Russia.

Ukraine merely exemplified the case of a country affected not only by lack of human constraint but, perhaps equally so, by geography, natural resources and abundant riches in general. Her antagonists would not have been interested in Ukraine had she been a huge desert. For this reason the failures of the Ukrainian leadership ought to be measured with these preexisting factors in mind, for even the most brilliant leadership could not eliminate all the geographical realities that could act either way. In 1918/1919 the geographical setting hampered Ukraine's national cause.

* * *

To implement effectively the policy of keeping Ukraine within Germany's economic sphere of interest, as outlined by the Imperial Economic Office and favored by the Foreign Office, several measures had to be taken. Among those were curtailing the purchase of grain by other buyers and restricting Ukraine's trade with other countries. Not only were the Ukrainian-Russian and Ukrainian-Georgian negotiations affected by this measure, but also neutral countries especially Denmark and Sweden which had shown interest in establishing trade relations with Ukraine.

Other steps in this regard extended to the control of the banking system and the circulation of Ukrainian currency (*karbovantski*), which was printed in Germany, hence restricted arbitrarily in quantity and the determination of exchange rates against Austrian and German currency.[15] The transportation of goods within Ukraine and to other countries depended on the railroad, rivers and other waterways, all of which were controlled by the German army. And finally, industrial plants being protected by the army remained *de facto* controlled and subordinated to German economic interest.

The Austrian policy in the South Ukraine after April 29 resembled rather a typical colonial-type pattern than that of a friendly country. The order to act in such a manner emanated from the highest authority, from Emperor Karl I himself as conveyed to General Alfred Krauss:

> The Emperor told me in May that I was to be considered a dictator for the exploitation of Ukraine for the Monarchy as the only means to save the Monarchy. He informed me about the wretched conditions in the Monarchy. . . . For these reasons and by disregarding the Ukrainian government, the army should confiscate grain and deliver it to the Monarchy. To this end an energetic and unscrupulous will must be applied.[16]

The Ministry of Foreign Affairs subsequently instructed him "to maintain peace and order in our zone of occupation, to exploit Ukraine for the Monarchy, especially grain and livestock and to secure a favorable trade agreement with Ukraine.[17]

The installation of the new regime in Kiev did little to change the attitude of the German and Austrian authorities in Ukraine. Although initial expectations did not come to pass, at least not immediately, their reaction nevertheless could not conceal the real intentions of the actual power brokers in Ukraine. The exchange of views concerning the Hetman's future, his ability to govern and to meet the Central Powers' wishes took place on May 6 at the meeting with Walter Princig, the Austrian Consul General in Kiev and General Groener.[18] There it was agreed to postpone any definite decision as to the Hetman's future for the time being. The ongoing negotiations between the Hetman and the socialist parties would determine the future discourse with a new regime. Otherwise, as Groener suggested, "a different arrangement can be made—at the insistence of some political parties a military *coup* can be staged to remove the Hetman and install a new government with ministers acceptable to us."[19] The issue of a new government, as has been seen by Groener and Princig, had been reduced to just two items: conclusion of a financial agreement and supply of foodstuffs. With the conditions spelled out, Groener earlier had told the socialist representatives that they should negotiate with the Hetman.

Negotiations indeed took place with the Hetman displaying some willingness to compromise, however, the socialists' insistence on a majority in the government including the positions of prime minister, foreign and agricultural ministries, precluded any hope of the two sides to reconciling their differences. Failure to form a government of national unity made it easier for the Central Powers to hold Ukraine tightly in their grip and subsequently contributed much to Ukraine's inability to become more forceful vis-a-vis the Central Powers.

Princig, on his part and without losing time, reminded the visiting Hetman on May 7 of Austria's exclusive interest in receiving Ukrainian grain and reaching appropriate financial agreement. Mumm's previously submitted recommendation for land reform in order to pacify the peasantry was seconded by Princig with the added suggestion of excluding from his government individuals with pro-Russian sympathies. The Hetman assured him of his desire to form "a liberally-governed Ukrainian state."[20] The Hetman acknowledged the Central Powers' support for Ukraine and expressed the hope that their collaboration may enable him to lead Ukraine out of the crisis created by the revolution.

The proposed positions as well as Princig's views expressed in several reports, were approved by Foreign Minister Burian as documented by the

Ministry's circular of May 10, sent to Prince Hohenlohe in Berlin, Count Trauttmannsdorff in Baden and Princig in Kiev.[21] Burian agreed to support Skoropadskyi as long as he acted within the guidelines of the Central Powers, especially in regard to the agrarian policy, fearing the peasants' threat of sabotage in case of reverses intended by the Agrarian Minister Fedir Lyzohub. Although Burian praised the agrarian policy as politically and economically important he could not deny the equally vital role U-kraine held for the Central Powers' own interests.

Another report to the Austrian Supreme Command of the Army from Ermolli Boehm, of May 12, offers a glimpse of the prevailing conditions in Ukraine during the first three weeks of Skoropadskyi's regime. Expecting a significant governmental turn to the right, the landowners, mainly in the area under Austrian occupation, initiated actions to reclaim their lands. The dismantlement of the commissars' offices, replaced by Duma organs established back in 1916, often with the assistance of the Austrian army, created unrest in the provinces. The local press in numerous cities had been suspended and rumors about imminent strikes were spreading across the country.

The underlying message of the reports to Vienna contained subtle anti-Ukrainian bias and seemed to reflect the conditions in thoroughly russified Odessa. Accordingly,

> the Hetman's regime is seen there as a step toward reunification with tsarist Russia, a widely shared wish in Odessa. All the people think and speak Russian. Especially the intelligentsia, with some exception among the Jews, is for reunification. Russia needs Ukraine, for she will starve, and she must not be removed from the Black Sea.[22]

The rest of Boehm's report speaks of measures to be taken to secure industrial, financial and agricultural exploitation of the country, by introducing martial law, by disarming the general population and tightening control over the news media.

A far more objective report providing indepth analysis of the social and national conditions in Ukraine was submitted by the Austrian military intelligence service by the end of May and made available to Burian.[23] This eleven page-long document offers the historian a rare insight into the state of mind and attitudes of all major ethnic groups that were instrumental in the shaping and determining of Ukraine's future.

As a consequence of the prolonged Russian rule over Ukraine and of the policy of an intensive Russification, most of the larger Ukrainian cities, such as Odessa, Kharkiv and Kiev, became bastions of Russianism, especially after the Bolshevik revolution when large numbers of Russian refugees fled into Ukraine. Additionally, the cities included high percentages of Jews, who during the tsarist period were not allowed to reside in Russia and therefore settled predominantly in the so-called border provinces —Ukraine, Belorussia, Lithuania, and Poland. However, most of the Jews were culturally russified, making them either neutral or even hostile to the national aspirations of the non-Russian peoples. Being well educated and skilled in the various professions, the Jews became highly visible and active in political affairs and parties, especially within the Russian Social Democratic Workers' Party and the Social Revolutionaries Party.

The Poles, the third group involved, with six to fourteen percent of the population in the gubernias of Volyn, Podolia, and Kiev represented mainly landlords, estate agents, and intelligentsia in cities. The Russian minority in all social classes and in the political parties rejected the concept of an independent Ukraine and remained either extremely hostile or just neutral. The Poles, on the other hand, were ready to accept Ukrainian statehood and to collaborrate with the Ukrainian government hoping to protect their interest. Since a large number of the Polish nobility were the offsprings of the polonized Ukrainian aristocracy, re-assimilation was less difficult and many of them were willing to offer their knowledge and experience in the building of the Ukrainian state. Only the short-lived experience of Ukraine's independence prevented this useful process from being realized.

The secret report also suggested that a majority of the Russians would rather submit to the Bolsheviks' power than be subjects in a Ukrainian national state. The presence of "internal enemies" willing to collaborate either with the tsarist generals or with Soviet Russia, estimated at about twenty percent of the population could have been effectively controlled and suppressed only with an able and reliable police force and with an all-Ukrainian solidarity and consensus. That such was not the case was due much to the basic weaknesses of the two Ukrainian governments of the period and the unsupportive armies of the Central Powers. On the contrary, in the months to come their behavior contributed much to the internal unrest and widespread dissatisfaction. Besides, as some reports correctly observed, by 1917 Ukrainians found themselves, as a consequence of prolonged statelessness, with only a tiny intelligentsia, "not large enough to immediately provide national leadership in the various areas of state building."[24] The "theoretical idealists" were not given time to mature, to learn and to prepare the masses of the peasantry for the task ahead.

Realizing the importance of the peasants, who made up to seventy-five percent of the Ukrainian population, the secret report dealt extensively with their condition and aspirations. Relentless agitation, followed by the outbreak of the revolution, made peasants restive, aggressive and susceptible to the most radical slogans spread across the former tsarist Russia by the Russian and Ukrainian Social Revolutionaries. The report pointed to the politicians' failure to inspire the peasantry with the national feelings that "were present at the beginning of the revolution. The Central Rada was unable to meet this challenge . . . . Resolving the agrarian question will determine the future of the state."[25]

After April 29, the fate of the Ukrainian state fell into the hands of Hetman Skoropadskyi whose efforts were contingent on the interest of the foreign armies, and handicapped by his domestic policy opposed by the Ukrainian socialist parties. By the end of May measurable signs of the undercurrent of social unrest began to foretell the coming eruption. The Austrian observer Forgach described the symptoms and suggested preventive treatment as follows:

> The agitation and unrest of the peasants spreading into various parts of the country is becoming noticeable . . . . The violence of the restless peasants necessitated energetic measures by the government's and the Central Powers' armies. While government actions were limited to issuing orders prohibiting the agitators' activities, the suppression of unrest and the destruction of the bands is left to the troops of the Central Powers. In that regard, the German troops became very active across the country . . . . The Austrian troops concern themselves with the cities, especially with Odessa where strict censorship has been imposed. In the countryside wherever Ukrainian troops sympathizing with the peasants are stationed, Austrian troops remain on alert.[26]

Referring to the memorandum of Symon Petliura, Chairman of the All-Ukrainian Council, protesting the massive arrests of the members of the local councils, Forgach suggested to continue with these measures and to ignore his protest. The German Ambassador Mumm assured him of agreeing with the Austrian position and the actions taken.

Another extensive report by Forgach of June 11[27] deserves the special attention of students of Ukrainian history. He convincingly defended the presence of the Ukrainian conscience and identity among the general public and peasantry in particular, a fact not given enough weight in his previous reports. The myth about the national indifference of the masses present in some recent works does not do justice to the facts.[28] Forgach admitted that the process made enormous progress during the war and especially after the 1917 revolution. The emergence of the Central Rada symbolized and represented equally national and socialist aspects of the Ukrainian revolution. In the given historical situation the Rada represented and reflected the prevailing mood of the Ukrainian people. Its 900 members included representatives of the Jewish, Russian, and Polish minorities. In the months to come the Rada underwent a process of social radicalization under the pressure of the Ukrainian socialist parties and in response to the more radical Bolshevist propaganda. At the same time the drive for national independence climaxed with the proclamation of the Fourth Universal making Ukraine a sovereign state on January 22, 1918. Back in Kiev, with the help of the German army, the Rada's failings and insurmountable problems grew unabated: increased internal opposition of the propertied classes, failure to organize a strong army and an effective administration and inability to calm the agitated peasantry were all accelerating her downfall.

Forgach freely admitted that already in March he and the German military representatives became convinced that the Rada was unable to function properly and to meet the Central Powers' objective. He acknowledged their active role in the removal of the Rada commencing in early April by the formulation of guidelines to be imposed upon the future Ukrainian government. The agrarian reform reinstating private property was among the prime concerns. "Hetman Skoropadskyi having secured for himself the support of the Central Powers unconditionally accepted their leadership. . . . The present situation permits the Central Powers to exercise the power under the umbrella of the local government."[29] Ukrainian intelligentsia accused the Hetman not so much of being conservative but more for his pro-Russian stance by bringing into his government Russian-oriented individuals. Forgach, while advising the Hetman against a deliberate conservative course and against promoting the Russian element, felt that the Ukrainian state, though not the Ukrainian national ideal, would not be endangered. However, he concluded on a more pessimistic note: "As of now it is premature to predict for the present government or for an independent Ukraine a more promising horoscope."

Of special interest is Forgach's, and most certainly Vienna's, perception of the possible future of Ukrainian development. Accordingly, the preservation of an independent Ukraine under a moderate conservative government subservient to the politics of the Central Powers and complying with their economic priorities, was foremost in Austria's plans, in view of the danger presented by the revolutionary parties' propaganda which could dangerously infect the agrarian-socialist thinking in Galicia, Poland, and Hungary. "For us the most unfavorable prospect, however, would be the realization of a Russian federation making Ukraine no longer dependent on us by satisfying her national elements which in turn would actively pursue an irredenta policy."[30]

Forgach saw the prospect of a possible spillover of Ukrainian nationalism and agrarian socialism into the Dual Monarchy as a greater danger than the restoration of centralist and absolute Russia, for "the Ukrainian irredenta and the national idea would only weaken such a Russia."[31] His reasoning and conclusion were correct, for an independent Ukraine, like the Hungarian revolution of 1848/49, was the powderkeg to both empires and any Russian nationalist, and even Marxist Lenin would have had to agree and support Forgach.

As far as Germany's policy in regard to Ukraine was concerned some interesting insights can be gleaned from General Krauss' report to the Austrain Army Supreme Command:

> Germany pursues an exclusive economic-political aim in Ukraine. According to Waldbott's report, the surest road to Mesopotamia, Arabia, Baku and Persia was opened to them by the invasion of Ukraine. This road leads through Kiev, Iakaterinoslav and Sevastopol, and from here to Batum and Trapenzunt. For this reason, I feel, Germans will keep Crimea for themselves either as a protectorate or as a colony . . . . To maintain this road, their control of the railroad system and the coal supply from the Donets Basin must be

assured. Moreover, the Germans will exploit Ukraine as their granary and as a market for their industry.[32]

This view has been confirmed by Groener and referred to as an explanation of why the Germans accused the Dual Monarchy of violating all the previous agreements by Austria's unilateral actions in Ukraine. Also for this reason Germany took control of the entire Donets Basin and from Austria the Iakaterinoslav gubernia.

Having accused the Germans of recklessly pursuing their economic and political aims, Krauss complained about Vienna's inability to formulate clearly its objectives in Ukraine. He did not believe that the preponderance of the food supply could by itself become a political program. Unable to challenge Germany's aims in the East, "we must maximize for the Monarchy all advantages while marching together with Germany."[33]

While the Dual Monarchy's Ukrainian policy continued to sway between animosity and uncertainty, Germany's position by June remained tied to the preservation of a Ukrainian state, national in character, yet within Germany's sphere of interest. A top-secret memorandum prepared by the Supreme Command and the Foreign Office[34] revealed that Mumm handed over to the Hetman the Emperor's personal letter in which he insisted on the Ukrainization of the government. At the special meeting, attended by among others Prince Dymitri Urusov, Baron F. Steingell, and S. Kistiakovskyi, the replacement of all ministers except Doroshenko, Vasylenko and Rzepetskyi with men of Ukrainian identity (such as D. Dontsov, I. Feshchenko-Chopivskyi, S. Shelukhyn, M. Vasylenko, A. Nikovskyi, and N. Porsh, a Social Democrat) was seriously discussed. There is, however, no evidence as to the Hetman's position on that issue.

A new development, and even direct attempts to influence Germany's Ukraine policy, began to surface in early July. The initiative was generated by Russian emigrees fleeing into Ukraine, as revealed in Forgach's telegram to Burian:

From the Crimea, the Don Region and from Moscow stream to Kiev not only the leaders of the Kadet Party but also well known members of the Russian aristocratic circles. They get in touch with the German military and political representatives with the intent to secure their support in reestablishing the Russian monarchy . . . .

They deny Ukraine's right to exist. . . . In that situation, the Hetman's position is become increasingly difficult. At Germany's and Austria's insistence he is willing to proceed with the Ukrainization of the government and remove the Russians. The problem remains complicated due to the radical position of the Ukrainian national elements making their participation in the government difficult.[35]

On July 5 Forgach reported to Burian the widening of the conflicting views prevalent among the Russians and Ukrainians. Apart from the Hetman himself, his Prime Minister Fedir Lyzohub, and Dmytro Doroshenko who sought the support of the Ukrainian political parties, other members of the Cabinet and many administrators in the provinces freely exhibited their anti-Ukrainian sentiments, including suppression of the Ukrainian newspapers. Also, the reactivation of the feared Russian secret police and its infamous activities became noticeable.

On his part, the Hetman is aware of the situation and is officially committed to building a social foundation for the Ukrainian state by introducing Ukrainian as the language of instruction in schools, by opening Ukrainian universities and by creating the Ukrainian Academy of Sciences. Furthermore, making Ukrainian the official language for the administration, promulgating the law on Ukrainian citizenship and the formation of a Ukrainian army remain on his agenda. The process of complete Ukrainization is hampered only by the existence of the tiny number of intelligentsia needed for the task and by its negative attitude toward the Hetman regime and the presence of Russians in governmental institutions.[36]

Forgach did not fail to notice that the election of the Russian Metropolitan Antonius to the Kievan and Halich Archbishoprics deeply antagonized the Ukrainians, especially after Antonius held a requiem mass for Tsar Nicholas II who was executed by the Bolsheviks. The service subsequently turned into a Russian monarchist demonstration. Equally offensive for the national-minded Ukrainians was the Hetman's decree permitting Russian officers to wear their uniforms in public. In some cases, the Germans returned some Russian officers back to Russia because of their questionable loyalty and suspicious anti-Ukrainian activities.

Forgach further singled out Russian political parties such as the Kadet party led by Paul Miliukov that together with the Ukrainian Kadets resigned themselves to the existence of a Ukrainian state and of a Russia in alliance with the Central Powers. Personally, Forgach did not trust Miliukov and suspected him of intending to organize the Russians and at the right time return to his all-Russian position and pro-Entente policy. He also suggested that the Entente purposely wanted to organize the Russian elements in Ukraine to use them later for the restoration of Russia and for the destruction of Ukrainian statehood. To prevent such an occurrence, Forgach proposed to remove Miliukov from Ukraine since he seemed to be the main instigator and his expulsion would only please Ukrainians.

Finally, he regreted the continued animosity between the government and the Ukrainian political parties, especially in view of the danger of a peasant rebellion that could affect the availability of foodstuffs for the Central Powers. He concluded with the prospect of prolonged occupation of Ukraine, "desired by the Russian conservative circles as the protection against the Socialists and Revolutionaries and by the Ukrainians as a guarantee against Great Russian expansion."[37]

While the hostile stance of the Russian as well as Ukrainian Bolsheviks and many of the Jews need little analytical elaboration and explanation, the case of the Ukrainian opposition to the Hetman regime and to the Central Powers warrants closer attention. After all, the Ukrainians consisted of over seventy percent of the population and they could have become the determining factor in any situation. One of the more crucial decisions affecting the fate of Ukraine during Hetman Skoropadskyi's rule, as Vynnychenko himself admitted, was the refusal of the Ukrainian moderate and left-oriented parties to participate in his government.

> One must admit that the Hetman in the first days in power intended to give his government an exclusive national Ukrainian character. His Prime Minister Ustynovych had turned to the Ukrainian bourgeois parties, including the Social-Federalists, proposing to them that they form a new government. But they refused. From a psychological vantage one can understand them, considering that they were Central Rada members dispelled by the Hetman. However, from the point of view of the national interest they had no reason to decline, considering the fact that the Social-Federalists were against the

socialization of the land. Other political parties had urged the Federalists to accept the offer before the bourgeoisie got everything into their hands.[38]

Having declined to negotiate with the Hetman, the Social Democrats together with the Social Revolutionaries officially involved the Germans in the internal affairs, thereby giving Groener an even more influential position. On May 2 their delegation handed Groener their conditions for participation in the government asking for a complete change of the government, a different agrarian policy, and the creation of a State Council representing all social classes in Ukraine. The demands, in fact, amounted to the restoration and implementation of the Rada policy. That policy was responsible not only for the internal chaos and the failure to defend the country, but certainly for the presence of the foreign armies in Ukraine, invited by the Rada. Groener, now in control of the situation and acknowledged by the left-wing parties as the arbiter, offered them only three or four ministries, rejecting all other points.[39] Not without a note of arrogance he wrote to his wife: "The leaders of the left-socialist parties would like to stash ministers' salaries into their pockets. They are running into my house putting forth such silly demands that makes it impossible to help them."[40] In his own account, he continued on this point: "In that country one goes farther only with the knout."[41]

Vynnychenko, the well known Ukrainian Social Democrat, rebuffed Groener in his way:

> The issue is not Skoropadskyi or his bourgeois cabinet, Lyzohub or the Protofis.[42] The central issue centers on German-Austrian imperialism and the German generals in Ukraine . . . . Because German imperialism needs the legality to justify its exploitation, it used the Hetman and his government's activities to create the impression that the Ukrainian state in fact exists, its people enjoying their national culture, language, peace and order.[43]

Some insights into the nature of the Austro-Hungarian and German economic policies in Ukraine are provided by the Protocol of the June 17 meeting in Berlin.[44] The meeting became the setting for accusations of each other's cover-up of exporting goods to their respective countries. For example, the Germans accused Austria of illegally smuggling goods across the border with Ukraine. Under the terms of existing agreements,[45] Austria-Hungary was obliged to maintain the distribution of cattle delivered by a ratio of 60 to 40. Instead of 40 percent going to Austria, on the order of Austrian authorities all cattle went for use of the Austrian army. Much of the foodstuffs intended for the needs of the Austrian army in Ukraine was shipped to Austria. The Austrians, on their part, accused the German Military Command of buying directly 10,000 heads of cattle and 10,000 puds (1 pud = 36.07 lbs.) of bacon at higher prices than agreed upon, making it easier for the Ukrainian government to remove itself from its obligation to be the sole supplier of goods and turning the task over to private enterprises. Germany failed to report to the Central Economic Council in Kiev two shipments of 28 and 66 railway cars loaded with cattle and lard.[46]

A few days later, on June 21, the German newspaper *Deutsche Orient-Korrespondenz* reported: "Anyone traveling in Ukraine feels that one cannot speak anymore about pro-German sympathy among the people." The article recommended that Ukraine be supplied with industrial goods and other essentials in exchange for foodstuffs in order to assure the people of the beneficial economic relations with Germany.

The most illustrative example of Germany's Ukrainian policy during Hetman Skoropadskyi's period is the Military and Economic Agreement between Germany and Ukraine signed on September 10, 1918. The draft of the agreement was prepared by the German representatives in Kiev and submitted by Mumm to Chancellor Hertling on June 1.[47]

Numerous provisions of the agreements offer a view into the future situation and intention in case of the Central Powers' victory. Articles 2 and 3 of the Military Agreement were to secure the German army's control of the country by reserving the right to maintain peace and order in Ukraine, including the imposition of censorship and control of identification papers restricting the movements of the population. The period during which German troops were to be stationed in Ukraine was to be decided by the Supreme Army Command. Since in both cases no participation of the Ukrainian army or political institutions was envisaged, the agreement in fact institutionalized the occupational control of the country for an indefinite time. Article 4 provided for the organization and equipment of the Ukrainian army with the assistance of the German Supreme Command, which in turn together with the Austria-Hungary would decide its size and deployment. Ukrainian troops engaged in the suppression of domestic unrest were to be placed under German command. The movement of the Ukrainian troops, the supply of weapons and their production had to have the German Command's approval. The subsequent articles of the agreement (fifteen in all) determining judicial, logistic, transport facilities, and economic aspects further extended the German army's authority, virtually controlling Ukraine's internal affairs.

The one-sidedness of the agreements was equally prevalent in its economic provisions, as Mumm, too, admitted in a letter to the Foreign Office. The first section dealt with transportation and tariffs, facilitating the incorporation of the Ukrainian railway system with the German railroad network, connecting the Baltic seaports with Black Sea harbors. Part Two of the agreement covered general trade exchange and was to remain in force until 1925. By the terms of the agreement the Central Powers would receive surplus grain and livestock not needed for domestic consumption. Ukraine was allowed to export some surplus to Russia only with the permission of the Central Powers. The prices for goods for the next two years was not to exceed current prices. Afterwards world market prices would be accepted. Articles 11 and 12 restored the prior Russian-German treaty's provisions concerning the export of metals for German industry and as a compensation to German nationals for their economic losses in Ukraine. Another provision legalized Germany's seizure of the British telegraph lines spanning across Ukraine and of the sea-cable connecting Odessa with Constantinople. Firmly in control of Ukraine, with peace on the Eastern front and still in a strong position on the Western front, the Germans looked confidently into the future. The degree of optimism can be measured by their willingness to reveal future plans embodied in the concept of *Ostpolitik.*

As far as Ukraine was concerned, Mumm's letter of June 1 to the Ukrainian government typifies and illustrates both the German intentions and the prevailing state of mind.[48] It began with the assertion that the Brest-Litovsk Treaty established a close relationship between Germany and the Ukrainian state. Consequently, Germany had fulfilled her obligation toward the endangered Ukraine by dispatching her troops, thereby saving Ukraine from imminent collapse, and providing a solid base for the political and economic life. Germany's action made it possible for Ukraine to function as an independent state in negotiations with Russia. As before, Germany remained ready to assist with her military and economic resources in Ukraine's peaceful development. A list of Germany's cited attributions was followed by a number of expected equivalents to be rendered in military and economic areas, which were specified in the enclosed draft of the agreement.

Additional expenditures of Germany's military assistance, not mentioned in the agreement, were enumerated in Mumm's letter. The monthly cost in support of the German troops was estimated at 110 million marks for sixteen infantry divisions, two cavalry divisions, in addition to fifty-eight batallions, twenty-nine squadrons and sixteen artillery batteries and a special divisional unit. The cost of future operations and of maintaining all logistic functions had not been even estimated, including the cost of equipping the two Ukrainian divisions. Finally, the document suggested a mode of payment as follows: (1) Ukrainians would recompense Germany's expenditures, with Germany willing to extend interest bearing loans, the rates of which would be determined by the German Central Bank. (2) Germany's expenditures and navigational systems would be settled in a separate agreement. (3) Ukraine was not permitted to undertake any other financial obligation until indebtedness to Germany was full repaid. In case the German claims could not be made in gold payments compensation in kind would be acceptable. The Austro-Hungarian claims were to be settled in a separate agreement.

The draft of the agreement, which was to determine not only Ukraine's economic position but, more importantly, her exclusive dependence on the Central Powers with Germany in control, encountered lengthy negotiations. The Hetman government, having achieved a measure of internal stability, was not about to remain completely submissive as Groener had expected. Moreover, Germany's serious setbacks at the Western front together with declining prospects for winning the war had only strengthened Kiev's hand and made German pressure less and less effective. At the same time, the growing prospect of an Entente victory began to alienate the pro-Russian and conservative elements in Ukraine, leading to further isolation of the Germans, who were already facing hostilities from the left-oriented parties and groups.[49] Finally, the Central Powers' failure to deliver the promised quantity of industrial products and their insistence on a free export from Ukraine while maintaining control over the import of goods into Ukraine contributed to the delays in the negotiations and even to significant changes in the final text of the Economic Agreement for the fiscal year 1918/1919, signed on September 10, 1918.[50]

With its twelve parts, the agreement covering all aspects of economic, financial, trade and organizational agreements, was to remain in force until June 30, 1919.[51] The Ukrainian government would not commit itself for a longer period, as originally intended in the draft submitted in June. Nonetheless, despite numerous changes achieved by the Ukrainian government, the agreement still reflected Germany's determination to use Ukraine as a bridgehead for gaining access to Russian markets.[52] Otherwise, it also underscored the Central Powers' declining influence in Ukraine, yet without any intention of breaking with Germany at that uncertain time. Skoropadskyi's trip to Germany in September and his meeting with Emperor William II, was indicative of his intention of raising the level of the relationship from subordination to a partnership of equals. His commitment to achieve a wider margin of freedom for Ukraine, however, was running short of time and could only partially be realized in the shadow of the approaching German defeat. According to his Minister for Foreign Affairs Dmytro Doroshenko, the hetman, facing the obstacles of the German military in Ukraine in the formation of a Ukrainian army and the unwillingness to return the Black Sea fleet to the Ukrainian government, hoped to seek the Emperor's support.[53]

The remaining three months of the Central Powers' occupation of Ukraine witnessed few new developments. The reports of their representatives in Kiev centered mainly on economic problems, concerns about obtaining and exporting as many goods as possible. The increasing level of local unrest and strikes commanded their attention, contributing to their growing conviction that the control of the existing conditions was beyond their abilities. The presence of the armies ceased to be an effective instrument of policy, apart from delaying Soviet Russia's attack on Ukraine. The assassination of Fieldmarshal Eichhorn in Kiev on July 30 by Russian Social Revolutionaries only exemplified the vulnerability of the occupying army and pointed to the internal instability in Ukraine, which was becoming a safe haven for Russian refugees committed to the destruction of Ukraine.

Equally so, the advantageous agreement of September 10 ensuring thirty-five percent of Ukraine's agricultural crops for the fiscal year

1918/19 amounting to 105.35 million puds (644,000 tons),[54] was in jeopardy and ultimately never fulfilled. Yet it pointed to Ukraine's economic potential and its vital importance to the Central Powers.

It was precisely Ukraine's vast agricultural riches and abundant natural resources combined with her strategic location that caught Groener's special attention in his vision and scheme of avoiding Germany's defeat. Having observed during his stay in Berlin in late September signs of defeatism among the industrialist-capitalist circles and their unwillingness to release more German workers for military service and also their tendency to consider Ukraine as an exclusive supplier of raw materials, Groener began to reconsider his own position. In his speech to the German officers in Kiev on October 3,[55] Groener outlined a new policy toward Ukraine which, if implemented in case of victory, could have had an enormous impact upon German-Ukrainian relations and would have changed the fate of Ukraine for decades to come. In case of a prolonged war and in the face of limited German industrial capacity he urged changing Ukraine into an industrialized country in order to relieve Germany's limits. This was to be done in spite of the objections of the German industrialists who were employing two million workers and could then have made available some 800,000 more men for the armed forces. Since Ukraine possessed plenty of coal, iron ore, and the necessary workforce, there would have been no need for transporting all of the resources to Germany. "We must produce here."[56] Groener's main objective in these consideratioms was the uninterrupted flow of goods between Germany and Ukraine's huge economic potential.

To alter Germany's Ukrainian policy he envisioned supporting the Ukrainian state so as to deprive the "Russian bear of its tastiest morsel." Germany's foremost task was to make Ukraine an economically and militarily capable ally. Groener concluded:

> We remain with our military, political, and economic Ukrainian policy on a doubled base, on two pillars. The first one is for the support of our immediate war aims and to endure the period of war and transition, and the second is intended for future development, which cannot be foreseen at this time.[57]

Groener's program as seen from the Ukrainian perspective would have granted Ukraine independence within the sphere of German influence to develop into a modern industrial society. This in turn could easily have made Ukraine a less dependent country under the leadership of a new generation. From a retrospective view, Ukraine would have been saved from Russia's domination and the subsequent dreadful Soviet policy with its social experiments costing some ten million lives and atrocious suffering affecting all Ukrainians. The theory of the "lesser evil" could have proven to be justifiable under certain conditions. Yet in Groener's words: "As of now Ukraine is not a monarchy, what will come nobody can predict."[58]

Precisely this state of unpredictability was the dominant characteristic of the Brest-Litovsk Treaty and of its consequences to all sides involved. After the nine months long presence of the German and Austrian armies, Ukraine's future and chance to stay independent had improved little; on the contrary, internal weakness and divisiveness and the external enemy, Soviet Russia, overshadowed the German presence in Ukraine. Thus, the Central Powers' expectations of exploiting Ukraine in the future failed to materialize, although ties with the Central Powers had from the beginning determined the future of Ukraine. All other factors remained of secondary significance.

One can also argue that Ukraine's fate was predetermined by the Central Rada's failure to steer the social revolution into the direction of a national one, relying on the Ukrainians' ability to create a strong defense. Such a task, in the face of the collapsing tsarist regime and the still unstable Bolshevik power in Russia was not beyond potential realization. Failure to do so led to placing Ukraine's future into the hands of foreign powers that were guided, first of all, by their own self-serving interests. To them Ukraine was of secondary importance. Therefore, placing most of the blame on Vienna and Berlin would not make a convincing case before the historians' jury.

Moreover, in the absence of any consensus between the Foreign Office, the Economic Office, and the Supreme Command of the Army the nature and aims of Germany's *Ostpolitik* remain unclear. Borowsky, while in agreement with Fritz Fischer, and aware of existing differences, casts the Foreign and Economic Offices as being "more imperialist" than the Supreme Command in the implementation of Ukrainian policy.[59] While priorities of "guilt" offer an exercise in scholasticism, the fact remains that the highly visible imperialist nature of Germany's policy only alienated the Ukrainian masses, making them more receptive to the radicalism of the Bolshevik propaganda, which minimized the importance of the national cause and extolled the attractiveness of socialism. In that regard the Ukrainian Social Democrats' as well as the Social Revolutionaries' contribution should not be underestimated. Therefore, Skoropadskyi's regime succumbed with Germany's defeat. Had he understoood his place in history, he could have saved himself the embarrassment of proclaiming a federation with nonexistent All-Russia. After only eight months in power, Skoropadskyi signed the document of abdication and left for Germany, having failed in his difficult role of hetman in the presence of a foreign army and in his role as leader of the nation during its difficult period of transition and rebirth.

On December 14 the forces of the Directory, led by Colonel Evhen Konovalets, entered Kiev setting up the government of the Directory to pick up the pieces of Ukrainian statehood. To glue them back together was not an easy task either, considering the past problems, failures and the aggressor waiting to attack from the North. Nonetheless, the Ukrainian national movement, having been granted a year's time to mature and to affect the masses, had gained more strength to persevere in the years to come even under Soviet Russian domination.

CHAPTER XII

THE BREST-LITOVSK TREATY IN THE LIGHT OF GERMAN, AUSTRIAN, UKRAINIAN, AND AMERICAN LITERATURE

The German Reichstag's enthusiastic approval of the treaty with Ukraine on February 22, tied to high economic and military hopes, had found equal support from the German news media, from experts, and from the public at large. A similarly positive attitude prevailed among the Ukrainians of national orientation. Both sides equally shared the treaty's provisions, even if for different reasons and expectations. The central point of departure between the Ukrainian and German perceptions in the case of the Brest-Litovsk Treaty and its aftermath rests with the varied expectations. Most of the Ukrainians seriously believed that the Central Powers, and Germany in particular, had sent their armies into Ukraine out of an overriding motive to help the Central Rada restore Ukraine's independence. In fact, however, the first and foremost concern of the Central Powers was to secure the flow of foodstuffs. The misplacement of expected priorities has been well documented in the voluminous literature available including the most recent works.

A sampling of German newspapers reflecting the main stream of political affiliations and views could be considered as reflective of the prevailing public opinion. Except for the left-radical voices, the main body of the political spectrum supported the government's policy and the signing of the treaty with Ukraine. There was much sympathy for Ukraine and even much knowledge of it.

The well known German Ukrainophile Paul Rohrbach had his best hour publishing his article "Peace with Ukraine" in *Stuttgarter Neues Tageblatt* on February 12: "Germany has peace and friendship with a country of 40 million people, a great united nation bordering our ally Austria-Hungary and whose name and importance until recently was unknown to us. This suggests that Russia and eastern Europe were known to our political thinking only superficially. However, there were 'Russian experts' who recently claimed with authority that the Ukrainian movement has no future, it has officers but no soldiers and there is no Ukrainian nation." He reminded the readers about his own publications and those of others and concluded, "We have known exactly what we expect from the Ukrainian peace. But we, as well as Ukraine, know what thanks she ought to give and what she can expect from us. German and allied weapons destroyed the chains keeping Ukrainians, Finns, Poles, and other non-Russian peoples in tsarist Russia. The destruction of Russia became an event of world-wide importance in the present war."

He, like Axel Schmidt, criticized German institutions, political as well as military, and Ambassador Mumm, for their inability to understand the problems of a Ukrainian internal situation caught between socialist and nationalist fervor. Consequently, by supporting Hetman Pavlo Skoropadskyi, Germany allied herself with the class of the large landowners; mainly Russians and Poles, who gravitated toward the restoration of the Russian empire and of the former feudal system.[1]

Another Stuttgart newspaper *Der Beobachter,* representing liberal views, published a lengthy article on February 11 "Peace with Ukraine," including the text of the treaty. Commenting on its importance, the article stressed Russia's removal from the Straits and from South-East Europe, which in turn would become the domain of the Central Powers. Of equal importance, as far as Ukraine was concerned, was the availability of her natural resources and agricultural products, which previously were utilized by the Russian Empire. Commenting on the significance of an independent Ukraine within the international context could only lead to increased public interest and sympathy. The subsequent issues continued to bring news about Ukraine on a daily basis, including the text of the Supplementary Agreement and the arrival of the Ukrainian delegation in

Berlin on February 18 that was seeking Germany's military help in the liberation of Ukraine from the Russian invasion.

Similar approbations were expressed in other German newspapers including *Kölnische Nachrichten, Leipziger Neueste Nachrichten,* and *Deutsche Politik.* The Austrian press joined the German in welcoming the treaty. *Neue Freie Presse* printed favorable articles by Julius Andrassy and Professor Hans Übersberger. *Die Zeit,* in a series of articles from February 14 through 17 defended the Kholmland settlement as the price of obtaining Ukrainian deliveries, and the *Wiener Allgemeine Zeitung* of February 19 pointed to the release of the Ukrainian prisoners of war as proof of the termination of the Austro-Hungarian war on the eastern front.

Neither the German nor the Austrian press could possibly completely comprehend all the complexities prevailing in Ukraine nor foresee events there in the immediate future. Lacking realistic foresight the press as well as the public in general expected too much too soon while enjoying the bright prospect of an end to years of deprivation and suffering.

The Brest-Litovsk Treaty also became the subject of monographs and memoir literature by the leading political and military personalities, among them Ottokar Czernin, Gustav Gratz, Richard Schüller and General Alfred Krauss on the Austrian side and the generals Erich Ludendorff, Max Hoffmann, and Wilhelm Groener and Richard Kühlmann on the German side. The first German monograph *Ukraina*[2] by Heinrich Lanz offers basic information on geography, population, economy, history, and culture. The treaty is seen as the first step toward friendly German-Ukrainian relations. The memoirs provide much detailed information on a daily basis of the opinions of the respective personalities. Most of the memoirs exhibit a rather friendly sentiment toward Ukraine and the treaty, but all of them are critical of the Central Rada, especially those of Krauss and Groener.

In the post-World War One literature the work of the publicist Karl Friedrich Nowak, *Der Sturz der Mittelmächte,*[3] discusses the treaty with Ukraine in the first chapter, using exclusively Czernin's and Hoffmann's memoirs. He sided with Czernin's dislike of the young Ukrainian delegates for their uncompromising demands on the Kholmland question and insistence on the creation of the young Ukrainian Crownland within the Habsburg empire. Kühlmann's sympathy for Ukrainians has drawn only biting remarks, while Czernin and Hoffmann have remained immune to any criticism. Nowak's account, flawed by his ignorance of the real conditions in Ukraine combined with his disregard of Ukrainian interests, hardly can be accepted as an objective assessment of the treaty as to its significance and potential.

From among German memoirs published immediately after the war, General Erich Ludendorff's views are reflective of German military thinking. He saw the value of Ukraine as an additional force against the Russian Bolshevism and as a supplier of needed foodstuffs without which the war itself could be jeopardized. Hence the military occupation of Ukraine was not exactly an act of political generosity, but was necessary to secure the economic advantages of the treaty. To Ludendorff there was no other alternative. Consequently, he as much as the German Supreme Command, welcomed the fall of the weak Central Rada and Skoropadskyi's *coup d'état*, seeing in him a more effective and useful ruler. Ludendorff equated a strong Ukraine with Germany's vital interest—a military ally against Soviet Russia. Within this context of expectations the treaty found Ludendorff's approval. He appreciated Ukraine's supply, even if it was not in the amount expected.

As for Hoffmann's and Groener's memoirs, there is much similiarity in the views typical of German army reasoning and priorities. The desire to maintain an independent Ukraine with a strong but submissive government sympathetic to Germany's economic needs and incorporated into her future economic sphere was their first priority. This priority coincided very closely with the German Economic Office in Berlin and with the business community at large. In that regard, British, and especially French, attitudes and policies toward Ukraine before the signing of the Brest-Litovsk Treaty and after the collapse of the Hetman regime did not differ significantly. The desire to dominate Eastern Europe, and Ukraine in particular, was shared equally by all Great European Powers. Germany was no exception. Perhaps the degree of pressure would have differed, but the underlying intentions remained.

The reasoning and actions of the German military had been equally shared by Fritz Werttheimer,[5] who witnessed the events in Ukraine in the Spring of 1918. To him the significance of the treaty revealed itself in the German army's liberation of Ukraine from the Bolshevik occupation, an act poorly understood by the socialist Rada. His support of Skoropadskyi's *coup* was genuine and in the interest of Ukraine, and in compliance with the Central Power's economic interest.[6]

The German historian of the post-World War One period, Volkwart John credits the treaty with being more balanced and reciprocal in terms of advantages than the Versailles Peace Treaty. Moreover, "Ukraine here appeared after a lengthy period of political dependence for the first time as an independent and recognized state. Ukraine achieved at Brest-Litovsk ideals for which the Ukrainian people fought for centuries."[7] Otherwise, Germany's defeat and her internal problems in the interwar period, together with the emergence of Nazism could hardly foster continuous interest in Ukraine. Apart from Axex Schmidt's two sympathetic publications,[8] Ukraine ceased to be the topic of interest. Only the Ukrainian Research Institute in Berlin remained a source of information for the German public with its monographs and serials in addition to the journal *Die Ukraine* published by the German-Ukranian Society, organized in 1918 by Paul Rohrbach and Axel Schmidt.

For the next decade and until 1945 German scholarship and the German people were forced to see Ukraine exclusively through Hitler's *Mein Kampf*, and the estranged Ukrainians to experience the second encounter with the Germans through Nazism with all the horrifying consequences. The Brest-Litovsk Treaty was not even mentioned by either side, though for very different reasons. Schmidt's book, *Ukraine, Land der Zukunft*, was wisely taken out of circulation.

Germany's second defeat in World War II and the total collapse of German *Ostpolitik* inspired more intensive studies of the Ukrainian issue within the context of Germany's drive to the East leading to national catastrophe, and the expulsion of German nationals from the whole of Eastern Europe. The availability of archival material stored in Vienna, Koblenz, Freiburg and Bonn as well as the pressing need for understanding Germany's failures made the appearance of scholarly studies possible and justifiable as well. Two scholars in particular, George Stadtmüller and Hans Koch, both residing in Munich, were the first to reactivate links with the past interest in Ukraine within the Federal Republic of Germany.[9] From among the post-World War Two generation Dietrich Geyer's contribution signaled a new rise of interest in Ukrainian subjects.[10] The first one, however, to discuss the German-Ukrainian relations of 1918 was the historian Hans Beyer. His short booklet *Die Mittelmächte und die Ukraine, 1918* (Munich, 1956, 58pp.) utilizing only a limited number of sources, mainly Austrian, and a few German, Ukrainian and American published monographs, fell short of becoming a standard work. While appreciating his familiarity with historical facts, Beyer's underlying intention was to discredit the Ukrainian presence at Brest-Litovsk, to disregard the conditions in which Ukraine found herself after the collapse of the tsarist regime and to confer immunity on the Germans involved in Ukrainian affairs. He accepts uncritically the negative comments of his countrymen without analyzing their motives, intentions, and the degree of their factual knowledge of the circumstances.

Beyer's argument that the "Rada was not in a position to secure deliveries promised in Brest-Litovsk" obviously should have been conditioned by the time factor and by the totality of objective factors. In the given situation any other government would have needed more time to establish itself and to gain effective control of a country passing through social and economic upheaval. The Rada was given less than two months to perform a most difficult task in the face of the impatient Central Powers who were interested only in their own welfare. At that time, more than ever before or since, the Rada indeed needed a genuine friend. Instead, the Rada was afflicted by requisitionists who only contributed to the rise of dissatisfaction and chaos, and indirectly helped the Bolsheviks in spreading their propaganda which was directed towards confusing the peasantry in particular. For this reason perhaps a more just assessment of the blame could be more defensible by equally sharing in the failure to implement the treaty in its best intention.

Within such a context and sequence of causes, intentions, and consequences Winfried Baumgart's contribution[11] must be seen as more objective and balanced. It is in the best tradition of Leopold Ranke's dictum: "*wie es eigentlich gewesen ist.*" This source-based study treats the Ukrainian aspect within the broader frame of the German *Ostpolitik* in a special chapter "German Policy in South Russia (Ukraine, Don Region and Crimea)." Baumgart's assertion that "the main purpose of the Peace Treaty was to provide Germany and especially Austria-Hungary with foodstuffs and raw materials," reveals the shortsightedness of the Central Powers in ignoring any long-term political strategy aimed at gaining friends and allies. By that time the Ukrainians were in no hurry to embrace the replacement of tsarist Russia's colonialism with that brought by the armies of the Central Powers. The consequences were unmistakably identified by Baumgart: "The work and rule of the German occupational army reduced the political status of Ukraine to an occupied area, to a 'general-government,' though the Foreign Office in Berlin maintained a fiction of Ukraine being a friendly state. Since the military held the bridles in their hands, they did not care about political guidelines given to the diplomatic representative in Kiev. . . . Groener characterized conditions in Ukraine with the phrase: 'We do what we consider to be good and needed and do not ask what the Wilhelm Street in Berlin, Erzberger and comrades would say.' Groener was the one who approved the Austrian troops' practices of forceful requisitions of foodstuffs. The Austrian representative Forgach, an essentially anti-Ukrainian individual, caught Groener's ear with his infamous resolution reducing the Ukrainian government's importance to only a *Mantel* (outercoat), and "nothing else."[13]

About the sequence of events leading to the overthrow of the Central Rada, Baumgart concluded: "Now (after April 23–S.H.) events set into motion proceeded with blow after blow. In fact, since April 6, there was no more talk about respect for the sovereignty of the Ukrainian state, especially after Fieldmarshal Eichhorn's order concerning the planting of crops. . . . On April 23, Ludendorff gave his consent to use either "a powerful pressure' to force the Rada to speed up deliveries or to remove her."[14] Obviously Beyer's statement that Skoropadskyi's *coup* in its planning and execution took place without any German participation and support remains groundless and misleading.

Yet the most comprehensive study of the German-Ukrainian encounter of 1918 had to wait until 1970 with the appearance of Peter Borowsky's monograph *Deutsche Ukrainepolitik 1918,*[15] which coincided with the American study by Oleh S. Fedyshyn.[16]

Borowsky, a former student of the German historian Fritz Fischer, modeled his work on his teacher's. Fischer directed German historiography into a more critical view of Germany's war aims and of *Ostpolitik* as well, especially in his book *Griff nach der Weltmacht: Die Kriegspolitik des kaiserlichen Deutschland 1914-1918* (1964).[17] Fischer's critical and somewhat revisionist account of Germany's war policy has found some response in Borowsky's discussion of the German attitude toward Ukraine. This, however, did not affect him in his research, analysis, and conclusions.

Unlike Beyer, Borowsky visibly abstains from judgments before establishing facts, and even then he does it sparingly, leaving the reader to come to his own conclusion. His assessment of the treaty is sound and goes beyond an exclusively economic stereotype: "The first peace settlement of the World War and therefore its psychological impact upon the war-weary and exhausted people in Germany and Austria-Hungary cannot be over-estimated."[18] Moreover, "the Peace Treaty with Ukraine speeded up the signing of the treaties with Russia and Romania, the treaty bestowed Germany's prospect on the much desired supply of foodstuffs and made it possible to realize Germany's war aims in the East as formulated since 1914. However, Austria-Hungary was burdened with the difficulties of the agreement. Czernin even afterwards, had to admit that without this *Brotfrieden* with Ukraine and, despite the limited quantity of the foodstuffs received, Austria-Hungary would not have been able to survive until the new harvest."[19] On the other hand, Austria-Hungary's compromise on the Kholmland and promise of the Ukrainian crownland created "the dangerous explosives for the right to self-determination of the nations in that multi-national empire."[20]

Borowsky answers the claim that Germany's intention was misplaced in concluding the peace treaty with the Ukrainians at a time when the real power of the Central Rada was limited to a small area in Volhynia, or as Trotsky cynically observed to their quarters in Brest-Litovsk, with Hoffmann's assurance that the German army was capable at any moment of reinstating the Ukrainian government in Kiev. Henceforth, "such military intervention offered the advantage for Germany to implement intended political and economic control of the country."[21] Having quite correctly established Germany's motives, Borowsky provided the crucial and original frame of reference against which future German policy and events in U-kraine can be explained and understood. In fact, most of his study and arguments revolve around this central thesis affecting the relationships of the two unequal partners: the strong Central Powers and the weak Central Rada.

While time and external conditions provided a unique chance for a new chapter in German-Ukrainian relations, several other equally essential factors, such as the general weakness of the Rada, its socialist policy, and especially Germany's failure to implement a more benevolent policy towards Ukraine, have overshadowed the significance of the external factors. Borowsky concludes his critical inquiries into the complex German-Ukrainian encounter and disappointment by placing the Ukrainian case into the broader context of Germany's war aims. Accordingly, he sees the Foreign

Office's main aim in weakening Russia by separating the borderlands, and creating conflicts between Russia and the important agricultural and industrial regions of the former tsarist empire, especially Ukraine. The acceptance of the Bolshevik regime in Russia and support of Skoropadskyi in Ukraine was in line with Kühlmann's intention to weaken Russia, at least for the duration of the war. In fact, he, as well as Ludendorff and Wilhelm II in their projection of the long-term post-war eastern policy, visualized the possibility of a unified Russia in alliance with Germany. The Foreign Office as well as the Economic Office (RWA) already were considering such a possibility while expecting the Entente Powers to continue the economic blockade of Germany after the war. Ukraine was also projected as a bridgehead to the Russian market. Even during the war officials from the Office of Economics worked at bringing the Ukrainian economy under German influence in order to affect not only the supply of foodstuffs but equally so the banking system, transportation and heavy industry. The Office also urged private commercial and industrial enterprises to become involved in the Ukrainian economy. Finally, Borowsky in summarizing Germany's often conflicting aims states: "In the final analysis the interdependence between the German *Ostpolitik* and the war's outcome contributed significantly to the failure of the German Ukraine policy. Considering the Brest-Litovsk Treaty solely as *Brotfrieden* secured by the military occupation of Ukraine, failure came as early as May 1918. Such understanding of the treaty and of the German occupation of Ukraine by Ludendorff and Czernin does not do justice to Germany's goals. The failure to deliver the anticipated grain from Ukraine in 1918 should not be equated with the failure of the German Ukraine policy."[23]

Indeed, Borowsky offers a more convincing line of argument for Germany's failure to benefit from the Brest-Litovsk Treaty. "During 1918 Germany failed to establish a counterforce against the Bolsheviks with Ukraine as the cornerstone for the formation of an anti-Bolshevik Russia. Up to the time of the withdrawal of the German troops the German military as well as the civil representatives of the German empire was in Kiev and so the Hetman regime did not gain the confidence of the Ukrainian people. On the contrary, opposition against Skoropadskyi grew from month to month; his government fell due to the German army's unwillingness to support him."[24] Hence, "the failure of the German Ukraine policy is the consequence of the military defeat in the West."[25] At the same time Borowsky submits that had the Allies permitted Germany to maintain her position in the East on the basis of the Brest-Litovsk Treaty, Germany would have been in a position to maintain the occupation of Ukraine for a longer period of time making possible German plans to build and to maintain "bridgehead Ukraine."

Borowsky's scenario extending the significance of the Ukrainian treaty beyond 1918, as related to Ukraine, deserves the historian's attention. The nullification of the Brest-Litovsk treaties with Ukraine and with Soviet Russia on March 3, 1918 by the Entente Powers, spelled out in the Armistice terms of November 11, 1918, served only the Bolshevik regime in Russia, contributing not only to its chances of survival but enabling it to invade Ukraine for the second time in 1919/1920.

Borowsky's scenario omits no substantial facts and factor which is reasonable and convincing: 1) Article IV of the treaty with Soviet Russia obliged the Soviet government to recognize Ukraine's treaty with the Central Powers, to withdraw Soviet troops and to conclude a peace treaty with Ukraine. 2) The Soviet Russian-Ukrainian Agreement of June 12, 1918 terminated war conditions between the two countries and also provided for the exchange of consulates and the renewal of transportation. 3) At British urging the German Free Corps unit was to remain in the Baltic region after 1918 thereby laying the groundwork for the emergence of free states—Estonia, Latvia and Lithuania. Similarly, an extended presence of the German army in Ukraine under certain provisions could have prevented the Soviet Russian invasion. Moreover, it could have given additional time for French and British military intervention utilizing Ukraine as an important factor in their attempts to overthrow the communist regime in Russia. Within such a flow of events the Brest-Litovsk Treaty could have achieved its historical significance and have redirected European history in a very different destiny.

The treaty found only limited interest among Austrian historians, despite the large archival resources available, including memoirs and newspaper accounts. The disintegration of the Dual Monarchy and the tumultuous events of the post-World War I period could hardly offer Austrian scholarship an environment in which to concentrate on such depressing events. The first scholarly treatment of the subject appeared only in 1970 by Wolfdieter Bihl.[26] The Ukrainian Treaty is discussed in Chapter 12, "Der Friedensvertrag mit der Ukraine" together with several documents listed in the Annex.

Bihl's short chapter concentrates mainly on the economic aspects of the treaty. Article 7, Paragraph 1 of the treaty binding Ukraine to deliver agricultural surplus to the Central Powers together with the Agreement of April 9 specifying quantities of items to be delivered before July 31, were of exclusive interest to Austria-Hungary. Vienna, under the pressure of the Poles, decided not only to annul the Secret Crownland Protocol of February 8, but also decided against ratifying the Peace Treaty precisely because of Ukraine's failure to deliver on time the promised quantity of foodstuff. Bihl accepts Vienna's arguments as valid and justifiable reasons and at the same time offers a reasonable explanation. Among the causes he cites were the Central Powers' overestimation of the quantity of surplus available in Ukraine, the war and the Bolshevik plundering during the 1917/18 winter, the agrarian revolution, general lawless conditions and the peasants's unwillingness to plant the crop. On the other hand, the government and the state's apparatuses were too ineffective to meet their responsibilities.[27] These sound reasons should have convinced Bihl and the government in Vienna that the Central Rada was not unwilling to comply, but unable. Given the problems of the Central Rada, the Vienna government should not have used delays in supply for political punitive action and should not have tolerated the Austrian army's forceful requisition of grain and other articles, including livestock and natural resources. The requisitions in turn encouraged passive resistance, making it only more difficult for the Ukrainian government to live up to its obligations. The Rada having signed the treaty and having requested military assistance became a friend of the Central Powers and not an adversary, a reasoning totally absent in Bihl's line of arguments. After all, prior to November Ukraine delivered 400,000 tons of foodstuffs to the Central Powers without which many Viennese would have probably died of starvation.

Nonetheless, Bihl's overall view on the Ukrainian treaty remains sound: "The importance of the Brest-Litovsk Treaty with Ukraine can be summarized as follows: It was the first peace treaty of the World War, the first step toward general peace, to the end of the bloodshed and for this reason it should be seen from the humane vantage as a positive accomplishment. The Ukrainian nation achieved with this treaty the recognition of her restored national independence, which it lost with the Pereiaslav Treaty of 1654."[28]

On the other hand, Bihl's apologetic defense of Austria-Hungary's policy toward Ukraine[29] seems to be the weakest part of his contribution, for the Ukrainian delegation in Brest-Litovsk naturally was motivated by Ukraine's and Ukrainians' national interest, as was instructed by Mykhailo Hrushevskyi, Chairman of the Central Rada. Accordingly, the fate of Ukrainians in Galicia and Bukovina was a legitimate concern to the Ukrainian state on the Dnieper. Vienna's troubles with the Poles and with other nationalities as well, was not of the Central Rada's making but of the Habsburg's centuries-old policy. Therefore, Bihl's sympathy for the Habsburg Empire reflect only his personal feeling and not the judgment of the uncommitted historian.

Reaction, responses and verdicts on the Brest-Litovsk Treaty among Ukrainians differed along ideological-political lines. The non-communist interpretation and understanding of the events of 1918 in Ukraine, in many instances, does not differ significantly from the Western views. However, the official historiography of the Ukrainian Soviet Socialist Republic—while negating the national-oriented scholarship—sees and interprets events in terms of the Marxist historical dialectic adjusted to the official lines spelled out by the Communist Party of the USSR. This is not to say that Soviet historiography has erased the Brest-Litovsk Treaty and the Central Powers' involvement in Ukrainian affairs from the pages of history. On the contrary, the post-World War II Soviet U-krainian historiography exhibits a special interest in German-Ukrainian relations with twelve monographs and dozens of articles published since 1950.[30]

Such extensive concentration on the events of 1918 is more a result of World War II and is intended to portray Germany an historical enemy of the Ukrainian people. While tying Nazi crimes in Ukraine to Germany's policy and the presence of the German army in 1918, the Soviet authors equate and identify both cases as illustrations of the nature of "German imperialism, and arch-enemy of the Ukrainian people." Equally so, in both periods, Ukrainians in their struggle against Germany found "an ally in Russia." Any other Ukrainian orientation, save for the pro-Russian, is labeled as "conspiracy of the Ukrainian bourgeois-nationalists with the German imperialism," as for instance, was the case with the Brest-Litovsk Treaty.[31] Having identified the Socialist Central Rada as "bour-geois-nationalist" S. N. Sazheniuk lowered the Rada to an instrument of the "counterrevolution" with the understanding that the Ukrainian Bolshevik *coup d'etat* in Kharkiv was the real representative of the U-krainian revolution, despite the fact that the Rada had emerged six months earlier as a popular organ of the workers and peasants of Ukraine. More-over, the most often exaggerated facts about Bolshevik-led attacks against the German army are being presented as the struggle of the Ukrainian people. Neglected are the activities, position and popularity of the two largest Ukrainian radical parties; the Ukrainian Social Democrats and the Ukrainian Social Revolutionaries. None of the Soviet publications admits that the uprising against Skoropadskyi in late November 1918 was prepared and executed by the Ukrainian socialist parties with the assistance of the Galician military unit "Sichovi Striltsi" led by the Di-rectory composed of such individuals as Volodymyr Vynnychenko and Symon Petliura.

And so Trotsky's official recognition of the Central Rada's delegation to the Brest-Litovsk negotiations became merely "Trotsky's act of treason which made it possible for the imperial diplomacy to resolve the complex issue of the Central Rada's representatives as the legal "souvereign" delegation, a fact which favored the realization of the German imperialists' plan and of the Ukrainian bourgeois-nationalists."[32] To Chervinkin-Koraliov the treaty's intention was two-fold: "as means to suppress Soviet power in Ukraine" and "an act against Soviet Russia and the Polish people," by giving Kholmland and Pidlasha to Ukraine. There is no mention of the ethnographic composition of the regions where Ukrainians comprised significant majorities. However, at the same time the Central Rada was blamed for signing the Secret Protocol with Austria-Hungary because "the agreement divided for ever the Ukrainian terri-tories and proved to be still another exposure of the bourgeois-national-ists' treason." Furthermore, " 'the peace treaty' with the Central Rada has been exploited by the German imperialists in their realization of invasion plans in regard to Soviet Russia."[34] Summarizing the conse-quences of the treaty, the Soviet author concludes that it provided an official excuse for the march of the German-Austrian armies into Ukraine, which amounted to the loss of the territory and equally so the very existence of Soviet power. In that situation the Leninist orientation on peace became the only right decision in signing the treaty on March 3, 1918 between Soviet Russia and the Central Powers. "The terms and the separate 'agreement' between the Austro-German imperialists and the Central Rada became especially intolerable for Ukraine, for she was temporarily breaking away from the Russian Federation. However, considering the need for survival and development of the socialist revolution, the working men of the Ukrainian SSR supported the signing and ratification of the Brest-Litovsk Treaty with Soviet Russia."[35]

Condemning the Ukrainian treaty with the Central Powers as an evil act, Soviet historiography found Soviet Russia's treaty with these same "imperialists"justifiable, wise and approved even by the "Ukrainian working men." Evidence indicating where and when Ukrainians did approve Lenin's policy is missing. In fact, they never had been consulted and never had dispatched a supporting note to Moscow with a list of signers.

Quite a different opinion prevailed on the opposite ideological and political side in Ukraine. In the absence of a consensus the varied views reflect the multiplicity of interpretations and reasonings. Volodymyr Vynnychenko, a Social Democrat and the first Prime Minister of the General Secretariat (government) until January 29, 1918, in his memoirs devoted a special chapter to the peace treaty with the meaningful subtitle "Apology to the Allies."[36] Being an ardent radical socialist, his political sympathy rested with the Entente Powers, however, he realized that England and France were not motivated by an honest desire to support the Ukrainian cause. Their only concern was to maintain the eastern front against the Central Powers and have others "pull the chestnuts from the fire" for their selfish interest. Ukraine found herself between two imperialistic interests represented by the Central Powers and the Entente with the Russian Bolsheviks attacking from the north. In Vynnychenko's understanding of that crucial period of history, "the German imperialism proved to be closer to the immediate interest of Ukraine." The initiative to negotiate with the Central Powers "was not ours." The Russian Bolsheviks were the first to sign an armistice with the Central Powers and at the same time they continued their hostilities against the Central Rada. Vynnychenko did not have any illusions about Germany's intentions in signing the treaty with the Rada, yet neither did he have illusions about the Rada's position: "In summary, that treaty could have been of enormous advantage for the Ukrainian state and its government, . . . provided the treaty was not a result of all favorable circumstances, but the result and the consequence of our own strength and our will, our ability to implement and to take advantage of the treaty's provisions. Only under such conditions could the treaty, of course, have become most advantageous."[37]

While the soundness of Vynnychenko's reasoning hardly can be argued, paradoxically enough it was he who most vigorously defied the formation of the Ukrainian army. Believing that the magic of socialism will peacefully resolve all the national and territorial conflicts, he, as well as too many Ukrainian socialists like him, disarmed their own socialist revolution.

Pavlo Khrystiuk, the historian of the Ukrainian revolution and one of the leaders of the Ukrainian Social Revolutionary Party, admitted that "Ukrainian socialist-revolutionaries and Ukrainian social-democrats were the children of the Ukrainian revolution,"[38] instead of becoming the leaders of the revolution, like Lenin and the Bolshevik Party in Russia. Khrystiuk's view of the Brest-Litovsk Treat is thoroughly positive reflecting well upon the yong Ukrainian diplomacy:

> The peace treaty concluded with Ukraine possibly represents the only agreement concluded during the war, and at the end of the great imperialist war under the dictate of the Entente Powers, which is not imperialistic in substance. This treaty was achieved, in fact, without annexations and indemnities. For Ukrainians it implemented the principle of national self-determination. Yes, Galicia remained within Austria-Hungary, however, an additional agreement provided for the free national development of the Ukrainian people in Galicia. Likewise from the economic aspect the treaty was agreeable and convenient for the Ukrainian People's Republic. The economic relationship was placed on the principle of mutuality. The conclusion of the treaty and its provisions are testimonies to the great accomplishment of building statehood by the Ukrainian nation of peasants and workers during the revolution. The Ukrainian achievements in the national-political struggle were possible also due to the fact that the Entente Powers as well as the Central Powers found it necessary to recognize the Ukrainian Republic and to establish, in one form or another, diplomatic relations . . . . The fact that the Brest-Litovsk Treaty with the Central Powers had not

been utilized and that the wheel of history had run over the destroyed it does not minimize its significance in the history of the national struggle and building of the statehood of the Ukrainian people.[39]

The "wheels of history" had crushed the Brest-Litovsk Treaty and an independent Ukraine had been rolled over by the Versailles Peace Treaty, a treaty which nullified many other agreements reached after World War One. Moscow's march did not end with the conquest of Ukraine leaving only to history the possibility of "stopping the wheels" at the borders of Ukraine.

Another Ukrainian historian, and former minister of Foreign Affairs in Hetman Skoropadskyi's government, Dmytro Doroshenko, the author of *History of Ukraine, 1917-1923,*[40] provides a clearly balanced and informative account of the negotiations based on Ukrainian, Austrian, and German sources and literature available to him. While abstaining from personal views, Doroshenko's treatment of the subject implies his approval. Doroshenko did not fail to notice that "Ukrainians in Galicia and Bukovina have greeted the Brest-Litovsk Treaty with enthusiasm. In Lviv (Lemberg) a large demonstration took place. Ukrainian newspapers warmly welcomed the treaty."[41]

Several years later the West Ukrainian journalist and editor of the special volume commemorating the Brest-Litovsk Treaty,[42] Ivan Kedryn (Rudnytskyi) offered a retrospective evaluation of the treaty which certainly reflected the views of the West Ukrainians living in Poland. By that time erstwhile enthusiasm gave way to the weighing of pros and cons. Kedryn lists on the negative voucher such losses as 42,000 railroad cars of grain for Austria-Hungary and not much less for Germany, the scandalous removal of the Central Rada, the shameful arrest of Vsevolod Holubovych, Prime Minister of the Ukrainian government, by the German army, and the never achieved separation of Galicia. Moreover, as a result of the treaty and the invitation of the German army, Ukrainians were labeled Germophiles, which hurt the Ukrainian cause at the Paris peace conference dominated by the victorious Allies.

On the ledger's credit side he registered the extension of Ukrainian statehood made possible with the assistance of the German army, and without which the short-lived independence of Ukraine would have become even shorter. The overall Ukrainian gains during the seven months long Hetmanate only increased Ukrainian potential and made it stronger *vis-a-vis* Soviet Russian policy in Ukraine in the 1920s and afterwards. Kedryn is no less impressed with the performance of the Ukrainian delegation at Brest-Litovsk which in spite of the weakness of the Ukrainian People's Republic, achieved considerable diplomatic success including the recognition of the Ukrainian statehood by the European powers. The treaty also reestablished the historical link of the Kholmland with Ukraine and improved the Ukrainian position in the Dual Monarchy. Yet "the greatest importance of the treaty lies in its affirmation of the Dnieper Ukrainians' concern about the fate of the West Ukrainian lands. Thus, the treaty became the first shiny signpost for national ideology; the fate of the Galician Land's issue became inseparably tied with the future of the Dnieper Ukraine. The liberation of Galicia hinged on the strength of the all-Ukrainian national center on the Dnieper."[43]

A different perception of the Brest-Litovsk Treaty and Germany's involvement in Ukrainian affairs in 1918 is offered by the Ukrainian American author Ihor Kamenetskyi. To him, "intervention and the presence of the German army in Ukraine had an impact on the implementation of German policy in Eastern Europe, dramatically extending Germany's expansionist ambition and securing greater influence of militaristic and ultra-patriotic circles of the German society on the formation of the foreign policy. There was born a prototype of the later expansionistic plans of the Third Reich and specific conceptions of its colonial policy despite significant differences in German policies in 1918 and in the years 1941-1944."[44]

As far as the Brest-Litovsk Treaty with Ukraine is concerned, English language scholarship and American in particular, remains virtually barren. Just the fact that there is no single monograph on that subject available and among more than one thousand history or political science Ph.D. dissertations on Russia and Eastern Europe none deals with that treaty.[45] However, half a dozen monographic studies on modern Ukrainian history relate to the treaty, especially those produced by John S. Reshetar, Oleh Fedyshyn, and Oleh S. Pidhainy.

Pidhainy's study,[46] in the Chapter "Recognition of the Ukrainian Republic by the Central Powers, and the Brest-Litovsk Conference" reflects Ukrainian thinking. In justifying the Rada's decision to conclude the peace treaty and its policy upon returning to Kiev in the presence of of the Germany army, he becomes too defensive of the Rada's policy and too reproachful of the Central Powers. He is not exactly correct in suggesting that Ukraine's *de facto* independence ceased with the occupation, which must be seen first of all as a welcome military operation, which only later turned into a kind of "friendly occupation." Perhaps one should speak rather of a limited sovereignty, especially after the removal of the Rada's government. Nonetheless, he speaks of the treaty on a positive note: "In this manner, Ukraine was recognized by the Central Powers and a mutually advantageous agreement was reached at Brest-Litovsk; above all, independence, freedom and peace were to become a reality."[47]

The signing of the treaty and liberation of Kiev by the Ukrainian troops led by Petliura,[48] with the German army behind, in Pidhainy's view, made it possible "to explore new ways for the Ukraine to develop as a state within the family of nations, a family still bitterly divided and at the high point of the immense conflicts of the First World War and the East European Revolution. The Ukrainian National Republic, having developed internally in constitution and externally in diplomacy, and having in the process consolidated its sovereignty had completed its period of formation and entered as an equal into the world community of states."[49]

Pidhainy seems to suggest that the Rada by its own strength "consolidated its sovereignty" on the territory of Ukraine, which obviously was not true. Moreover, the mere presence of the large foreign armies of some 750,000 men, imposed limits upon the Rada's freedom of action. It was exactly the Rada's failure to defend the borders of Ukraine that brought about the situation over which it had no control. Pidhainy, however, is correct in his insistence on Ukraine's *de facto* recognition by France and Great Britain; a fact disputed by John S. Reshetar.[50] The latter's rather narrow definition of the *"de facto* recognition cannot be upheld in the face of available documentary evidence.

Reshetar in his work *Ukrainian Revolution* succinctly summarizes the Rada's motives in sending a delegation to Brest-Litovsk:

> The Ukrainians found themselves in an unpleasant and difficult situation; the Bolsheviks had concluded an armistice with the Central Powers on December 15 in the name of the whole of Russia,

including Ukraine. In addition they were confronted with a dilemma: if they refused to conclude a peace with the Central Powers the armies of the latter would invade Ukraine; if they did conclude a separate peace they would antagonize the Entente Powers who, although not in a position to render any effective aid, were insistent upon continued Ukrainian participation in the war.[51]

The forcefulness of his arguments rests on the logic of analytical insights into the events as they unfolded and prevailed. Consequently, Reshetar's approval of the treaty, though not without reservations, remains convincing:

> Although the Rada lost Kholm for all practical purposes, it did obtain legal recognition from Germany, Austria-Hungary, Bulgaria, and Turkey or, in Vinichenko's words, the treaty gave to Ukraine "the opportunity to strengthen and legalize our statehood on the international plane." The price paid for this recognition was high: it required forfeiture of the "recognition" which has been accorded the Rada by the Entente, and it made Ukraine a German satellite.[52]

Oleh Fedyshyn's is the only study on Germany's *Ostpolitik* with exclusive concentration on Ukraine.[53] In it he devotes much space to the Brest-Litovsk Treaty and its aftermath. In fact, Germany's active interest in Ukraine surfaced late and only as a result of the Bolshevik revolution in Russia and Lenin's decision to conclude an armistice with the Central Powers. This fact should have dispelled any suspicion of a German or Ukrainian conspiracy. Initial German hesitation to deal officially with Ukraine melted only slowly. "It is generally agreed that the Germans welcomed the Ukrainians at Brest mainly because they believed that their presence would enable them to put pressure on the Soviet delegation, and perhaps force them to accept the Central Powers' terms."[54]

As for the Ukrainian decision to enter ongoing negotiations in Brest, Fedyshyn explains it as a consequence of Soviet Russia's peace propaganda and the Bolshevik menace to Ukraine. He does not fail to notice that the Ukrainian delegation acted with a satellite mentality; on the contrary:

The representatives of the Central Powers, including Count Czernin (even though he felt humiliated on being forced to deal with the 'young men' from the Ukraine), took the Ukrainian delegates quite seriously and acted as though they were dealing with equal partners. Both Kühlmann and Hoffmann had genuine admiration for the young Rada negotiators at Brest.[55]

Fedyshyn rebuffs the negative appraisals of John W. Wheeler-Bennet's exclusively pro-Entente view,[56] Axel Schmidt's insistence on the absence of any positive results for Ukraine,[57] and certainly Soviet writings branding the treaty as an "act of treason." His concluding comment appears judicious:

In light of all this (and one may add that the final outcome of World War I was then still in doubt), the Ukraine's acceptance of a separate treaty with the Central Powers—a treaty which, despite some obvious dangers, was rather advantageous for Kiev—can only be viewed as making the best of a bad situation.[58]

Outside of the above cited works, the treaty found very little attention, if any, in American literature. The only passing reference to the treaty comes from Richard Pipes in his standard work *The Formation of the Soviet Union*[59] which implies that Ukraine's treaty with the Central Powers "provided for the latter's occupation of the Ukraine."[60] The wording is not exactly correct, for the treaty itself did not stipulate the possibility of "occupation." German intervention came about by the appeal of the Ukrainian government to assist in the liberation of the country.

Another American work on Ukraine is Robert S. Sullivant's book on the Soviet politic[61] which incorrectly states in a passing reference to the Brest treaty that "German spokesmen, despite Russian objections, admitted representatives from the Central Rada as the official delegation from the Ukraine."[62] The truth is that it was Trotsky, a Foreign Commissar, who extended the official recognition to the Rada's delegation. Before him Stalin, on December 12, 1917, repeated Russian recognition of the Central Rada's legitimacy.[63]

Numerous American textbooks of Russia/USSR history give no indication of the treaty and its place in history. Adam Ulam's four-line reference

"They (the German generals) concluded a separate peace with Ukrainian nationalists, and their armies would occupy the Ukraine on behalf of the latter," sounds more like propaganda than serious scholarship. Donald W. Treadgold writes: "On February 9 Hoffmann produced a peace treaty with the Ukrainian Rada—at the moment, as it happened, when the Bolsheviks were occupying Kiev."[65] Not much more attention to the treaty is given in Basil Dmytryshyn's textbook.[66] His statement of fact, "On February 9, 1918, the talks with Trotsky . . . culminated in a separate treaty. In return for recognition and support, the Ukrainians pledged to place their surplus of foodstuffs and agricultural products (estimated to be some 1,000,000 tons) at the disposal of the Central Powers,"[67] explains nothing and adds only to confusion of the student of East European history.

CHAPTER XIII

CONCLUSIONS

The Central Rada's decision to conclude a peace treaty with the Central Powers and to bring the war to an end created new ramifications that affected deeply not only Ukraine's role in Eastern Europe, but equally so intensified events affecting the possibility of a quick end to the bloody, exhaustive war. It also directly complicated the Polish problem and certainly had an enormous impact on the Soviet Russian-Ukrainian encounter both internally as well as externally. The Brest-Litovsk treaty undeniably marked another turning point in European history.

To better understand the Rada's motives a deeper insight into the prevailing conditions should be most helpful. The coincidence of factors such as the Bolshevik seizure of power in Russia, the ongoing war, the spread of social unrest, and last but not least, the growing national consciousness reaching for self-determination, could only accentuate the difficulties and complexities facing the Rada. Having committed itself to social democracy, the Ukrainian government received no support from Lenin and only token sympathy from France and England. This was not enough to protect Ukraine from the invasion from the North in collaboration with the local Bolsheviks. The latter's challenge to the Rada's power did not present great danger, however the armies of Antonov-Ovsiienko and of Muraviev meant the end to the Ukrainian road toward statehood. The Rada's sincere commitment to socialism and pacifism was hardly sufficient to defend the northern frontiers. That and the Allies' inability to help left little choice for the Rada. Under these circumstances the former enemy across Ukraine's western border appeared as the only logical ally. But even in that crucial period this was not the Rada's original intention. It came about only as a reaction to the Soviet Russian decision to send a delegation to Brest-Litovsk to sign an armistice with the Central Powers on December 15, 1917, and to claim to act on behalf of the "whole of Russia," including Ukraine.

The Bolshevik usurpation of the right to represent Ukraine, while unanswered, would have amounted to the Rada's renunciation of its right to act as the legal representative of the Ukrainian people. Within this sequence of events, not the Ukrainian government, but the Russian Bolsheviks deserted the common front against the Central Powers, leaving the burden of war entirely on the shoulders of the Allies.

Unlike tsarist Russia and the Russian Provisional Government, Ukrainians had no interest whatsoever in the war that was forced upon them by the regime which oppressed them for more than one hundred fifty years. To have to die at the frontlines for the control of the Straits, for the victory of the oppressor, or to kill Germans because they were Germans hardly could motivate the Ukrainian soldiers in Russian uniforms, especially at the time of the Bolshevik advance into Ukraine. Hence, reclassifying friends and enemies was bound to come as a natural process of national identity and for the realization of immediate aims.

This self-awareness should not have been left to the control or intention of any outsider, including the Entente Powers, for their interest in preserving the Russian empire only extended Ukraine's subjugation. The Western democracies' commitment to save the Russian colonial realm, coupled with their cool and reserved treatment of the democratic Central Rada and subsequently of the Directory, must have felt like a cold shower for the young, enthusiastic Ukrainian intelligentsia inexperienced in *Realpolitik*. Although they had been characterized by foes and friends as being naive and romantic, they did not impose upon the Ukrainian people a tsarist *Okhrana* or Lenin's *Cheka*. In its commitment to social democracy the Rada neglected to build a strong army and to organize a police force as an instrument of government, thereby bringing on its own demise which led through Brest-Litovsk.

With Muraviev's offensive toward Kiev, the signing of the peace treaty with the Central Powers and the subsequent request for their military assistance the Rada government did what any other governing body would have done to save the country from imminent destruction. This was not an action to indicate its pro-German or pro-Austrian preference. Of course, there was a price to be paid: the obligation to deliver one million tons of foodstuffs, which meant a respite for the Dual Monarchy and a prolonging of the war. But there were also worthy achievements in regard to the Kohlmland and to Vienna's expressed commitment to create a Ukrainian Crownland within the Empire. For the young and inexperienced delegation it was an impressive accomplishment.

The Brest-Litovsk Treaty was, in the final analysis, nothing more and nothing less than the product of the reciprocal interests of the parties involved. Each one of them desired to achieve maximum political, economic, and military gains. It seemed to be a good agreement for all and it should be judged as such first of all. Polish indignation about the "fourth partition" of Poland was more pretentious than substantial, for the population of the Kholm region was Ukrainian in the majority and the Polish overlordship in East Galicia was nothing more than the remnants of the earlier colonial-type exploitation of the Ukrainian masses. Bolshevik propaganda was handicapped by its own doings. Especially damaging was its support of the principle of self-determination of the peoples, Trotsky's official recognition of the Rada's delegation, and its own peace offensive culminating in the conclusion of an armistice with the Central Powers long before February 9, 1918.

The Allies' refusal to recognize the Ukrainian treaty remains understandable but only when viewing it from the vantage of their own interests. Nonetheless, their dissatisfaction should have been directed primarily against Soviet Russia. The chain of events leading to Brest-Litovsk was unlocked· in Moscow and not in Kiev. Besides, France and England, too, conspired to divide the borderlands of the Russian empire into "spheres of action" as agreed upon at the Paris Anglo-French convention of December 23, 1917. The French sphere included Ukraine, Bessarabia, and the Crimea; that of England consisted of the Don and Kuban regions, as well as the Caucasus. Innocence and altruism were not the primary virtues of either side. The difference depended on the ability to prevail, and in the given period this was reserved for the Central Powers, thereby determining the fate of Ukraine. Anglo-American historiography might arrive at a different reasoning but it cannot change the facts.

Germany, clearly the strongest partner, easily prevailed in her relationship to Ukraine and consequently reversed the former partnership into domination, reflecting the substance and intention of Berlin's *Ostpolitik* intertwined with its war aims. Exactly the fusion of both, exemplified by Ludendorff and Groener, affected Ukraine adversely. This in turn had to create widespread anti-German feelings that could only hamper the long-term political goals of Germany's presence and influence in Eastern Europe. In this regard, the rather irresponsible treatment of the Central Rada, its downfall and the restrictions imposed upon Hetman Skoropadskyi's regime, including the denial of a strong Ukrainian army, served neither Germany's nor Ukraine's interest. Moreover, Austria-Hungary's essentially inconsistent policy subordinated mainly to its economic priorities, did little to solidify the progress of Ukrainian statehood. Instead, it fostered internal dissatisfaction that Bolshevik propaganda effectively utilized by portraying Ukraine as an agent of the foreign occupying powers.

Further to the North, by taking advantage of the March 3 peace treaty with the Central Powers, Soviet Russia was granted not only an important respite, but also almost unlimited opportunity to solidify the Bolshevik regime and to proceed with the building of an army for future engagements. Occupied by foreign armies, Ukraine had no similar advantage and remained, in fact, dependent on the victory or defeat of the Central Powers. The Brest-Litovsk treaty promised only a chance to survive, but failed to deliver on its promise.

The search for causes determining Ukraine's failure to maintain independence after 1919, however, ought not to be limited to external factors exclusively such as those mentioned before, but equally to other interrelated events. Among them the Polish attack on the Western Ukrainian Republic in November 1918, weakened considerably the Ukrainian potential and ability to face the renewed Soviet Russian offensive in late 1919. An additional antagonist of Ukrainian independence appeared in the form of the Russian Volunteer Army under General Anton Denikin, operating on the territory of Ukraine since mid-June 1919. His offensive against Kiev and its short-lived seizure in late August from the Ukrainian Galician Army that had expelled the Bolsheviks from the city created another setback for the Ukrainian struggle. By the same token, it made the Bolsheviks' final victory easier.

During that crucial period the Allies in Paris, including the American Secretary of State, Robert Lansing, categorically refused to recognize U-kraine's independence and to extend any assistance to the Ukrainian army. The Allies regarded Kolchak and Denikin as exclusive spokesmen for the whole of Russia.[1] The Directory, the Ukrainian democratic government since December 1918, was rebuffed by the Western democracies who preferred to support the remnants of the tsarist Russian autocratic regime. By doing so, the Allies' direct contribution to Lenin's final triumph became a fact clearly recorded by history.

This unfortunate Ukrainian scenario leads to another consideration—the quality of the Ukrainian leadership in that crucial period of national history. Under the conditions inherent in the almost two centuries of Russian autocratic rule over Ukraine, the Ukrainian intelligentsia was not only few in the predominantly peasant-agrarian society, but also lacked basic experience in the building of statehood and its functioning. Their commitment to social issues, though sincere and understandable, proved to be insufficient in reconstructing a national state that could provide the conditions for social and economic reforms. Just such a misplacement of priorities proved to be the decisive factor in rendering the Central Rada ineffective. The attempt to build a nation and a new social order without the protection of an army and blindly trusting declarative slogans consequently forced the Rada to seek the protection of foreign armies. The price tag attached to this action proved to be very costly for the Rada and Ukraine as well.

Individually, neither the historian Mykhailo Hrushevskyi nor the Social Democrat writer Volodymyr Vynnychenko together with their compatriots showed little understanding of the complexities of building and maintaining the state. Those representing nationalist concepts such as Mykola Mikhnovs'kyi and his followers from the Revolutionary Ukrainian Party and subsequently the Ukrainian Socialist-Federalist Party were too few in number of counter the influence upon the masses of the Social Revolutionaries and Social Democrats.

General Pavlo Skoropadskyi, certainly nationally conscious and not without a commitment to the concept of Ukrainian statehood, would have been in place in a different period of Ukraine's history, in a more tranquil time. The prevailing passion tearing the society apart in the presence of uncooperative foreign armies overpowered his ability to bring internal consolidation. Although he successfully preserved the skeleton of a Ukrainian state, he failed to revive it with a national consensus. Perhaps his enemies from the left should be equally brought to account for his desperate act of federation with yet-to-be-restored Russia, having refused to collaborate with him in the early period of his rule.

In case this line of reasoning and conclusion has any merit, then obviously the responsibility for Ukraine's defeat by the end of 1919 can be explained as a result of three simultaneously contribuing chief causes: the unpreparedness of the Ukrainian political leadership for the swiftly moving events after 1917, the policy of the Central Powers during the occupation of Ukraine, and the failure of the Allies to correctly assess the existing conditions and to foresee the consequences of their policy in regard to Soviet Russia and to Ukraine in particular after the withdrawal of the German army from Eastern Europe.

Unlike the Americans, Italians and Bulgarians, the Ukrainians in their struggle for national independence in the final analysis had to depend exclusively on their own strength. While the Poles, the South Slavs and the Czechs had been given a chance to erect their independent states in time of an appropriate political vacuum without enemies lurking on their borders, the Ukrainians were faced with one too many adversaries, particularly Soviet Russia. Within that context of events the Brest-Litovsk treaty in its intention remains a bright spot on the scene of Ukraine's history.

APPENDIX A

FOURTH UNIVERSAL
of January 22, 1918, proclaiming the independence
of the Ukrainian National Republic

People of Ukraine,

By your strength, will, and word a Free Ukrainian National Republic was established on the Ukrainian Land. The former old dream of your fathers, fighters for freedom and the rights of the working people has come true.

But the freedom of Ukraine was reborn in a difficult hour. Four years of vicious war have weakened our country and the population. Factories are not producing goods, works at the plants are coming to a stand still, the railroads are dislocated, the money is losing its value, the bread has grown scarcer—hunger is approaching. Bands of robbers and thieves sprang up throughout the country, especially when Russian troops pulled back from the front, causing carnage, disorder and ruin in our land.

For these various reasons the elections to the Ukrainian Constituent Assembly could not take place at the time designated by our previous Universal and the meeting designed for this day could not be held so that the Assembly could take over from us the temporary revolutionary authority in Ukraine, to establish order in our National Republic, and to organize a new government.

In the meantime, the Petrograd Government of People's Commissars, in order to place the free Ukrainian Republic under its authority, has declared war against Ukraine and is dispatching troops into our land—the Red Guard, the Bolsheviks who rob bread from our peasants and carry it off to Russia without any compensation, not sparing even the grain prepared for planting; they kill innocent people and everywhere they spread disorder, thievery, and chaos.

We, the Ukrainian Central Rada, made every effort to avoid the fratricidal war between the two neighboring nations but the Petrograd government did not do likewise and continues the bloody fight with our people and the Republic. Furthermore, the very same Petrograd Government of People's Commissars is delaying the peace efforts and calls for a new war, naming it "holy." Once more the blood will flow, again the unfortunate working people are to lay down their lives.

We, the Ukrainian Central Rada, elected by the congresses of peasants, workers, and soldiers of Ukraine, cannot agree to this and will not support any war because the Ukrainian Nation desires peace and a democratic peace should come as soon as possible.

And so that neither the Russian government nor any other should place obstacles for Ukraine in establishing the desired peace and to lead our country to order, to a creative work, to strengthen the revolution and our freedom we, the Ukrainian Central Rada, inform all citizens of Ukraine of the following:

From this day on the Ukrainian National Republic becomes an independent, subordinated to none, free, sovereign State of the Ukrainian Nation.

With all neighboring states such as Russia, Poland, Austria, Romania, Turkey and others we want to live in peace and friendship but none of them can interefere with the life of an independent Ukrainian Republic. Its authority will belong only to the People of Ukraine and in its name, until the Ukrainian Constituent Assembly convenes, we the Ukrainian Central Rada, the representatives of working peasants, workers, and soldiers, shall govern together with our executive organ which as of today shall have the name of Council of National Ministers.

And this first of all we direct the government of our Republic, the Council of National Ministers to do, as of this day to conduct peace negotiations with the Central Powers, which already had begun, completely independently and to bring them to a conclusion, disregarding any obstacles from any other part of the former Russian Empire and to establish peace so that our country can begin life in peace and harmony.

Regarding the so-called Bolsheviks and other aggressors who are destroying our country we direct the Government of the Ukrainian National Republic to take firm and decisive measures against them and we call upon all citizens of our Republic to defend the welfare and the freedom without regard for their life. Our National Ukrainian State should be cleared of the attackers sent from Petrograd who trample the rights of the Ukrainian Republic.

Immeasurably hard war, started by the bourgeois government, exhausted our Nation, already destroyed our country, ruined the economy. Now all of this must come to an end.

At the time when the army will be demobilized, we direct that some soldiers are to be released to their homes and after the peace treaties had been ratified, to dissolve the army completely; then, instead of a permanent army to create a national militia so that our troops would serve in the defense of the working people rather than the desires of the ruling strata.

Localities ruined by the war and demobilization are to be reconstructed with the help of our state treasury.

When our soldiers reach home, the people's councils—borough and county—and the city dumas are to be reelected at a prescribed future time so that also our soldiers would have a chance to vote. In order to establish a local authority which would enjoy the confidence and which would find support from all revolutionary democratic segments of the population, the Government should invite the cooperation (with the bodies of local self-government) of the councils of peasants, workers, and soldiers deputies, elected from among the local population.

In the matter of land, the commission elected at our last session, has already worked out a law concerning the transference of land to the working population without compensation, having accepted as the basis the abolishment of ownership and the socialization of land according to our resolution at the eighth session. This will will be examined in a few days by the plenary Central Rada. The Council of National Ministers will use all means to see to it that the transfer of land into the hands of working people through the land committees will definitely take place before the spring works.

The forests, waters, and all underground wealth, as a property of the Ukrainian working population, is placed at the disposal of the Ukrainian National Republic.

The war has also claimed for itself all the working forces of our country. The majority of plants, factories and shops have been producing only what was necessary for war and the population was left entirely without goods. Now the war is over. Therefore we direct the Council of National Ministers to take immediate measures to adjust all plants and factories to peacetime conditions, for the production of goods needed, first of all by the toiling masses.

This very same war has given birth to hundreds of thousands of unemployed as well as invalids. In an Independent National Republic of Ukraine not one worker should suffer. The Government of the Republic is to upraise the industry of the State, has to initiate the construction work in all branches in which all unemployed would be able to find work and to utilize their force, and to make every effort to provide security for the maimed and those who have suffered from the war.

In the time of the old regime traders and various middle men had amassed great capital at the expense of the poor, suppressed classes. From this day on the Ukrainian National Republic is taking over the most important branches of trade and all profits will be returned for the benefit of the people. Our State will supervise the import and export of foods in order to prevent the high costs which are suffered by our poorest classes because of the speculators. For the execution of this directive we instruct the Government to prepare and submit for approval a law dealing with this as well as a law concerning the monopoly on iron, leather, tobacco, and other products and goods from which most profits were taken from the working classes for the benefit of non-working people.

Also we direct to establish state-national control over all banks which with credits and loans helped the non-working classes to exploit the working classes. From this day on help in the form of bank loans is to be given mainly for the support of labor and for the development of national economy of the Ukrainian National Republic rather than for speculation and various exploitation and gain on the part of the banks.

Founded on disorder, uneasy life and the lack of goods dissatisfaction is growing in some parts of the population. Various dark forces take advantage of this dissatisfaction and prod the ignorant people toward the old regime. These dark forces want once more to submit all free nations to a unified tsarist yoke of Russia. The Council of National Ministers should fight decisively against counter-revolutionary forces. And anyone who will urge an insurrection against the Independent Ukrainian National Republic, to return to the old regime, should be punished for state treason.

All democratic freedoms proclaimed by the Third Universal, the Ukrainian National Republic reaffirms and especially proclaims: in the Independent Ukrainian National Republic all nationalities enjoy the right of national-personal autonomy, recognized by us through a law of January 20.

If we, the Ukrainian Central Rada, will not be able to accomplish in the following weeks the goals listed in this Universal, they will be completed by the Ukrainian Constituent Assembly.

We order our citizens to conduct the election to it very carefully: to take every measure to count the votes as quickly as possible, so that in a few weeks our Constituent Assembly—the supreme master and arranger of our Land—would strengthen liberty, order and welfare by a constitution of the Independent Ukrainian National Republic for the benefit of the entire working population, for the present and for the future.

This highest body is to decide the matter of federative union with the national republics of the former Russian state.

Up to that time we call upon all citizens of the Independent Ukrainian National Republic to stand firmly on guard of the gained freedom and the rights of our nation and to defend with every effort the liberty from all enemies of the Independent Ukrainian Republic of peasants and workers.

In Kiev, 22 January 1918.   Ukrainian Central Rada

APPENDIX B

THE TREATY OF PEACE BETWEEN THE UKRAINIAN NATIONAL REPUBLIC AND THE CENTRAL POWERS*
(Brest-Litovsk, Februry 9, 1918)

Whereas the Ukrainian People has, in the course of the present world war, declared its independence, and has expressed the desire to establish a state of peace between the Ukrainian People's Republic and the Powers at present at war with Russia, the Governments of Germany, Austria-Hungary, Bulgaria, and Turkey have resolved to conclude a Treaty of Peace with the Government of the Ukrainian People's Republic; they wish in this way to take the first step towards a lasting world peace, honourable for all parties, which shall not only put an end to the horrors of the war but shall also conduce to the restoration of friendly relations between the peoples in the political, legal, economic, and intellectual spheres.

To this end the plenipotentiaries of the above-mentioned Governments, viz.

For the Imperial German Government: Imperial Actual Privy Chancellor Richard von Kühlmann, Secretary of State of Foreign Affairs:

For the Imperial and Royal Joint Austro-Hungarian Government: His Imperial and Royal Apostolic Majesty's Privy Councillor Ottokar Count Czernin von and zu Chudenitz, Minister of the Imperial and Royal House and Minister for Foreign Affairs;

For the Royal Bulgarian Government: Dr. Vassil Radoslavoff, President of the Council of Ministers; the Envoy M. Andrea Tosheff, the Envoy M. Ivan Stoyanovich; the Military Plenipotentiary Colonel Peter Gantcheff; and Dr. Theodor Anastassoff;

For the Imperial Ottoman Government: His Highness the Grand Vizier Talaat Pasha; Ahmet Nessimi Bey, Minister for Foreign Affairs; His Highness Ibrahim Hakki Pasha; and General of Cavalry Ahmet Izzet Pasha;

---

* Reprinted from Texts of the Ukraine "Peace." Washington, D.C; United States Department of State, 1918.

For the Government of the Ukrainian People's Republic: M. Alexander Sevruk, M. Mykola Liubinsky, and M. Mykola Levitsky, member of the Ukrainian Central Rada;–have met at Brest-Litovsk, and having presented their full powers, which were found to be in due and proper form, have agreed upon the following points:

Article I

Germany, Austria-Hungary, Bulgaria, and Turkey on the one hand, and the Ukrainian People's Republic on the other hand, declare that the state of war between them is at an end. The contracting parties are resolved henceforth to live in peace and amity with one another.

Article II

1. As between Austria-Hungary on the one hand, and the Ukrainian People's Republic on the other hand, in so far as those two Powers border upon one another, the frontiers which existed between the Austro-Hungarian Monarchy and Russia, prior to the outbreak of the present war, will be preserved.

2. Further north, the frontier of the Ukrainian People's Republic starting at Tarnograd, will in general follow the line Bilgorav, Szozebrzeszyn, Krasnostav, Pugashov, Radzin, Miedzyzheche, Sarnaki, Melnik, Vysokie-Litovsk, Kameniec-Litovsk, Prujany, and Vydonovsa Lake. This frontier will be delimited in detail by a mixed commission according to the ethnographical conditions and after taking the wishes of the inhabitants into consideration.

3. In the event of the Ukrainian People's Republic having boundaries coterminous with those of another of the Powers of the Quadruple Alliance, special agreements are reserved in respect thereto.

Article III

The evacuation of the occupied territories shall begin immediately after the ratification of the present Treaty of Peace.

The manner of carrying out the evacuation and the transfer of the evacuated territories shall be determined by the Plenipotentiaries of the interested parties.

Article IV

Diplomatic and consular relations between the contracting parties shall commence immediately after the ratification of the Treaty of Peace.

In respect to the admission of consuls on the widest scale possible on both sides, special agreements are reserved.

Article V

The contracting parties mutually renounce repayment of their war costs, that is to say, their State expenditure for the prosecution of the war, as well as payment for war damages, that is to say, damages sustained by them and their nationals in the war areas through military measures, including all requisitions made in enemy territory.

Article VI

Prisoners of war of both parties shall be released to their homeland in so far as they do not desire, with the approval of the State in whose territory they shall be, to remain within its territories or to proceed to another country. Questions connected with this shall be dealt with in the separate treaties provided for in Article VIII.

Article VII

In has been agreed as follows with regard to economic relations between the contracting parties:

I

The contracting parties mutually undertake to enter into economic relations without delay and to organize the exchange of goods on the basis of the following stipulations:

Until July 31 of the current year a reciprocal exchange of surplus of their more important agricultural and industrial products, for the purpose of meeting current requirements, is to be effected according to the following provisions:

(a)   The quantities and classes of products to be exchanged in accordance with the preceding paragraph shall be settled on both sides by a commission composed of an equal number of representatives of both parties, which shall sit immediately after the Treaty of Peace has been signed.

(b)   The prices of products to be exchanged as specified above shall be regulated on the basis of mutual agreement by a commission composed of an equal number of representatives of both parties.

(c)   Calculations should be made in gold on the following basis: 1000 German imperial gold marks shall be equivalent to 462 gold rubles of the former Russian Empire (1 ruble = 1/15 imperial), or 1000 Austrian and Hungarian gold kronen shall be equivalent to 393 karbovantsi 76 grosh gold of the Ukrainian People's Republic, or to 393 rubles 78 copecks in gold of the former Russian Empire (1 ruble = 1/15 imperial).

(d)   The exchange of goods to be determined by the commission mentioned under (a) shall take place through the existing Government central offices controlled by the Government.

The exchange of such products as are not determined by the above-mentioned commissions shall be effected on a basis of free trading, arranged for in accordance with the conditions of the provisional commercial treaty, which is provided for in the following Section II.

II

In so far as it is not otherwise provided for under Section I hereof economic relations between the contracting parties shall be carried on provisionally in accordance with the stipulations specified below until the conclusion of the final Commercial Treaty, but in any event until a period of at least six months shall have elapsed after the conclusion of peace between Germany, Austria-Hungary, Bulgaria and Turkey on the one hand, and the European States at present at war with them, the United States of America and Japan on the other hand:

A

For economic relations between the German Empire and the Ukrainian People's Republic, the conditions laid down in the following provisions of the Germano-Russian Commercial and Maritime Treaty of 1894-1904, that is to say:

Articles 1-6 and 7 (including Tariffs "a" and "b"), 9-10, 12, 13-19; further, among the stipulations of the final Protocol (Part I), paragraphs 1 and 3 of addendum to Article I; paragraphs 1, 2, 4, 5, 6, 8, 9 of addenda to Articles I and 12 addendum to Article 3, paragraphs 1 and 2 of addendum to Article 5; addenda to Articles 5, 6, 7, 9, and 10; addenda to Articles 6, 7, and 11; to Articles 6-9; to Articles 6 and 7, paragraphs 1, 2, 3, 5, of addendum to Article 12, further in the final Protocol (Part IV), paragraphs 3, 6, 7, 12, 12b, 13, 14, 15, 16, 17, 18 (with the reservations required by the corresponding alterations in official organizations), 19, 20, 21, and 23.

An agreement has been arrived at upon the following points:

1. The General Russian Customs Tariff of January 13-26, 1903, shall continue in force.

2. Article 5 shall read as follows:

"The contracting parties bind themselves not to hinder reciprocal trade by any kind of import, export, or transit prohibitions, and to allow free transit.

"Exceptions may only be made in the case of products which are actually, or which may become, a State monopoly in the territory of one of the contracting parties; as well as in the case of certain products for which exceptional prohibitory measures might be issued, in view of health conditions, veterinary police, and public safety, or on other important political and economic grounds, especially in connection with the transition period following the war."

3. Neither party shall lay claim to the preferential treatment which the other party has granted, or shall grant to any other State, arising out of present or future Customs Union (as, for instance, the one in force between the German Empire and the Grand Duchy of Luxembourg), or arising in connection with petty frontier intercourse extending to a boundary zone not exceeding 15 kilometers in width.

4. Article 10 shall read as follows:

"There shall be reciprocal freedom from all transit dues for goods of all kinds conveyed through the territory of either of the parties, whether conveyed direct or unloaded, stored and reload during transit."

5. Article 12(2) shall be revised as follows:

"(a) With regard to the reciprocal protection of copyright in works of literature, art, and photography, the provisions of the Treaty concluded between the German Empire and Russia on February 28, 1913, shall prevail in the relations between Germany and the Ukrainian People's Republic.

"(b) With regard to the reciprocal protection of trade-marks, the provisions of the Declaration of July 11-23, 1873, shall be authoritative in the future."

6. The provision of the final Protocol to Article 19 shall read as follows: "The contracting parties shall grant each other the greatest possible support in the matter of railway tariffs, more especially by the establishment of through rates. To this end both contracting parties are ready to enter into negotiations with one another at the earliest possible moment."

7. Paragraph 5 of Part IV of the final Protocol shall read as follows:

"It has been mutually agreed that the customs houses of both countries shall remain open on every day throughout the year with the exception of Sundays and legal holidays."

B

For economic relations between Austria-Hungary and the Ukrainian People's Republic, the agreements shall be valid which are set forth in the following provisions of the Austro-Hungarian-Russian Commerical and Maritime Treaty of the 15 February, 1906, being Articles 1, 2, and 5 (including Tariffs "a" and "b"); Articles 6, 7, 9-13; Article 14, paragraphs 2 and 3; Articles 15-24 further, in the provisions of the final Protocol, paragraphs 1, 2, 4, 5, and 6 of addenda to Articles 1 and 12; addenda to Article 2; to Articles 2, 5, 6, and 7; to Article 17, and likewise to paragraphs 1 and 3, Article 22.

An agreement has been arrived at upon the following points:

1. The General Russian Customs Tariff of January 13-26, 1903, shall remain in force.

2. Article 4 shall read as follows:

"The contracting parties bind themselves not to hinder reciprocal trade between their territories by any kind of import, export, or transit prohibition. The only permissible exceptions shall be:

"(a) In the case of tobacco, salt, gunpowder, or any other kind of explosives, and likewise in the case of other articles which may at any time constitute a State monopoly in the territories of either of the contracting parties:

"(b) With respect to war supplies in exceptional circumstances;

"(c) For reasons of public safety, public health, and veterinary police;

"(d) In the case of certain products for which, on other important political and economic grounds, exceptional prohibitory measures might be issued, especially in connection with the transition period following the war."

3. Neither party shall lay claim to the preferential treatment which the other party has granted or shall grant to any other State arising out of a present or future Customs Union (as, for instance, the one in force between Austria-Hungary and the Principality of Liechtenstein), or arising in connection with petty frontier intercourse, extending to a boundary zone not exceeding 15 kilometers in width.

4. Article 8 shall read as follows:

"There shall be reciprocal freedom for all transit dues for goods of all kinds conveyed through the territory of either of the contracting parties, whether conveyed direct or unloaded, stored and re-loaded during transit."

5. The provsion of the final Protocol to Article 21 shall read as follows:

"The contracting parties shall grant each other the greatest possible support in the matter of railway tariffs, and more especially by the establishment of through rates. To this end both contracting parties are ready to enter into negotiations with one another at the earliest possible moment."

C

In regard to the economic relations between Bulgaria and the Ukrainian People's Republic, these shall, until such time as a definitive Commercial Treaty shall have been concluded, be regulated on the basis of most-favored-nation treatment. Neither party shall lay claim to the preferential treatment which the other party has granted or shall grant to any other State arising out of a present or future Customs Union, or arising in connection with petty frontier intercourse, extending to a boundary zone not exceeding 15 kilometers in width.

D

In regard to the economic relations between the Ottoman Empire and the Ukrainian People's Republic, these shall, until such time as a definitive Commercial Treaty shall have been concluded, be regulated on the basis of most-favored-nation treatment. Neither party shall lay claim to the preferential treatment which the other party has granted or shall grant to any other State arising out of a present or future Customs Union, or arising in connection with petty frontier intercourse.

III

The period of validity of the provisional stipulations (set forth under Section II hereof) for economic relations between Germany, Austria-Hungary, Bulgaria, and the Ottoman Empire on the one hand, and the Ukrainian People's Republic on the other hand, may be prolonged by mutual agreement.

In the event of the periods specified in the first paragraph of Section II not occurring before June 30, 1919, each of the two contracting parties shall be entitled as from June 30, 1919, to denounce within six months the provisions contained in the above-mentioned section.

IV

(a) The Ukrainian People's Republic shall make no claim to the preferential treatment which Germany grants to Austria-Hungary or to any other country bound to her by a Customs Union and directly bordering on Germany, or bordering indirectly thereon through another country bound to her or to Austria-Hungary by a Customs Union, or to the preferential treatment which Germany grants to her own colonies, foreign possessions, and protectorates or to countries bound to her by a Customs Union.

Germany shall make no claim to the preferential treatment which the Ukrainian People's Republic grants to any other country bound to her by a Customs Union and bordering directly on the Ukraine or bordering indirectly thereon through any other country bound to her by a Customs Union, or to colonies, foreign possessions, and protectorates of one of the countries bound to her by a Customs Union.

(b) In economic intercourse between territory covered by the Customs Convention of both States of the Austro-Hungarian Monarchy on the one hand, and the Ukrainian People's Republic on the other hand, the Ukrainian People's Republic shall make no claim to the preferential treatment which Austria-Hungary grants to Germany or to any other country bound to her by a Customs Union and directly bordering on Austria-Hungary, or bordering indirectly thereon through another country which is bound to her or to Germany by a Customs Union. Colonies, foreign possessions, and protectorates shall in this respect be placed on the same footing as the mother country. Austria-Hungary shall make no claim to the preferential treatment which the Ukrainian People's Republic grants to any other country bound to her by a Customs Union and directly bordering on the Ukraine, or bordering indirectly thereon through another country bound to her by a Custom Union, or to colonies, foreign possessions, and protectorates of one of the countries bound to her by a Customs Union.

V

(a) In so far as goods originating in Germany or the Ukraine are stored in neutral States, with the proviso that they shall not be exported, either directly or indirectly, to the territories of the other contracting party, such restrictions regarding their disposal shall be abolished so far as the contracting parties are concerned. The two contracting parties therefore undertake immediately to notify the Governments of the neutral States of the above-mentioned abolition of this restriction.

(b) In so far as goods originating in Austria-Hungary or the Ukraine are stored in neutral States, with the proviso that they shall not be exported, either directly or indirectly, to the territories of the other contracting party, such restrictions regarding their disposal shall be abolished so far as

the contracting parties are concerned. The two contracting parties therefore undertake immediately to notify the Governments of the neutral
States of the above-mentioned abolition of this restriction.

Article VIII

The establishing of public and private legal relations, and the exchange
of prisoners of war and interned civilians, the amnesty question, as well as
the question of the treatment of merchant shipping in the enemy's hands,
shall be settled by means of separate Treaties with the Ukrainian People's
Republic, which shall form an essential part of the present Treaty of
Peace, and, as far as practicable, come into force simultaneously therewith.

Article IX

The agreements come to in this Treaty of Peace shall form an indivisible
whole.

Article X

For the interpretation of this Treaty, the German and Ukrainian text
shall be authoritative for relations between Germany and the Ukraine; the
German, Hungarian, and Ukrainian text for relations between Austria-
Hungary and the Ukraine; the Bulgarian and Ukrainian text for relations
between Bulgaria and the Ukraine; and the Turkish and Ukrainian for relations between Turkey and the Ukraine.

Final Provision

The present Treaty of Peace shall be ratified. The ratifications shall be
exchanged in Vienna at the earliest possible moment.

The Treaty of Peace shall come into force on its ratification, in so far as
no stipulation to the contrary is contained therein.

In witness whereof the plenipotentiaries have signed the present Treaty
and have affixed their seals to it.

Executed in quintuplicate at Brest-Litovsk this 9th day of February
1918.

(L.S.)

F. v. Kühlmann   Al. Ssewrjuk
Hoffmann   M. Ljubynskyi
                                                       M. Lewitskyi

APPENDIX C

**Secret Crownland Agreement of February 8, 1918
between Austria-Hungary and Ukraine: Secret
Integral Part of the Treaty of Peace of February 9, 1918***

By signing the Treaty of Peace between Germany, Austria-Hungary, Bulgaria and Turkey and the Ukrainian People's Republic, the Foreign Minister of the Dual Monarchy, Count Czernin, and the representatives of the Ukrainian People's Republic decided to reach agreement on the following:

The Representatives of Austria-Hungary and the Ukrainian People's Republic agreed upon that both parties wish to maintain among them a close and friendly relationship.

Expecting that this relationship will become even better when the national minorities residing in both States and being of interest to both of them, will be assured the freedom of national and cultural development, the Foreign Minister of the Dual Monarchy is acknowledging that the laws of the Ukranian People's Republic shall guarantee the rights of the Polish and German minorities in Ukraine, as well as the rights of the Jewish people.

The Plenipotentiaries of the Ukrainian People's Republic acknowledge on their part His Majesty the Emperor's effort announced in His Crown Declaration to pursue with all means within the existing arrangements national and cultural development of the Ukrainian people living in Austria leading to additional guarantees.

In order to achieve this aim, the Austrian government will submit to both chambers of the Reichsrat a bill, which will provide for East Galicia populated by a majority of Ukrainian people and in unification with Bukovina a common Crownland.

---

* Translation based on the German translation by Volkwart John, *Brest-Litowsk*, pp. 80-81, and on the Ukrainian text in Doroshenko, *Istoriia Ukrainy*, II, pp. 215-16.

The Austrian government promises to implement the plan no later than July 31, 1918.* To this end all legal means will be taken to assure the passing of the bill to be enacted as the law.

The High Parties are in agreement that this Declaration remains an integral part of the Peace Treaty and its validity shall expire in case of nonfulfillment of any of the provisions of said treaty.

This document and its contents shall remain secret.

Brest-Litovsk, 8 February 1918.

Oleksander Sevriuk   Ernst Ritter v. Seidler
Mykola Liubyns'kyi   Graf Ottokar Czernin
Mykola Levyts'kyi

---

* Volkwart John gives July 20 as the correct date.

UKRAINE
IN 1918

- - - Eastern Front, December 1917
-·-·- German advance in the East in 1918
·····-· Boundaries of the Ukrainian State in 1918

NOTES

Notes to Chapter I

1. Discussed by M. D. Bychvarov and V. S. Hors'kyi, *Ukrainobolhars'ki filosofski zviazky* (Kiev, 1966).

2. *Ukraine: A Concise Encyclopedia,* Edited by Volodymyr Kubijovyć, vol. 1, (Toronto: University of Toronto Press, 1963), p. 685b.

3. Dmytro Doroshenko, *Die Ukraine und das Reich: Neun Jahrhunderte deutsch-ukrainischer Beziehungen* (Leipzig, 1942).

4. Bruno's chronicle was published in *Monumenta Poloniae historica,* vol. 1.

5. His most interesting account, *Tagebuch des Erich Lassota von Steblau,* edited by Reinholdt Schottin, was published in Halle, 1854. It remained a significant source of Cossack history.

6. Especially in his *Einleitung zu der Historie der vornehmsten Reiche und Staaten* (Frankfurt, 1684).

7. On his and other chroniclers' and authors' contributions see Doroshenko, *Die Ukraine,* pp. 1-38.

8. Published in *Archiv zur neueren Geschichte, Geographie, Natur und Menschenkenntnis,* vols. 4, 6, and 8. Also Doroshenko, *Die Ukraine,* pp. 29-34.

9. Johann Benedikt Scherer, *Histoire raisonnée du commerce de la Russie* (Paris, 1788). (Chapter V: "Commerce de la Petite-Russe ou l'Ukraine.")

10. Mykhailo Hrushevskyi, *Istoriia Ukrainy-Rusy,* vol. 8, Pt. 2; Borys

Krupnitzky, *J. Chr. Engel und die Geschichte der Ukraine* (Berlin, 1931), pp. 33, 46-47; Doroshenko, *Die Ukraine*, pp. 69-79.

11. Doroshenko, *Die Ukraine*, pp. 106-147.

12. Eduard von Hartmann, "Russland und Europa," *Gegenwart* (Berlin), no. 1-3, 1888.

13. Doroshenko, *Die Ukraine*, pp. 159-178.

14. On Ukrainian experiences under Austrian rule see Kost' Levyts'kyi, *Istoriia politychnoi dumky halyts'kykh ukraintsiv 1848-1914* (Lviv, 1926); Ivan L. Rudnytsky, "The Ukrainians in Galicia under Austrian Rule," *Austrain History Yearbook*, 3:2 (1967): 394-429; Andrei S. Markovits and Frank E. Syssyn, eds., *Nationbuilding and the Politics of Nationalism: Essays on Austrian Galicia* (Cambridge, MA: Harvard Ukrainian Research Institute, 1982).

15. R. Dyminskyj, ed., *Handbuch der Ukraine: Wirtschaftsleben* (Leipzig, 1941); Peter Borowsky, *Deutsche Ukrainepolitik 1918 unter besonderer Berücksichtigung der Wirtschaftsfragen* (Lübeck and Hamburg, 1970), pp. 21-25.

16. Doroshenko, *Die Ukraine*, pp. 179-216; Borowsky, *Deutsche*, pp. 13-14, 40-41; Paul Rohrbach, *Um des Teufels Handschrift: Zwei Menschenalter erlebter Weltgeschichte* (Hamburg, 1953).

17. Rohrbach authored dozens of articles in various newspapers and journals in addition to two monographs: *Der Krieg und die deutsche Politik* (Dresden, 1914); and *Russland und wir* (Stuttgart, 1915).

18. Doroshenko, *Die Ukraine*, pp. 182-203.

19. *Die Unabhängigkeit der Ukraine als einzige Rettung von der russischen Gefahr* (Munich and Leipzig, 1915).

20. *Die Ukraine: Beitrag zur Geschichte, Kultur und Volkswirtschaft* (Berlin, 1916).

21. *Die Ukraine und die ukrainische Bewegung: Kriegshefte aus dem Industriebezirk* (Essen, 1916).

22. Axel Schmidt, *Das Ziel Russlands: Mit einem ökonomisch-politischen Kapitel von G. Hermann* (Stuttgard, 1916).

23. Albrecht Penck, "Ukraine," *Zeitschrift der Gesellschaft für Erdkunde zu Berlin*, (1916), pp. 1-36.

Notes to Chapter II

1.   For instance in Inokentii Gizel's *Sinopsis ili kratkoe sobranie* (1674). More in Dmytro Doroshenko, "A Survey of Ukrainian Historio-graphy," *The Annals of the Ukrainian Academy of Arts and Sciences in the U.S.* 5-6 (1957): 38-59.

2.   *Putieshestviie v Malorosiiu akad. Gildeshtedta i kn. Dolgurukavo 1817* (St. Petersburg, 1842 [?]).

3.   A. *Lenshin, Pisma z Malorosii* (St. Petersburg, 1816).

4.   Johann G. Kohl, *Moscow, Kharkoff, Riga, Odessa, the German Provinces, the Steppes, the Crimea, and the Interior of the Empire* (London, 1844), pp. 527-29.

5.   Dmytro Doroshenko, *Ukrainskyi rukh 1890kh rr. v osvitlenni avstriiskoho konzula v Kyievi* (Warsaw, 1938), pp. 63-65.

6.   S. N. Shchegolev, *Ukrainskoe dvizheniie kak sovremennyi etap iuzhnorusskogo seperatizma* (Kiev, 1912).

7.   Ivan Lysiak-Rudnyts'kyi, *Mizh istorieiu i politykoiu* (New York, 1973), p. 45.

8.   Mykhailo Drahomanov, *Vybrani tvory: zbirka politychnyckh tvoriv z prymitkamy*, vol. 1 (Prague, 1937).

9.   Ibid., pp. 31-32.

10.   Ibid., p. 305; also his pamphlet, *Shevchenko, ukrainofily i sotsial-izm*, (1878).

11.   Ivan Lypa, "Braterstvo Tarasivtsiv," *Literaturno-Naukovyi Visnyk*, 1925.

12.   Sherii Shemet, "Mykola Mikhnovs'kyi," *Khliborobs'ka Ukraina*, 1924-25.

13.   Iaroslav Orshan, "Rozvytok ukrains'koi politychnoi dumky za sto lit (nacherk kursu)," *Almanakh: Idea v nastupi*, 1938: 78-79.

14.   On this aspect see Ivan L. Rudnytzky. "The Ukrainians in Galicia under Austrian Rule," *Austrian History Yearbook*, III: 2 (1967): 394-429; Kost' Levyts'kyi, *Istoriia politychnoi dumky halyts'kykh ukraintsiv, 1849-1914* (Lviv, 1926).

15.   Orshan, "Rozvytok," op. cit., p. 82.

16.   On the composition of the RSDRP in Ukraine see Ralph Carter Elwood, *Russian Social Democracy in the Underground: A Study of the RSDRP in the Ukraine, 1907-1914* (Assen, 1974).

17. John S. Reshetar, *The Ukrainian Revolution, 1917-1920: A Study in Nationalism* (Princeton, NJ, 1952), p. 142.

18. Selected titles on modern Ukrainian history: Dmytro Doroshenko, *Isstoriia Ukraine,* 2 vols. (Uzhhorod, 1932-33); Basil Dmytryshyn, *Moscow and the Ukraine, 1918-1953* (New York, 1956); John S. Reshetar, *The Ukrainian Revolution, 1917-1920: A Study in Nationalism (Princeton,* NJ, 1952); Arthur Adams, *Bolsheviks in the Ukraine: The Second Campaign, 1918-1919* (New Haven, CT, 1963); Oleh S. Fedyshyn, *Germany's Drive to the East and the Ukrainian Revolution, 1917-1918* (New Brunswick, NJ, 1971); Taras Hunczak, ed., *The Ukraine 1917-1921: A Study in Revolution* (Cambridge, MA, 1977).

19. Dmytro Doroshenko, *Istoriia Ukrainy,* I, p. 42.

20. Ibid., p. 43.

21. Ibid., pp. 179-181; Reshetar, *The Ukrainian Revolution,* pp. 89-91; Oleh S. Pidhainy, *The Formation of the Ukrainian Republic* (Toronto, 1966), pp. 204-205.

22. Doroshenko, *Istoriia Ukrainy,* I, pp. 264-68.

Notes to Chapter III

1. Reshetar, *The Ukrainian Revolution,* p. 97; Alexander Shulgin (Choulguine), *L'Ukraine contre Moscou (1917)* (Paris, 1935), p. 161.

2. Doroshenko, *Istoriia Ukrainy,* I, pp. 23-25; Shulgin, *L'Ukraine,* p. 53.

3. Doroshenko, *Istoriia Ukrainy,* p. 235.

4. Ibid., p. 236.

5. Reshetar, *The Ukrainian,* p. 99.

6. Doroshenko, *Istoriia Ukrainy,* p. 236.

7. *Nova Rada,* no. 207, 1917.

8. Erwin Hölzle, *Der Osten im ersten Weltkrieg* (Leipzig, 1944), p. 44.

9. Doroshenko, *Istoriia Ukrainy,* p. 230.

10. Ibid., p. 296.

11. On S.V.U. political activities see Wolfdieter Bihl, "Österreich-Ungarn und der Bund zur Befreiung der Ukraine," *Österreich und Europa: Festgabe für Hugo Hantsch zum 70. Geburtstag* (Graz, Vienna, Cologne, 1965), pp. 505-526; Theophil Hornykiewicz, *Ereignisse in der Ukraine*

1914-1922; deren Bedeutung und historische Hintergründe, vol. I (Philadelphia, 1966), pp. 160-245.

12. Konstantyn Levyskyi, *Velykyi zryv* (Lviv, 1931).

13. Wolfdieter Bihl, "Beiträge zur Ukraine-Politik Österreich-Ungarns 1918," *Jahrbücher für Geschichte Osteuropas* 14:1 (1966):51-62.

14. Kost' Levyts'kyi, *Istoriia vyzvolnykh zmahan halyts'kykh ukraintsiv z chasu svitovoi viiny, 1914-1918* (Lviv, 1928-30), p. 314.

15. Matthew Stakhiv and Jaroslaw Sztendera, *Western Ukraine at the Turning Point of Europe's History, 1918-1923,* vol. I (New York, 1969), pp. 82-85.

16. Hans Beyer, *Die Mittelmächte und die Ukraine 1918* (Munich, 1956), pp. 307.

17. Ibid., p. 4.

18. Op. cit.

19. Bogdan Graf von Hutten-Czapski, *Sechzig Jahre Politik und Gesellschaft,* 2 vols. (Berlin, 1936), especially vol. II, p. 157.

20. Beyer, *Die Mittelmächte,* p. 6.

21. On Germany's policy toward Ukraine see Ihor Kamenetskyi, "Nimetska polityka suproty Ukraine v 1918 rotsi ta ii istorychna geneza," *Ukrainskyi istoryk,* 17-20(1968) and 21-23(1969). Reprint available.

22. Ibid., Reprint p. 12.

23. Alfred Milatz, "Der Friede von Brest-Litovsk und die deutschen Parteien" (Ph.D. dissertation, Hamburg University, 1949), p. 36.

24. Beyer, *Die Mittelmächte,* pp. 1819.

25. Ibid., p. 19.

26. Ibid., pp. 23-24.

27. Ibid., p. 26.

Notes to Chapter IV

1. Theophile Hornykiewicz, comp., *Ereignisse in der Ukraine,* Vol. I, Doc. no. 119, Erwin Hölzle, *Der Osten im ersten Weltkrieg,* p. 64.

2. Oleh S. Fedyshyn, *Germany's Drive to the East and the Ukrainian Revolution, 1917-1918,* p. 61.

3. A. O. Chubarian, *Brestskii mir,* p. 128.

4. Max Hoffmann, *Der Krieg der versäumten Gelegenheiten,* p. 256.

5. Complete text of the Note in J. Kreppel, *Der Friede im Osten*, pp. 72-73; *Europäischer Geschichtskalender*, Jhrg. 33/II, pp. 41-43.

6. The text of the ultimatum in William H. Chamberlain, *The Russian Revolution*, I, pp. 486-87. See also John S. Reshetar, *The U-krainian Revolution*, pp. 89-97; Richard Pipes, *The Formation of the Soviet Union: Communism and Nationalism, 1917-1923*, pp. 114-124.

7. On the Soviet accounts of events see S. M. Korolivskii, *et. al.*, *Pobeda sovetskoi vlasti na Ukraine* (Moscow, 1967); *Z istorii borot'by za vstanovlennia radians'koi vlady na Ukraini* (Kiev, 1957).

8. Volkwart John, *Brest-Litovsk, Verhandlungen und Friedensverträge im Osten, 1917-1918*, p. 21.

9. Mykola Zalizniak, "Moia uchast' u myrovykh perehovorakh v Berestiu Lytovs'komu," in Ivan Kedryn, comp., *Beresteis'kyi myr. Z nahody 10-tykh rokovyn 9.II.1918-9.II.1928*, p. 83.

10. This particular notion has been laid to rest, too, by O. Fedyshyn, *Germany's Drive*, p. 63.

11. On the Ukrainian participation and conduct of negotiations see the attached bibliography.

12. Karl Nowak, *Der Sturz der Mittelmächte*, p. 8.

13. Erich von Ludendorff, *Ludendorff's Own Story*, II, pp. 525-26.

14. Max Hoffmann, *Die Aufzeichnungen des Gen. Major Max Hoffmann*, II, p. 200.

15. Edmund Glaise-Horstenau, *Die Katastrophe*, p. 145.

16. Bergen's Note to Kühlmann in Brest-Litovsk of January 9, GFOA, no. 110; Fedyshyn, *Germany's Drive*, p. 65.

17. O. Sevruik, "Beresteis'kyi myr," in Kedryn, *Beresteis'kyi myr*, p. 151.

18. Op. cit.

19. Zalizniak, "Moia uchast," pp. 104-5.

20. John W. Wheeler-Bennett, *The Forgotten Peace: Brest-Litovsk, March 1918*, p. 158.

21. Sevriuk, "Beresteiskyi myr," p. 152.

22. Chubarian, *Brestskii mir*, p. 128.

23. Zalizniak, "Moia uchast'," pp. 90, 93.

24. Complete text in Dmytro Doreshenko, *Istoriia Ukrainy*, II, pp. 264-48.

25. Text in Kreppel, *Der Friede im Osten*, p. 163; Zalizniak, "Moia Uchast'," pp. 104-7.

26. Zalizniak, op. cit., p. 108.

27. Ibid., pp. 108-15; Doroshenko, *Istoriia Ukrainy*, I, pp. 308-13,; Reshetar, *The Ukrainian Revolution*, pp. 107-9.

28. Kreppel, *Der Friede im Osten*, p. 187; Doroshenko, *Istoriia Ukrainy*, I, pp. 313-14.

29. Hoffmann, *Die Aufzeichnungen*, II, p. 212.

30. Zalizniak, "Moia uchast'," p. 119.

31. Ottokar Czernin, *Im Weltkriege*, p. 315.

32. Zalizniak, "Moia uchast'," p. 120.

33. Ibid., pp. 121-22.

34. Peter Borowsky, *Deutsche Ukrainepolitik 1918 unter besonderer Berücksichtigung der Wirtschaftsfragen*, p. 58.
Note: By that time Czernin had been informed of the economic importance of Ukraine in a special study prepared for him by the Army's Supreme Command (AOK), highlighting the economic-geographic aspects of Ukraine, the historical-political development of the Ukrainian national movement, the status of the Ukrainian Republic and its war against Soviet Russia, and the status of the Ukrainian army. The study, among other information, estimated the Ukrainian harvest for 1910 with 215 million tons of foodstuffs and 26 million of livestock. (Hornykiewicz, *Ereignisse in der Ukraine*, II, pp. 298-313. Doc. no. 124.)

35. Max Hoffmann, *Der Krieg der versäumten Gelegenheiten*, p. 123; Fedyshyn, *Germany's Drive*, pp. 73-74.

36. Fedyshyn, *Germany's Drive*, p. 74; Kühlmann's telegram no. 19 to the Imperial Chancellor, February 1, 1918. GFOA, no. 3634.

37. Czernin, *Im Weltkriege*, p. 272.

38. Protocols of the *Reichswirtschaftsamt* from February 5, 1918. vols. 1-2 (Einfuhr aus der Ukraine), nos. 1136-1137; Borowsky, *Deutsche Ukrainepolitik*, pp. 58-59.

39. Zalizniak, "Moia uchast'," pp. 124, 127-29.

40. Sevriuk, "Beresteis'kyi myr," pp. 163-64.

41. John, *Brest-Litovsk*, pp. 131-38.

42. Borowsky, *Deutsche Ukrainepolitik*, pp. 59-60.

43. Hornykiewicz, *Ereignisse in der Ukraine*, II, pp. 208-209.

44. Text in Hornykiewicz, II, pp. 209-211; John, *Brest-Litovsk*, pp. 80-81.

45. Zalizniak, "Moia uchast'," pp. 134-47.

46. Ibid.
47. Ibid., pp. 137-38.
48. Ibid., p. 139.
49. Ibid.

Notes to Chapter V

1. Hornykiewicz, *Ereignisse in der Ukraine*, II, pp. 211-12, Doc. no. 243.
2. *Reichgesetzblatt*, Jhrg. 1918, no. 107; Hornykiewicz, op. cit., p. 1009 ff; English translation is provided in Annex.
3. Zalizniak, "Moia uchast'," p. 142.
4. Op. cit., pp. 139-41.
5. Doroshenko, *Istoriia Ukrainy*, I, pp. 317-19.
6. Op. cit., I, pp. 319-22.
7. Hornykiewicz, *Ereignisse in der Ukraine*, II, pp. 229-275, Doc. nos. 246-295.

The Kholmland together with Podlachia, already in the ninth and tenth centuries, were populated by Ukrainian tribes within Kiev Rus'. In 1018, the Polish king Boleslaw the Brave (Chrobry), crossed the Vistula River and occupied the whole area including Kholmland. Twelve years later, the Kievan Grand Prince, Iaroslav the Wise, recovered Kholmland which remained under Rus' until the collapse of Kiev Rus' in the middle of the thirteenth century. Thereafter, Kholmland became a part of the Galician-Volhynian Kingdom. King Danylo founded the city of Kholm, where he spent several years. In 1352, the Polish king Casimir the Great claimed the Galician-Volhynian kingdom as his fiefdom, creating the so-called "Rus' voivodship." In 1809, Napoleon incorporated Kholmland into the Duchy of Warsaw, to be given to Russia by the Congress of Vienna. In 1910, the Russian Duma, at the urging of the Poles, established a separate "Kholm Government" consisting of Kholmland and Podlachia. According to the Russian census of 1919, the new government included 1,800,000 people with the following distribution for Kholmland:

Kholmland	District	Ukrainians	Poles	Jews
	Kholm city	48.16%	28.56%	10.94%
	Konstantyniv	70.82	14.20	14.94
	Bila	60.48	15.60	23.35
	Voladova	64.97	14.80	15.52
	Hrubeshiv	57.31	25.91	16.22
	Tomashiv	46.71	41.07	12.22
	Samostie	29.01	52.36	18.08
	Bilhorai	38.56	49.00	11.43

(Source: Hornykiewicz, *Ereignisse in der Ukraine*, II, p. 272, Doc. no. 295.

8.   Doroshenko, *Istoriia Ukrainy*, I, p. 320.
9.   Hornykiewicz, *Ereignisse in der Ukraine*, II, pp. 29-30, Doc. no. 246.
10.   Op. cit., Doc. nos. 247-295.
11.   Op. cit., Doc. nos. 261-264.
12.   Op. cit., Doc. nos. 263, 264.
13.   Telegram from Vienna, February 11, 1918 in Doroshenko, op. cit., p. 321.
14.   This view is shared by Ihor Kamenetskyi, "Nimets'ka politika," Reprint, p. 26; by Borowsky, *Deutsche Ukrainepolitik*, p. 62; and Fedyshyn, *Germany's Drive*, p. 84.
15.   Volodymyr Vynnychenko, *Vidrodzhennia natsii*, II, pp. 214-18.
16.   Borowsky, *Deutsche Ukrainepolitik*, p. 61.
17.   Op. cit., p. 295.
18.   Op. cit., pp. 61-62.
19.   Czernin, *Im Weltkriege*, p. 338.
20.   Reference is made to views expressed by Fritz Fischer, Peter Borowsky and Hans Beyer.

Notes to Chapter VI

1.   Fedyshyn, *Germany's Drive*, p. 85.
2.   Borowsky, *Deutsche Ukrainepolitik*, pp. 63-65; Winfried Baumgart, *Deutsche Ostpolitik 1918. Von Brest-Litowsk bis zum Ende des ersten Weltkrieges* (Vienna, Munich, 1966), pp. 24-28.

3. Erich Ludendorff, *Meine Kriegserinnerungen 1914-1918* (Berlin, 1919), p. 448.

4. Text in Doroshenko, *Istoriia Ukrainy*, I, pp. 334-35.

5. Ibid.

6. Ibid.

7. Ibid., pp. 335-37.

8. Ibid.

9. Ibid.

10. *Istoriia SSSR sudrevneishikh vremen do nashikh dnei* (Moscow, 1967), I, p. 350.

11. I. I. Minz and R. Ejdeman, eds., *Die deutsche Okkupation der Ukraine Geheimdokumente* (Strassburg, 1937), pp. 37-39.

12. On the Soviet version of events leading to the signing of the peace treaty see A. O. Chubarian, *Brestskii mir*, pp. 165-190.

13. Ibid., p. 186.

14. Text in Doroshenko, *Istoriia Ukrainy*, I, pp. 264-68.

15. Ibid., pp. 286-90; *Narodna volia*, no. 21, March 2, 1918.

16. Philips Price (former correspondent of the *Manchester Guardian* in Russia), *My Reminiscences of the Russian Revolution* (London, 1921), p. 160.

17. Pavlo Khrystiuk, *Ukrains'ka revoliutsiia: zamitky i materialy do istorii ukrains'koi revoliutsii 1917-1920* (Vienna, 1922) II, p. 128.

18. Reshetar, *The Ukrainian Revolution*, p. 120.

19. Khrystiuk, *Ukrains'ka revoliutsiia*, II, p. 124; Doroshenko, *Istoriia Ukrainy*, II, pp. 290-92.

20. V. Antonov-Ovseenko, *Zapiski o Grazhdanskoi voine* (Moscow, 1924), I, p. 153.

21. Doroshenko, *Istoriia Ukrainy*, I, p. 294.

22. Ibid., I, pp. 341-42.

23. Ibid., II, p. 5.

24. Ibid., pp. 6-7.

25. Fedyshyn, *Germany's Drive*, p. 105.

26. Wilhelm Groener, *Lebenserinnerungen* (Göttingen, 1957), pp. 385-86.

27. Fedyshyn, *Germany's Drive*, pp. 102-3; Doroshenko, *Istoriia Ukrainy*, II, pp. 7-9.

28. *Vistnyk*, no. 14, p. 21.

29.   Ibid., p. 15.

30.   Hoffmann, *Die Aufzeichnungen*, II, p. 227.

Notes to Chapter VII

1.   On the Bolsheviks' activities in Ukraine during 1918, and as seen in recent Soviet literature, see V. E. Tymchyna, *Borot'sba proty nimets-kykh okupantiv i vnutrishnioi kontrrevoliutsii na Ukraini u 1918 r.* (Kharkiv, 1969); M. I. Suprunenko, *Ukraina v period inozemnoi inter-ventsii i hromadians'koi viiny (1918-1920)* (Kiev, 1951); I. K. Rybalka, *Vidnovlennia radians'koi vlady na Ukraini (1918-1919rr.)* (Kharkiv, 1957); I. I. Chervin-Koroliov, "Pro zmovu nimets'koho imperializmy z central-noiu Radoiu u Brest-Lytovs'ku v 1918r.," *Ukrains'kyi istorychnyi zhurnal* 3 (1983): 17-28.

2.   Khrystiuk, *Istoriia ukrains'koi revoliutsii*, II, p. 187.

3.   Doroshenko, *Istoriia Ukrainy*, II, pp. 16-17.

4.   Hoffmann, *Die Aufzeichnungen*, I, p. 189.

5.   "Tagebuch und Aufzeichnungen Wilhelm Groeners" in Winfried Baumgart, ed., *Von Brest-Litovsk zur deutschen November-Revolution* (Göttingen, 1971), p. 283.

6.   Alfred Krauss, "Die Besetzung der Ukraine," in Hugo Kerschnawe, *et. al.*, eds., *Die Militärverwaltung in den von den österreichisch-ungari-schen Tuppren besetzten Gebieten* (Vienna, 1928), pp. 366-73).

7.   Krauss, "Die Besetzung," pp. 372-73.

8.   Complete text in *Haus-und-Hof- und Staatsarchiv*, (Vienna), Liasse XI-dl, Folio 1-887, Karton 152, Doc. no. 3629. (Henceforth, HHS).

9.   The text of the "Ukraineabkommen" in Stefan Horak, "Der Brest-Litowsker Friede zwischen der Ukraine und den Mittelmächten in seinen Auswirkungen auf die politsche Entwicklung der Ukraine," (Ph.D. dissertation, Erlangen University, 1949), pp. 42-44; Doroshenko, *Istoriia Ukrainy*, II, pp. 232-34; *Politsches Archiv des Auswärtigen Amtes* (Bonn), Ukraine, I vol. 6; (Henceforth PAA); HHA, Doc. no. 5215; BAK, R85, Aktenband 6999, *Ukraine-Abkommen vom 28.3.1918*.

10.   Borowsky, *Deutsche Ukrainepolitik*, pp. 74-75.

11.   Groener, *Tagebuch*, pp. 330-332.

12.   PAA, i, vol. 6; *Die deutsche Okkupation der Ukraine: Geheim-dokumente* (Strassburg, 1937), pp. 32-33.

13. Groener, *Tagebuch,* p. 330.

14. Ibid., pp. 332-33.

15. Borowsky, *Deutsche Ukrainepolitik,* p. 75.

16. Text in *Bundesarchiv Koblenz,* R85, Box 6995, no. 142. (BAK).

17. BAK, no. 156.

18. Pinson S. Koppel, *Modern Germany: Its History and Civilization,* 2nd ed., (New York, 1966), p. 318.

19. BAK, no. 183. See also Borowsky, *Deutsche Ukrainepolitik,* pp. 70-73.

20. BAK, Ibid.

21. Fedyshyn, *Germany's Drive,* pp. 97-98.

22. Ibid., p. 85; Doroshenko, *Istoriia Ukrainy,* II, p. 10.

23. HHS, no. 3629 ff.

24. Ibid.

25. Kerschnawe, *Die Militärverwaltung,* pp. 373-75.

26. HHS, doc. no. 3686.

Notes to Chapter VIII

1. Fedyshyn, *Germany's Drive,* p. 123.

2. Doroshenko, *Istoriia Ukrainy,* II, p. 17.

3. Text in Horak, "Der Brest-Litowsker Friede," p. 59.

4. Doroshenko, *Istoriia Ukrainy,* II, p. 1718; Horak, "Der Brest-Litowsker Friede," p. 59.

5. Doroshenko, Ibid., II, p. 18.

6. Vynnychenko, *Vidrodzhennia natsii,* II, p. 323.

7. BAK, R85, vol. 6997. Telegram, March 18, 1918.

8. Op. cit.

9. HHS, Telegram no. 80; Hornykiewicz, *Ereignisse in der Ukraine,* I, doc. no. 145. Texts of other telegrams on conditions in Ukraine and the related Austrian government's views in doc. nos. 146-159.

10. Among others, Winfried Baumgart, *Deutsche Ostpolitik 1918,* p. 124. "Operation and rule of the German occupational army reduced the status of Ukraine to an occupied area, a general-gouvernement, although the Foreign Office in Berlin still tried to hold to the fiction of a friendly state. Since the Militarists hold the bridles tightly in their hands, they did not care much about the political guidelines being entrusted to the diplomatic representative in Kiev."

11.   Groener, *Lebenserinnerungen*, p. 399, and note 43. Also in Baumgart, *Deutsche Ostpolitik*, p. 125.

12.   Baumgart, ed. *Von Brest-Litovsk*, pp. 335-36.

13.   PAB, Ukraine i, vol. 6.

14.   Hornykiewicz, *Ereignisse in der Ukraine*, I, doc. no. 148.

15.   BAK, Aktenband 6998, doc. no. 115. Telegram of April 6.

16.   Doroshenko, *Istoriia Ukrainy*, II, p. 30.

17.   BAK, R85, Aktenband 6998, telegram of April 9, 1918; Borowsky, *Deutsche Ukrainepolitik*, pp. 98-100.

18.   Statistical data on Ukraine's deliveries in Horak, "Der Brest-Litowsker Friede," pp. 147-154; Hornykiewicz, *Ereignisse in der Ukraine*, I, doc. no. 152; Borowsky, *Deutsche Ukrainepolitik*, pp. 189-94; BAK, Aktenband 6999, no. 59.

19.   PAB, Ukraine I, vol. 7.

20.   Borowsky, *Deutsche Ukrainepolitik*, pp. 98-99; *Friedensverträge*, p. 54ff.; Deutsches Zentralarchiv II. Merseburg, VI Europa. No. 23: Ukrainische Volksrepublic, vol. 1, 1918 (henceforth DZA). On March 29 the Ukrainian government asked for 201,000 plows and 27,000 harrows. Germany was able to supply only 10,000 plows and 1,000 harrows and Austria-Hungary 5,000 plows and 600 harrows.

21.   PAB, Ukraine 1. Vol. 7.

22.   Borowsky, *Deutsche Ukrainepolitik*, p. 101.

23.   M. Baron von Stolzenberg, Colonel, representative of the Prussian War Ministry.

24.   Baumgart, ed., *Von Brest-Litovsk*, p. 350; Bundesarchiv, Militär-archiv. Freiburg, N46/172 (henceforth BMF).

25.   Details in Fedyshyn, *Germany's Drive*, pp. 137-141; Doroshenko, *Istoriia Ukrainy*, II, pp. 30-32.

26.   Fedyshyn, op. cit.; Doroshenko, op. cit.; *Die deutsche Okkupation*, pp. 56-57; Groener, *Lebenserinnerungen*, pp. 398-99; HHS, Princig's telegram of April 25, 1918, no. 244.

27.   Borowsky, *Deutsche Ukrainepolitik*, p. 103; DZA I, RWA 1097, B1. 211 ff.

28.   On April 23 Ludendorff consented to the use of either "powerful pressure" to force the Rada to a speedy delivery of foodstuffs or to remove it altogether. He also rejected the Foreign Office's proposal for a meeting with the Supreme Command as an unneccesary loss of time.

(Ludendorff's letter to Groener, April 23, 1918 in Baumgart, *Deutsche Ostpolitik*, p. 127.)

29.   Borowsky, *Deutsche Ukrainepolitik*, p. 107.

30.   Summaries of agreements in Doroshenko, *Istoriia Ukrainy*, II, pp. 292-96; Reshetar, *The Ukrainian Revolution*, p. 176; Borowsky, *Deutsche Ukrainepolitik*, pp. 105-06.

31.   Biography in Doroshenko, *Istoriia Ukrainy*, II, pp. 22-28; Horak, "Der Brest-Litowsker Friede," pp. 62-63; Fedyshyn, *Germany's Drive*, pp. 140-41.

32.   As admitted by Skoropadskyi, "Uryvok zi spomyniv." *Khli borobs'ka Ukraina*, vol. 5, p. 65.

33.   *Die deutsche Okkupation der Ukraine*, Doc. no. 53, p. 133.

34.   Fedyshyn, *Germany's Drive*, p. 140. There is no mention in Borowsky's book either.

35.   Borowsky, *Deutsche Ukrainepolitik*, pp. 107-08.

36.   PAB, Ukraine 1, vol. 8. Mumm's note to the Foreign Office, April 19, 1918.

37.   Borowsky, *Deutsche Ukrainepolitik*, pp. 107-08.

38.   Horak, "Der Brest-Litowsker Friede," p. 66; Hornykiewicz, *Ereignisse in der Ukraine*, III, pp. 204; DZA I, RWA 1097, B1. 80-83.

39.   Text in Doroshenko, *Istoriia Ukrainy*, II, pp. 32-33.

40.   Horak, "Der Brest-Litowsker Friede," p. 67.

41.   Ludendorff's *Meine Kriegserinnerungen*, p. 453.

42.   The text of Holubovych's report in Khrystiuk, *Ukrains'ka revoliutsiia*, II, pp. 167-69.

43.   Baumgart, *Von Brest-Litovsk*, pp. 127-28; Beyer, *Die Mittelmächte und die Ukraine*, p. 40; Reshetar, *The Ukrainian Revolution*, pp. 125-26; Borowsky correctly uses April 26 as the date of the meeting instead of April 24 as cited by Reshetar.

44.   Beyer's assertion that Groener did not "lend support to the *coup d'état*" cannot be sustained (Beyer, Die Mittelmächte, p. 40).

45.   Hornykiewicz, *Ereignisse in der Ukraine*, III, doc. no. 465, pp. 7-9; PAB, Ukraine 1, vol. 9.

46.   Borowsky, *Deutsche Ukrainepolitik*, pp. 111-12.

47.   Doroshenko, *Istoriia Ukrainy*, II, p. 34; Khrystiuk, *Ukrains'ka revoliutsiia*, II, pp. 169-74.

48.   Mumm's report to the Foreign Office, April 28, 1918; Borowsky, *Deutsche Ukrainepolitik*, pp. 112-14.

49.   Borowsky, op. cit., p. 113; AAB, Ukraine 1, vol. 9.

50.   Doroshenko, *Istoriia Ukrainy*, II, pp. 35-41; Reshetar, *The Ukrainian Revolution*, pp. 143-207; Hornykiewicz, *Ereignisse in der Ukraine*, III, pp. 6-7.

51.   Khrystiuk, *Ukrains'ka revoliutsiia*, II, pp. 174-81.

52.   Doroshenko, *Istoriia Ukrainy*, II, pp. 40-41.

53.   Krauss, "Die Besetzung der Ukraine 1918," *Die Militärverwaltungen*, p. 378.

54.   Kurt Fischer, *Deutsche Truppen und Entente-Intervention in Südrussland 1918/1919* (Boppard a. Rhein, 1979), p. 15.

55.   Hoffmann, *Die Aufzeichnungen*, pp. 194-95.

56.   Paul Rohrbach, "Warum ich Ukrainophile wurde," *Ukraine in Vergangenheit und Gegenwart* 1 (1952): 16-18.

57.   Baumgart, *Deutsche Ostpolitik*, p. 87.

58.   Baumgart, *Von Brest-Litovsk*, p. 357.

59.   Ibid., p. 358.

60.   Ibid., p. 359.

61.   HHS, Princig's telegram, May 6, 1918, no. 306.

Notes to Chapter IX

1.   Roppel S. Pinson, *Modern Germany: Its History and Civilization*, 2nd ed. (New York, 1966), p. 321.

2.   Surprisingly enough, American authors of German history textbooks failed to notice the significance of that treaty: John E. Rodes, *Germany: A History* (New York, 1964); Roppel S. Pinson, *Modern Germany*.

3.   Detailed composition in Pinson, *Modern Germany*, Appendix A.

4.   Ibid., p. 320.

5.   The completion of the ratification of the treaty took place only on July 24 with the exchange of ratification notes in Vienna. The first country of the Central Powers to ratify the treaty with Ukraine was Slavic Bulgaria (July 15), Turkey's ratification followed on August 22. Austria-Hungary under the pretext of Ukraine's failure to deliver goods on time refused to ratify the treaty. Source: *Verhandlungen des Reichstages. XIII Legislaturperiode, II. Session.* Band 311. *Stenographische Berichte*, Berlin, 1918.

Notes to Chapter X

1. V. Kubiiovych, *Heohrafiia ukrains'kykh i sumezhnykh zemel,* p. 396.

2. DZA I, RWA 1097, B1. 92; Borowsky, *Deutsche Ukrainepolitik,* p. 98, footnote no. 163.

3. The Central Powers were to pay for 16.36 kilograms of wheat 11.21 rubles and 9.39 rubles for rye. The exchange rate of 1 ruble = 1.175 karbovantsi (Ukrainian currency). In German currency, one ton of wheat, including shipping costs, was priced at 800 marks, rye at 675 marks, or double the price paid in Germany.

Notes to Chapter XI

1. For a more detailed treatment of the Skoropadskyi period see the works of John S. Reshetar, Oleh S. Fedyshyn, Dmytro Doroshenko and Peter Borowsky, including the Ph.D. dissertations of Stefan Horak and Taras Hunczak.

2. Fedyshyn, *Germany's Drive,* p. 158; Mumm's telegram to the Foreign Office, no. 836, June 3, 1918, General Foreign Office Archives. Washington, D.C. (Henceforth GFOA.).

3. Doroshenko, *Istoriia Ukrainy,* II, p. 132.

4. Ibid., p. 134.

5. Ibid., p. 135.

6. Text in GFOA, June 22, 1918.

7. Groener, *Lebenserinnerungen,* p. 403.

8. Fedyshyn, *Germany's Drive,* pp. 162-63.

9. Ibid., pp. 178-79.

10. For details see Fritz Fischer, *Germany's Aims in the First World War* (New York, 1967), Chapter XXI.

11. On Ukraine's foreign relations see Doroshenko, *Istoriia Ukrainy,* II, Chapters VIII, X, XI.

12. Fedyshyn, *Germany's Drive,* p. 183.

13. Reshetar, *The Ukrainian Revolution,* p. 180.

14. The members of the Directory were S. Petliura, F. Schvets, O. Andriievs'kyi, A. Makarenko, and V. Vynnychenko. For more on the Directory see Khrystiuk, *Ukrains'ka revoliutsiia,* III, p. 133ff.; Reshetar, *The Ukrainian Revolution,* Chapter V, "The Republican Revival."

15. Corresponding currency agreements with Germany and Austria-Hungary were concluded on April 26 and May 10. Text in GFOA, no. 37.

16. Krauss, *Ursachen unserer Niederlage,* p. 253.

17. Ibid., p. 254.

18. HHS, Princig's telegram of May 8, 1918, no. 7685.

19. Ibid.

20. Ibid., no. 7747.

21. Ibid., Referat I, Z 191, no. 523.

22. Ibid.

23. Ibid., Secret Report of the Army Supreme Command, May 21, 1918, no. 5636.

24. Ibid.

25. Ibid.

26. Ibid., Forgach's report to Burian, May 31, 1918, no. 5998.

27. Ibid., Forgach's report to Burian of June 11, 1918, no. 6337.

28. Reshetar, *The Ukrainian Revolution,* p. 331.

29. Ibid.

30. Ibid.

31. Ibid.

32. HHS, K.u.K. Armeekommando report to Burian, June 13, 1918, no. 805.

33. Ibid.

34. HHS, Doc. no. 835.

35. Ibid., telegram to Forgach, July 3, 1918.

36. Ibid.

37. Ibid.

38. Vynnychenko, *Vidrodzhennia natsii,* II, p. 29.

39. Details in Hornykiewicz, *Ereignisse in der Ukraine,* III, p. 18, 28-29; Reshetar, *The Ukrainian Revolution,* pp. 149-151; Horak, "Der Brest-Litowsker Friede," pp. 93-94; Doroshenko, *Istoriia Ukrainy,* II, pp. 54-55.

40. Baumgart, *Von Brest-Litovsk,* p. 360.

41. Ibid.

42. "Union of Industry, Commerce, Finance, and Agriculture."

43. Vynnychenko, *Vidrodzhennia natsii,* III, p. 55.

44. BAK, R85, Doc. no. 7003-265.

45. Agreements of February 2, March 28, April 23 and May 18, 1918. For details see Borowsky, *Deutsche Ukrainepolitik,* pp. 176-194.

46. Borowsky, op. cit.

47. AAB, Ukraine 1, Vol. 14; BAK, R85, no. 7004-Ukraine, 1179; Borowsky, op. cit., pp. 248-63.

48. BAK, R85, no. 7004-1179.

49. Ibid., Otto Wiedfeldt's report to the Office of Economics and Foreign Affairs Office of August 17, 1918.

50. Text in BAK, R85, no. 7013, Folio 1; Doroshenko, *Istoriia U-krainy*, II, pp. II-XXXV (Annex).

51. Detailed analysis of the agreement in Borowsky, *Deutsche Ukrainepolitik*, pp. 254-63.

52. Ibid., p. 262.

53. Doroshenko, *Istoriia Ukrainy*, II, pp. 381-86.

54. BAK, R85, no. 7085. Wiedfeldt's report of August 17, 1918.

55. Text in Groener, *Lebenserinnerungen*, p. 411ff.; Baumgart, *Von Brest-Litovsk*, pp. 425-37; *Deutsche Ostpolitik*, pp. 258-303, 377-79; Borowsky, *Deutsche Ukrainepolitik*, Chapter "Deutsche Ukraine-Politik im Zeichen der Niederlage."

56. Baumgart, *Von Brest-Litovsk*, p. 428.

57. Ibid., p. 430.

58. Groener's letter of October 20, 1918 to his wife.

59. Borowsky, *Deutsche Ukrainepolitik*, p. 298.

Notes to Chapter XII

1. Paul Rohrbach reiterated his views on Ukraine some thirty years later in an article, "Die ukrainische Frage," *Ukraine in Vergangenheit und Gegenwart*, 1, 3 (1952): 5-12.

2. Heinrich Lanz, *Ukraina* (Berlin, 1918), 94p.

3. Karl Friedrich Nowak, *Der Sturz der Mittelmächte* (Munich, 1921), 435p.

4. Ludendorff, *Meine Kriegserinnerungen*.

5. Fritz Wertheimer, *Durch Ukraine und Krim* (Stuttgart, 1918).

6. Ibid., pp. 126-28.

7. John, *Brest-Litowsk*, p. 97.

8. Axel Schmidt, "Das ukrainische Problem." Reprint from *Volk und Reich*, Heft 8. Berlin, 1933, and *Ukraine, Land der Zukunft* (Berlin, 1939).

9. For more details see Stefan Horak, "Die Geschichte der Ukraine und die deutsche Ostforschung," *Ukraine in Vergangenheit und Gegenwart,* 15, 43 (1968): 65-70.

10. Dietrich Geyer, "Die Ukraine im Jahre 1917. Russische Revolution und nationale Bewegung," *Geschichte in Wissenschaft und Unterricht,* 8, 1957: 670-93.

11. Baumgart, *Deutsche Ostpolitik.*

12. Ibid., p. 124.

13. Ibid., p. 125.

14. Ibid., pp. 126-27.

15. Borowsky, *Deutsche Ukrainepolitik.*

16. Fedyshyn, *Germany's Drive.*

17. Available in English under the title *Germany's Aims in the First World War* (New York, 1967), 625 p.

18. Borowsky, *Deutsche Ukrainepolitik,* p. 61.

19. Ibid., pp. 62-63.

20. Ibid.

21. Ibid.

22. Ibid., pp. 294-95.

23. Ibid., p. 297.

24. Ibid.

25. Ibid., p. 298.

26. Wolfdieter Bihl, *Österreich-Ungarn und die Friedensschlüsse von Brest-Litovsk* (Vienna, Cologne and Graz, 1970), 192p.

27. Ibid., p. 125.

28. Ibid., p. 128.

29. In his response to my Ph.D. dissertation, "Ukraine was for Austria-Hungary only an area for exploitation and nothing else." (Der Brest-Litowsker Friede zwischen der Ukraine und den Mittelmächten vom 9. Februar 1918 in seinen Auswirkungen auf die politische Entwicklung der Ukraine." Erlangen University, 1949).

30. For the most updated list of Soviet Ukrainian publications see V. E. Tychyna, *Borot'ba proty nimets'kykh okupantiv i vnutrishnioi kontrrevoliutsii na Ukraini u 1918 rotsi* (Kharkiv, 1969), 283p.; I. I. Chervinkin-Koroliov, "Z istorii Ukrains'koi RSR u period hromadians'koi viiny ta inozemnoi voiennoi interventsii: pro zmovu mimets'koho imperializmu z Tsentralnoiu Radoiu u Brest-Lytovs'komu v 1918 r." *Ukrains'kyi istorychnyi zhurnal,* 3 (March 1983): 17-28.

31. I. M. Teodorovych, *Zmova ukrains'kykh burzhuaznykh natsional-istiv z nimets'kym imperializmom v Brest-Lytovs'komu, liutyi 1918* (Kiev, 1969).

32. Chervinkin-Koroliov, "Z istorii Ukr. RSR," *Ukr. ist. zhurnal*, p. 21.

33. Ibid., p. 25.

34. Ibid.

35. Ibid., pp. 27-28.

36. Volodymyr Vynnychenko, "Myr z tsentralnymy derzhavamy: vybachennia pered soiuznykamy," *Vidrodzhennia natsii* (Vienna, 1920), Vol. II.

37. Vynnychenko, *Vidrodzhennia natsii*, vol. 3, p. 289.

38. Zhrystiuk, *Zamitky i materialy*, vol. 2, p. 35.

39. Ibid., vol. 1, p. 324.

40. Dmytro Doroshenko, *Istoriia Ukrainy*, 2 vols.

41. Ibid., vol. 1, p. 324.

42. Ivan Kedryn, ed., *Beresteiskyi myr. Z nahody 10-tykh rokovyn, 9.II.1918-9.II.1928 r. Spomyny ta materialy* (Lviv, 1928).

43. Ibid., p. 40.

44. Ihor Damenetskyi, "Nimets'ka polityka." Reprint from *Ukrain-s'ky istoryk*, 17-20 (1968); 21-23 (1969).

45. There are however, three Ph.D. dissertations on the Brest-Litovsk Treaty in the German language: Stefan Horak, "Der Brest-Litowsker Friede." Erlangen University, 1949; Peter Horban, "Die Mittelmächte und die Ukraine im ersten Weltkrieg." Heidelberg University, 1958; Taras Hunczak, "Die Ukraine unter Hetman Pavlo Skoropadskyi." Vienna University, 1960.

46. Oleh S. Pidhainy, *The Formation of the Ukrainian Republic* (Toronto, New York, 1966), 685p.

47. Ibid., p. 538.

48. Ukrainian military units advancing from Volhynia entered Kiev before the arrival of the German troops.

49. Pidhainy, *The Formation of the Ukrainian Republic*, p. 650.

50. For details on this subject see John S. Reshetar, *The Ukrainian Revolution*, pp. 98-103; Pidhainy, *The Formation*, Chapter 5: "Recognition of the Ukrainian Republic by the Allied Powers and the War."

51. Reshetar, *The Ukrainian Revolution*, p. 103.

52.   Ibid., p. 116.

53.   Fedyshyn, *Germany's Drive.*

54.   Ibid., pp. 63-64.

55.   Ibid., p. 79.

56.   John W. Wheeler-Bennett, *The Forgotten Peace,* p. 98.

57.   Axel Schmidt, *Ukraine, Land der Zukunft,* p. 191.

58.   Ibid., p. 81.

59.   Richard Pipes, *The Formation of the Soviet Union: Communism and Nationalism 1917-1923.* Rev. ed. (New York, 1968), 365p.

60.   Ibid., p. 130.

61.   Robert F. Sullivant, *Soviet Politics and the Ukraine, 1917-1957* (New York, 1962), 438p.

62.   Ibid., p. 37.

63.   Iosef V. Stalin, *Sochineniia.* Vol. 5, pp. 8-9.

64.   Adam Ulam, *A History of Soviet Russia* (New York, 1976), p. 22.

65.   Donald W. Treadgold, *Twentieth Century Russia,* 5th ed. (Boston, 1981), p. 133.

66.   Basil Dmytryshyn, *USSR: A Concise History,* 3rd ed. (New York, 1978), 646p.

67.   Ibid., p. 82.

Notes to Chapter XIII

1.   Arnold Margolin, *Ukraina i polityka Antanty,* p. 161; Reshetar, *The Ukrainian Revolution,* p. 285.

BIBLIOGRAPHY

SOURCES AND PERTINENT LITERATURE

Considering the topical limits of this monograph on the Ukrainian Brest-Litovsk treaty and its consequences, the list of documentary material and works has been narrowed accordingly to works directly pertaining to the subject matter. More extensive bibliographies on Ukraine's history of the period 1918-1920 can be found in works cited here. Preference has been given to books in English, German and Ukrainian which are available for further studies. Only a few titles published in the Soviet Union have been included as representative of the Soviet historiographical views on the subject matter.

I

Archives:

Die Akten des Auswärtigen Amtes über die Verhandlungen in Brest-Litowsk. Available on film in National Archives, Washington, D.C. Cited in the Notes as AAA.

Bundesarchiv-Bestand R 85 (Auswärtiges Amt) Koblenz. Cited as BAK; Bundes-archiv. Militärarchiv. Freiburg.

Deutsches Zentralarchiv, I. Potsdam; Deutsches Zentralarchiv II. Merseburg. Cited as DZA.

K.u.K. Armeekommando. Tagesmeldung 1918 für Seine Majestät über die Ereignisse auf den Kriegsschauplätzen. Staatsarchiv. Kriegsarchiv. Wien.

Österreichisches Staatsarchiv, Abteilung Haus,-Hof- und Staatsarchiv Wien: Politisches Archiv. Liasse XI-d1. Die Ukraine. Folio 1-887. Cited as HHS.

Politisches Archiv des Auswärtigen Amtes. Bonn. Cited as PAB.

II

Published Documents:

Horak, Stefan. *Die Ukraine in der internationalen Politik, 1917-1953: Verträge, Abkommen, Deklarationen, Noten und Interventionen. Zeittafel mit Quellen und Literaturangaben.* Munich: Verlag "Ukraine," 1957.

Hornykiewicz, Theophil, comp. *Ereignisse in der Ukraine, 1914-1944, deren Bedeutung und historische Hintergründe.* 3 vols. Philadelphia: W. K. Lypynsky East European Research Institute, 1966-1968.

Hunczak, Taras, ed. *Ukrains'ka revoliutsiia, dokumenty.* Vol. I: *1917-1918;* Vol. II: *1919-1921.* New York: Ukrainian Free Academy of Arts and Sciences in the USA, 1984-1985.

Letopis revoliutsii. Kharkiv, 1922-1928.

Dyminskyj, Roman, ed. *Handbuch der Ukraine. Wirtschaftsleben.* Leipzig: Harrassowitz, 1941.

Europäischer Geschichtskalender. Herausgegeben von Schulthess. Vol. 34 (1918) Parts I and II.

Dotsenko, Oleksander. *Litopys ukrains'koi revoliutsii: Materialy i dokumenty do istorii ukrains'koi revoliutsii.* 2 vols. Kiev-Lviv, 1923-1924.

Khrystiuk, Pavlo. *Zamitky i materialy do istorii ukrains'koi revoliutsii.* 4 vols. Vienna, 1921-1922.

Grazhdanskaia voina na Ukraine 1918-1920. Vol. I, Books 1: *Osvoboditelnaia voina ukrainskogo naroda protiv nemetsko-avstriiskikh okkupantov. Razgrom burzhuano-natsionalisticheskoi direktorii. Sbornik dokumentov i materialov.* Kiev, 1967.

Die deutsche Okkupation in der Ukraine. Geheimdokumente. Strassburg, 1937.

Mints, I. and Gorodetskii I., eds. *Dokumenty o razgrome germanskikh okkupantov na Ukraine v 1918 g.* Moscow, 1942.

Ludendorff, Erich, ed. *Die Urkunden der OHL über ihre Tätigkeit 1916-1918.* Berlin, 1922.

Kreppel, Jonas, ed. *Der Friede im Osten. Noten, Manifesto, Botschaften, Reden, Erklärungen, Verhandlungsprotokolle und Friedensverträge mit der Ukraine, Russland und Rumänien.* Vienna, 1918.

Friedensverträge mit der Ukraine, Russland und Finnland samt den dazugehörigen wirtschaftlichen Vereinbarungen, publiziert von General-Kommissariat für Kriegs- und Übergangswirtschaft im K. K. Handelsministerium Wien. Vienna, 1918.

Busemann, M., ed. *Der Friedensvertrag mit der Ukraine vom 9. Februar 1918, der Zusatzvertrag und der deutsch-ukrainische Handelsvertrag nebst der amtlichen Denkschrift: Die wirtschaftliche Bedeuting der Ukraine.* Berlin, 1918.

Verhandlungen des Reichstages. XIII Legislaturperiode. II. Session. Vol. 311. Stenographic report on the ratification of the Brest-Litovsk Treaty. Berlin, 1918.

Reichs-Gesetzblatt. Jahrgang 1918. No. 107. Berlin. Provides complete text of the Brest-Litovsk Treaty with Ukraine in German and Ukrainian.

III

Memoirs:

Baumgart, Winfried, ed. *Von Brest-Litovsk zur deutschen Novemberrevolution: Aus den Tagebüchern, Briefen und Aufzeichnungen von Alfons Paquet, Wilhelm Groener und Albert Hopman, März bis November 1918.* Göttingen, 1971.

Czernin, Ottokar von. *Im Weltkriege.* Berlin and Vienna, 1919. English edition, *In the World War.* London and New York, 1920.

Doroshenko, Dmytro. *Moi spomyny pro nedavne-mynule, 1914-1918.* 4 vols. Lviv, 1923-24.

Glaise-Horstenau, Edmund. *Die Katastrophe.* Zürich, 1929.

Gratz, Gustav and Schuller, Richard. *Die äussere Wirtschaftspolitik Österreich-Ungarns. Mitteleuropäische Pläne.* Vienna and New Haven, 1925.

Groener, Wilhelm. *Lebenserinnergungen.* Edited by F. F. H. von Gärtlingen. Göttingen, 1957.

Hindenburg, Paul von. *Aus meinem Leben.* Leipzig, 1920. In English, *Out of My Life.* London, 1920.

Hoffmann, Max. *Der Krieg der versäumten Gelegenheiten.* Munich, 1923.

Kedryn, Ivan, comp. *Beresteis'kyi myr. Z nahody 10-tykh rokovyn 9.II. 1918-9.II.1928 r.* Lviv, 1928.

Krauss, Alfred. *Die Ursachen unserer Niederlage.* Heidelberg, 1948.

Kühlmann, Richard von. *Erinnerungen.* Heidelberg, 1948.

Mazepa, Isaak. *Ukraina v ohni i buri revoliutsii, 1917-1921.* 2 vols., n.p., 1950.

Nazaruk, Osyp. *Rik na velykii Ukraini.* Vienna, 1920.

Nowak, Karl Fr., ed. *Die Aufzeichnungen des Generalmajors Max Hoffmann.* 2 vols. Berlin, 1929.

Price, Philip. *My Reminiscences of the Russian Revolution.* London, 1921.

Rohrbach, Paul. *Um des Teufels Handschrift: Zwei Menschenalter erlebter Weltgeschichte.* Hamburg, 1953.

Skoropadskyi, Pavlo. *Spomyny.* n.p., 1927.

Trotsky, Leon. *My Life.* New York, 1930.

Vynnychenko, Volodymyr. *Vidrodzhennia natsii.* 3 vols. Vienna, 1920.

Wilhelm II, German Emperor. *The Kaiser's Memoirs.* New York, 1922.

IV

Monographs:

Baumgart, Winfried. *Deutsche Ostpolitik 1918. Von Brest-Litovsk bis zum Ende des Ersten Weltkrieges.* Vienna and Munich: Oldenburg Verlag, 1966. 462p.

Beyer, Hans. *Die Mittelmächte und die Ukraine.* Munich: Isar Verlag, 1956. 58p.

Bihl, Wolfdieter. *Österreich-Ungarn und die Friedensschlüsse von Brest-Litovsk.* Vienna and Cologne: Verlag Böhlau, 1970. 192p.

Borowsky, Peter. *Deutsche Ukrainepolitik 1918 unter besonderer Berücksichtigung der Wirtschaftsfragen.* Lübeck and Hamburg: Mathiesen Verlag, 1970. 316p.

Borys, Jurij. *The Sovietization of Ukraine: The Communist Doctrine and the Practice of National Self-Determination.* Edmonton, Alberta: Canadian Institute of Ukrainian Studies, 1980. 488p.

Chamberlin, William H. *The Russian Revolution, 1917-1921.* 2 vols. New York: Macmillan, 1935.

Choulhuine, Alexander. *L'Ukraine contre Moscou.* Paris, 1935.

Chubarian, A. O. *Brestskii mir.* Moscow, 1964. 245p.

Dmytryshyn, Basil. *Moscow and the Ukraine 1918-1953: A Study of Russian Bolshevik Nationality Policy.* New York: Bookman Associates, 1956. 310p.

Doroshenko, Dmytro. *Istoriia Ukrainy 1917-1923.* 2 vols. Uzhhorod, 1930-32.

Doroshenko, Dmytro. *Die Ukraine und das Reich: Neun Jahrhunderte deutsch-ukrainischer Beziehungen im Spiegel der deutschen Wissenschaft und Literatur.* Leipzig, 1942. 216p.

Fedyshyn, Oleh. *Germany's Drive to the East and the Ukrainian Revolution, 1917-1918.* New Brunswick, NJ: Rutgers University Press, 1971. 401p.

Fischer, Fritz. *Griff nach der Weltmacht: Die Kriegspolitik des kaiserlichen Deutschlands, 1914-1918.* Düsseldorf, 1961. 411p.

Fischer, Kurt. *Deutsche Truppen und die Entente-Intervention in Südrussland 1918/19.* Boppard a Rhein, 1973. 160p.

Groener, Wilhelm. *Der Weltkrieg und seine Probleme.* Berlin, 1920.

Hölzle, Erwin. *Der Osten im erten Weltkrieg.* Leipzig, 1944.

John, Volwart. *Brest-Litovsk Verhandlungen und Friedensverträge im Osten, 1917 bis 1918.* Würzburg, 1937. 217p.

Kosyk, Wolodymyr. *La politique de la France ę l'égard de l'Ukraine, mar 1917-février 1918.* Paris: Publications de la Sorbonne, 1981. 304p.

Kulinych, Ivan M. *Ukraina v zaharbnyts'kykh planakh nimets'koho imperializmu, 1900-1944 rr.* Kiev, 1963.

Levyts'kyi, Kost. *Velykyi zryv: Do istrorii ukrains'koi derzhavnosty vid bereznia do lystopada 1918 r. na pidstavi spomyniv ta dokumentiv.* Lviv, 1931.

Likholat, A. B. *Razgrom natsionalisticheskoi kontrrevoliutsii na Ukraine 1917-1922.* Moscow, 1954.

Mints, I. and Eidelman, I., eds. *Krakh germanskoi okkupatsii na Ukraine.* Moscow, 1936.

Nowak, Karl. *Der Sturz der Mittelmächte.* Munich, 1921.

Pipes, Richard. *The Formation of the Soviet Union: Communism and Nationalism, 1917-1923.* Rev. ed. New York: Atheneum, 1968. 365p.

Pidhainy, Oleh S. *The Formation of the Ukrainian Republic.* Toronto: New Review Books, 1966. 685p.

Reshetar, John S. *The Ukrainian Revolution, 1917-1920: A Study in Nationalism.* Princeton, NJ: Princeton University Press, 1952. 363p.

Rohrbach, Paul and Schmidt, Axel. *Osteuropa, historisch-politisch gesehen.* Potsdam, 1942.

Schmidt, Axel. *Ukraine, Land der Zukunft.* Berlin, 1939.

Tychyna, V. E. *Borot'ba proty nimets'kykh okupantiv i vnutrishnioi kontrrevoliutsii na Ukraini u 1918 rotsi.* Kharkiv, 1969.

Wheeler-Bennett, John W. *The Forgotten Peace: Brest-Litovsk, March 1918.* New York, 1939.

Zastavenko, H. *Krakh nimetskoi interventsii na Ukraini v 1918 rotsi.* Kiev, 1959.

V

Doctoral dissertations:

Horak, Stefan. "Der Brest-Litowsker Friede zwischen der Ukraine und den

Mittelmächten vom 9. Februar 1918 im seinen Auswirkingen auf die politische Entwicklung der Ukraine." Erlangen University, 1949.

Horban, Peter. "Die Mittelmächte und die Ukraine im Ersten Weltkrieg (auf Grund der bisher gedruckten Quellen)." Heidelberg University, 1958.

Hunczak, Taras. "Die Ukraine unter Hetman Pavlo Skoropadskyi." Vienna University, 1960.

Kock, Heinrich. "Die Friedensverhandlungen von Brest-Litovsk im Spiegel der Wiener Presse." Hamburg University, 1937.

VI

Articles:

Bihl, Wolfdieter, "Beiträge zur Ukraine-Politik Österreich-Ungarns 1918," *Jahrbücher für Geschichte Osteuropas,* 14 (1966): 51-62.

Bihl, Wolfdieter, "Die österreichisch-ungarischen Dienststellen in der U-kraine 1918," *Mitteilungen des österreichischen Staatsarchivs,* 20 (1967): 379-388.

Borschak, Elie, "La Paix ukrainienne de Brest-Litovsk," *Le Monde Slave,* II: 4 (1929): 33-62; III: 7 (1929): 63-84; III: 8 (1929): 199-225.

Czubatyj, Nicholas, "The National Revolution in Ukraine, 1917-1919," *The Ukrainian Quarterly,* 1 (1944): 17-39.

Eudin, X. J., "The German Occupation of the Ukraine in 1918," *Russian Review,* 1 (1941/42): 90-112.

Horak, Stefan, "Der Friedensvertrag mit der Ukraine im deutschen Reichstag (1918)," *Ukraine in Vergangenheit und Gegenwart,* 11: 26 (1964): 18-25.

Meyer, Henry Cord, "Germans in the Ukraine, 1918. Excerpt from Unpublished Letters," *The American Slavic and East European Review,* 9 (1950): 105-115.

Paneyko, Basil, "Conditions of Ukrainian Independence," *Slavonic Review,* 2 (1923): 336-345.

Stentzel, Ernst, "Der Sturz der ukrainischen Rada-Regierung durch die deutschen Militärbehörden Ende April 1918," *Zeitschrift für Militärgeschichte,* 8 (1969): 41-49.

Velsen, Stefan von, "Die Ukraine und wir. Ein Rückblick auf die deutsche Okkupation," *Preussische Jahrbücher,* 176 (1919): 260-266.